Elections
& Erecti

D0335843

Also available by Pieter-Dirk Uys

Trekking to Teema

Elections & Erections

A Memoir of Fear and Fun

PIETER-DIRK UYS

With cartoons by

Zapiro

ZEBRA

Published by Zebra Press
an imprint of Struik Publishers
(a division of New Holland Publishing (South Africa) (Pty) Ltd)
PO Box 1144, Cape Town, 8000
New Holland Publishing is a member of the Johnnic Publishing Group

First published 2002

3 5 7 9 10 8 6 4 2

Publication © Zebra Press 2002
Text © Pieter-Dirk Uys 2002

Cover photographs © Pat Bromilow-Downing
Cartoons © Zapiro

PUBLISHING MANAGER: Marlene Fryer
MANAGING EDITOR: Robert Plummer
PROOF-READER: Ronel Richter-Herbert
COVER AND TEXT DESIGNER: Natascha Adendorff
TYPESETTER: Monique van den Berg

Set in 11 pt on 15 pt Adobe Garamond

Digitally imposed and imaged at Syreline Process
Printed and bound by CTP Book Printers

ISBN 1 86872 665 7

www.zebrapress.co.za

Log on to our photographic website www.imagesofafrica.co.za for an African experience

Contents

Acknowledgements

I have always been writing about other people's lives, either focusing on the baroque fantasy of the Bezuidenhout family, or the surreal reality of the Bothas and Bothalezis. This time round I have taken time out to write a memoir of moments in my life that reflect both the fear and fun of being a South African.

Starting with the first climax and building up to a holocaust, this journey retraces so many familiar areas: discovering sex, questioning authority both political and religious (in my case the same thing), discovering democracy late in life, and coming face to face with uncompromising decline and death through the threat of a virus that has no cure. But care is halfway towards a solution. And if anything must remain with the reader, it is the celebration of my hope and optimism for the future of South Africa and its remarkable people.

I must thank my lucky stars for those emotions, because some of my generation don't see the future with hope and optimism. Among my lucky stars are those whose wisdom and care guided me through the minefields of growing up. My parents are no longer visible, but are constantly felt as guardian spirits along the path. My sister and I are the only ones left of the Uyses from Homestead Way, Pinelands, Cape Town, South Africa, Africa, the World. And we're happy to be here!

Thanks also to Jonathan, the immortal Zapiro, who has enhanced this experience with his tongue so firmly in the cheeks of the nation. And let us not forget past and present South African politicians who, as unconscious scriptwriters, have written all my material. I could not have made up what I explore so eagerly. If hypocrisy is the Vaseline of political intercourse, let's hope all politicians learn to wear condoms of humour. Warm and grateful acknowledgements also to Robert Plummer of Zebra who, as my editor, has made sense of the nonsense that seemed to vomit out on the pages with every thought.

Introduction: Fear and Fun

Once upon a time, not so long ago, we had an apartheid regime in South Africa that killed people. Now we have a democratic government that just lets them die.

We are not sissies when it comes to viruses. We had one for over forty years, and it had no cure. Tens of thousands of South Africans died because of it. Millions had their lives violently changed forever. But eventually the virus of apartheid was neutralised. We found a cure called democracy.

Why did it take so long? Was it because the propaganda was so believable? 'Democracy is too good to share with just anyone!'

So simple. Our solution had been there all the time. And yet for so long we were not allowed to believe that it was effective. We had a president called PW Botha who repeatedly assured us that there would be no black multiracial rule. He would segregate voting so that whites stayed in charge. He was wrong. Today we have a president called Thabo Mbeki who denies the link between HIV and AIDS. He is also wrong. And the letters 'Thabo' can also spell the name 'Botha'!

Apartheid wasn't funny. The hypocrisy behind the civilised Christian façade of those who benefited from it made us laugh, because the fear that it elicited was exposed as ridiculous. Laughing at fear has become my secret cure: laugh at fear and put it into perspective. It's always going to be there, but once it has a name, it also has a place.

At least the virus of apartheid was visible. It certainly had a colour. Although neither white nor black are colours of the rainbow, one was the master and the other was the servant. The culture with a capital K that was so protected by legalised racism at least stank to high heaven, in spite of the perfume of so-called civilised Christian demeanours. And the signs were everywhere: WHITES ONLY, NO DOGS OR NATIVES ALLOWED. The signs warned us: beware of the virus. If you don't have the vaccine of a white skin, you will get it and your small dreams will die.

Recently a black family from Soweto visited Clifton Beach in Cape Town. The son is fourteen. Energetic and full of fun. More comfortable speaking English to his Xhosa father than the language of his roots. He prefers Michael Jackson to the Soweto String Quartet.

'Wow, Dad,' he said, 'this is a cool beach. You must've had such fun coming here for your holidays.'

His father smiled.

'Yes, it's cool. And no, I never came here when I was a boy.'

'Oh, but didn't you visit Gogo in Langa?'

'Yes.'

'And she never let you come to Clifton?'

'No, we weren't allowed.'

'Oh? Why?'

'There was a law.'

'Why?'

'It said this beach was for whites only.'

'Oh? Why?'

'Because that was the law. You got into terrible trouble if you were black and came to this white beach.'

'Was there a minefield to keep you off it?'

His father smiled.

'No. There was a sign.'

A *sign*?

Yes, for over forty years we did nothing because of the signs. Because of the fear. We believed the urban legends. We bowed down to the paraphernalia of Boer Power. We thought they knew what they were doing.

We were wrong. They didn't have a clue, because if they did, they would have killed their opposition early on. The Struggle for South Africa started 350 years ago. Maybe the greatest weakness of the Struggle and at the same time its unique strength was that both sides passionately loved the same thing. Their country. So, contrary to predictions, we did not become another Gaza, not another Vietnam, not another Rwanda, not another Belfast. Here, at the southern tip of nowhere, the world was cheated out of a major prime-time bloodbath and camera crews waddled off into the bloody Balkan sunrise with irritation and hopes of better angles.

So the news is good. South Africa is reborn with the greatest Constitution in the world. We have a Bill of Rights. We had an unforgettable Truth and Reconciliation Commission. We have been blessed with both a Nelson Mandela and a Desmond Tutu. But we also have the greatest incidence of HIV/AIDS in the world. While the First World is burying the lambs, the Third World is burying its babies.

2

So the minefield has moved: from politics to sex.

Can one do the tango in front of a firing squad again? Laughing at the fear of death? You come and then you go? And what's funny about HIV/AIDS?

The whole scenario begs for laughter. Firstly, leave the virus out of it. Just look at sex. If politics is funny, sex can be a scream! I think it's one of God's last little jokes. To furnish men with small soft things that must get bigger and hard and stick out to fit into the dark warm places that women have? That's sometimes like trying to get a limp piece of thread through the eye of a needle! Then we have to wobble up and down, pushing in and out, looking like small mammals trying to get rid of a flea biting us on the bum, then screaming a syllable or two – 'Yes! Yes! Yes!' – shuddering like a jellyfish, mumbling the name of someone else, and falling asleep! Go there with a smile and you end with a bellyache and a flopped experience. But when death is disguised as something we like – because let's face it, sex is nice! – this is going to be more difficult than ever.

During Virus No.1 we had a government with absolutely no sense of humour at all. And so it became my aim in life to make them so angry with humour, to drive them so crazy with laughter, that they had heart attacks and died. And I had some success. Now there is no PW Botha glaring out at me from the television news. There is no wagging of that finger and licking of those lips.

'Apartheid is just a pigment of the imagination!'

3

I'd mirror him on stage, although he never said something so clever. Nor did I, because I found that slogan on a toilet wall along with so many other memorable lines and phone numbers! I'd 'do' PW and people laughed. And when we realised that we were laughing at absolute power and were getting away with it, it made us feel stronger. Maybe it worked, because we're still here and most of those targets aren't.

The irony is that, after the bull's-eye target of apartheid, we are now faced with yet another government balls-up crying out for satirical stabs. Amid all the freedoms of speech, of expression, of sexual preference – for don't forget our Constitution even protects the rights of gay couples! – we have a leadership in denial.

Starting at the top with Comrade President Thabo Mvuyelwa Mbeki. A bright man who spent his life working for this job. A deeply disadvantaged member of the ANC executive, because poor Thabo was never jailed by the white supremacists. Maybe that's why he is so bitchy towards whiteys. They didn't put him on the Struggle T-shirts! So poor Thabo must sleep on the kitchen floor every Friday night just to keep up with the Cabinet! All the comrades in the ANC were in jail, following Nelson Mandela's example. And what a pertinent example is that for today's leaders? That politicians first go to jail and then into politics? And not the other way round!

So little Thabo threw stones at police cars and the police threw them back. Maybe they just thought he was a schoolboy with a pipe. So Thabo went into exile in 1962 to spend most of his life outside South Africa, longer than Mandela spent jailed inside South Africa. Young Mbeki went to the University of Sussex, where he studied and absorbed the best of what Britain had to offer political refugees. Then, to add to the profile of the comrade who nearly wasn't, he went to the Soviet Union, embraced their racism – also known as communism – and studied at the University of Moscow, returning to South Africa a stranger and a confirmed Stalinist. Just one of the many returned exiles trying to fit their square peg of dreams into the round hole of reality.

While Nelson Mandela dazzled the world with his genius for making friends of enemies, Thabo made enemies of friends, and when the choice for a successor to Mandela came up, there was only one left in the arena. All the other lions who had stayed and fought the Struggle from within had been eaten. The returned exiles took over the bridge and the chipmunk became king.

I met him during the years of his audition as Deputy President. A few times

I would be summonsed to dinners hosted by him in Pretoria, while Madiba was being hosted elsewhere. I would be given two ten-minute slots.

'And the Deputy President says, go for it!' they'd whisper.

Go for what? The silver? Would there be any left once my act was over?

He once said to me: 'Don't do PW Botha. Don't be safe. Be dangerous. Show us how to laugh at ourselves.'

Dazzled we were, me and my shadows. This bright young man with the twinkle in his eyes, brought up on *Monty Python* and *Not the Nine O'Clock News*, a veteran of the best of British satire, and on my side?

'Pieter, you will never do me on stage!'

'Yes, I will!'

'No, Pieter, I will make it very hard for you. I will not wear an ethnic Mandela shirt, Pieter. I will not wag my finger like PW Botha, Pieter. You will never do me on stage, Pieter.'

'Yes, I will do you on stage! You will be the President of South Africa. You'll also go mad.'

'No, Pieter, I'm not an Afrikaner!'

He was right. It's very difficult to 'do' Thabo Mbeki on stage because he's never here! Our virtual President. They say he was in South Africa last week on a state visit, but who knows when he'll be back. Of course it's difficult having to follow in the footsteps of our beloved old guardian angel, but as the days go by, are Nelson Mandela's footsteps getting larger, while Thabo's are getting smaller?

What an act to follow as a politician and statesman! At first Thabo looked good for the country. He was a crafty politician, a man who knew his business, having practised it for decades. A true professional. An apparatchik. A comrade, yet a Eurocentric in African mode. And from the first day, the one man in power who wore the red AIDS ribbon, long before anyone else did.

We hoped Thabo would carry the flame of awareness and care. We were wrong. I don't even think he knows what that red ribbon signifies.

Suddenly he stopped us all in mid-stride.

'Does HIV lead to AIDS?'

Hello? Does the sun rise? And why is he asking that question with sunglasses on?

'Is AIDS a disease, or just a syndrome?'

Can we move on to the dying people? But the leader has spoken and the sheep all bleat. The party line is drawn and cross it at your peril. The President of South Africa slowly transformed himself in the eyes of the watching world

5

from potential superstar to suspected loony. He gathered together dissidents and naysayers from all corners of the medical spectrum. He gave them press and media attention. He stopped the wheels of awareness turning. Everyone was confused. If HIV doesn't lead to AIDS, what does? What is HIV? If the President says it's not a proven reality, then is there a danger? Why use condoms, if there is no AIDS? Is it a white conspiracy to brand blacks sexually promiscuous?

The world shakes its head politely. Can't criticise a black leader who still stands in the aura of Mandela. To question is to be racist. Hope it will all just go away. And so the world happily concentrates on a Bosnian holocaust and the search for Milosevic, while Thabo flies around the world making speeches about everyone else's agendas.

Back home the rainbow nation shakes in terror.

'What is this Thing that's making my children sick and forces my husband into a corner of the shack where he dies?'

'Why are there all these funerals each week?'

'What is killing us? TB? Colds?'

Yes, actually, all of those things. Once the immune system is gone, anything can invade and destroy. So maybe Thabo was right. Maybe AIDS is the umbrella for the disaster that the virus invites? Did he get wrong advice from those highly paid, coked-up informers that surround the core of power?

Does he himself have HIV, which could explain his denial?

Is the South African government dying of AIDS? Surely not impossible when one recalls that when the ANC was celebrating victory over apartheid in the salons of Lusaka and Harare and Lagos and Dakar in the last days of the 1980s, they probably didn't use condoms?

So the urban legends multiply and find fertile ground in townships and ghettos, around dinner tables and in coffee shops. While the mutter of malice and concern mists up the clarity of daily life, penises get erect and semen mixes with blood and the virus gallops into the sunset of another life. And we are all frightened to death!

Fighting fear and political madness with humour has been my way of life since the 1970s. I always said that the previous government wrote my material for me. That's why I didn't pay taxes; I paid royalties. I repeat that today: the democratic government for which I voted is doing me proud. Never a dull moment. While democracy is not usually a laugh at life, our daily survival on the speed wobbles of careless government has turned South Africa into my favourite funny fair! And it's all the fault of elections and erections!

Today there are no answers left. After two planes flew into two towers and broke every rule and heart and law, anything is possible. No answers, just questions. Maybe somewhere along the line I lost the map leading to answers. I think I know that route by heart, having stared at it for so long. So, let me go back to the beginning of that map, when it was still crackly and new.

PART I

FOREPLAY

The First Coming

My background as a child growing up in South Africa was both ordinary and extraordinary. My father Hannes Uys was Afrikaans, my mother Helga Bassel German. Not ordinary, but not unusual in a country rife with international marriages. The fact that both parents were musicians was special. The secret that my mother was Jewish was extraordinary. She died when I was in my twenties, and only then did we find out that she was not just a refugee from Nazi Germany, but also a Jew. That makes me a Jew on the one side and an Afrikaner on the other: belonging to both chosen peoples!

I have a small framed letter next to my desk. I'm looking at it now, as I do every time I sit and work here. It is dated 19 August 1935, and addressed to Helga Bassel, Neue Kantstrasse 16, Berlin-Charlottenburg. It is from Dr Peter Raabe, President of the Reichs-Musikkammer. Although it is in official German and defies easy translation, the letter says the following:

> Because you are a member of the Jewish Race, you will no longer be allowed to practise your career as a pianist. No professional venue will be allowed to employ you. You may no longer perform in Germany.

She did perform in Germany for the next four years, playing Mozart, Beethoven, Liszt, Scarlatti and Chopin, flaunting her art and her contempt for the Nazis. Until 1938, when her frightened friends took her to Bremenhaven and put her on a boat, which eventually docked in Cape Town. One of her first engagements was with the Cape Town City Orchestra, playing a two-piano Mozart concerto with a young local pianist called Hannes Uys.

I look at this letter all the time. It's just a little letter. Like so many other little letters, powerful enough to end a dream and so often a life.

Our home in Pinelands was always devoid of racist labels. Even Pa would disguise the thought of 'kaffir' with expletives such as 'daardie dônner!' Maybe the experience of being Jewish in the Berlin of the late 1930s had left its mark on my mother, who would not tolerate name-calling. Kids call each other names: 'rooinek' for the English, 'boer' for Afrikaner and the bouquet of names that described blacks: 'kaffir, hotnot, meid, jong!' At school these words were part of our conversation. At home, verboten.

My sister Tessa and I were taught to play the piano. As soon as she could clutch at an octave with her small fingers, Tessa explored music. Although she also loved ballet and athletics, the day would come when music called the tune. I was too lazy to do all those Hannon exercises, and never went beyond my own version of 'Never On Sunday' and 'Moon River'.

Ma gave up and Pa shouted.

We'd take part in eisteddfods. Pa wanted us to win. Ma would drive us there and say: 'If you win you get an ice cream. If you don't, you get two ice creams!'

Tessa and I fought like cat and dog, as all siblings do. She was the apple of her father's eye and would always get the benefit of the doubt. I just played in the garden with my Dinky Toys and started collecting pictures of Sophia Loren. For a short period Sophia shared the wall with my hero, Prime Minister Hendrik Verwoerd, but her legs were better and, mercifully, so was her sticky tape. Verwoerd fell to the floor, and I was liberated.

I went to a white school, lived in a white suburb, travelled on white buses and white trains. I swam at white beaches and went to white cinemas. It was a white country. The greatest sin against God – for was He not also Afrikaans and white? – was to break the laws of racial divide. Especially the Immorality Act, which forbade sex between the races. We'd have a snigger session every Sunday when we scanned the papers and read about yet another Afrikaner dominee who'd been found with his pants around his ankles and his sexual parts exposed in the company of a large black naked 'meid/kaffir/hotnot/jong'! His suicide often added spice to the sensation. There was never a twinge of sympathy. How could this white man, the chosen of God, have done that with a black! Sis! It was against God's Law!

And then it came to pass that this boy left his childhood and boyishness behind and hair sprouted on his body in silly tufts and things went hard in the night and always on the bus! And sex happened.

Except I didn't even know what it was when it happened. And I was on my own!

It was 1959. I was fourteen years old and spent most of my time in the garden on my knees, playing with my Dinky Toys. No one spoke about sex in those days. South Africa had the best of both worlds. On one side, we had the cream of British education and the essence of British reserve, being still a member of the Commonwealth. We kids were told to 'hush'.

'Children should be seen and not heard!'

'Don't speak until you are spoken to!'

And if you asked anything that could be deemed sexual?

'Miss, what are those dogs doing?'

'Dirty little boy, how dare you ask things like that! Hush!'

On the other side there was Afrikaner Nationalism, Dutch Reformed Church morality and that all-powerful word, *sies*!

'Sies!'

Which is ten times worse than hush! So between 'sies' and 'hush' we didn't ask questions for forty years. Not about politics; definitely not about sex. Boys would use words in the locker room and the words sounded interesting. Just as the word 'democracy' must have had a certain fascination, but absolutely no meaning.

I would then ask my father, 'Pa? What does *naai* mean?'

'Sies!'

So I had to depend on what I heard from other kids, who also didn't have a clue. Or from teachers who knew, but pretended they didn't. We were once herded into the school hall. Boys sitting to the left, girls to the right, and Mr van Zyl, the PT teacher, patrolling the no-kids-land in between with a baseball bat in his clenched fists. Miss Reid came onto the stage and clasped her hands together in an awful display of control.

'Children, today we are going to talk about the facts of life.'

To us, this meant chocolates after school and radio serials before supper.

'We are going to tell you about the birds and the bees.'

That was it. Birds and bees. And storks.

So there I was, fourteen years old and on the verge of my first sexual experience. I didn't have a clue what was coming. Literally. At that time I had discovered the magic of reading. I loved books, and the Pinelands Library was always a place of magical stories, filled with a musty book smell. I'd read *Biggles* and *The Hardy Boys* and *Trompie* and *Saartjie* – also *Nancy Drew* – and then one day I discovered a French girl called Angelique. Every time I read about her, I felt a nice warm feeling Down There. I didn't know what it was. Hay fever! But nice! So I panted through *Angelique*, then *Angelique in Love*, followed by *Angelique in Revolt* and *Angelique and the King*. The books were set in the time of Louis XIV at Versailles, a period that appealled to me, and I soon also started reading biographies of other grand horizontals like Madame du Barry and Madame de Pompadour. But that was only after the first climax. Nothing could touch Angelique!

'Countess Angelique lay back on her chaise longue. Her negligée parted and exposed her alabaster skin. She was naked. Her golden hair cascaded over her luscious firm breasts …'

If you're hearing an acceptable English accent here, I'm misleading you. I spoke Afrikaans and German at home. Schoolboy English I learnt in the locker rooms! So, I carefully mouthed the big foreign words as Angelique exposed herself to me.

'Countess Angelique lay back on her … chaysielongie … her … neglageee parted and exposed her … alabuster skin she was naked her golden hair cascaded over her lussis furm breasts the pyrple nipples looked angryagainstthewhiteskin … the door opened and the Comt-e Joffrey de Peyrac limped into the room the moonlight shone on his one good eye he put out his hand and with his long tapered fingers touched the Countess Angelique on her naked stomach … allowinghis … his … his … handstogolowerandlowerandloweruntil SUDDENLY …'

SPLAT!

Wet sticky goo shit whatthefuckishappeninghere?!

Oh my God I'm dying! Something's wrong with me! My chameleon's just vomited on my tummy!

A fourteen-year-old nervous breakdown, and a wet patch on the sheet. So normal. It happens to everyone. Boys become men and girls become women. It's a fact of life. But if you don't know what it is, it can be the most frightening thing imaginable. And in 1959 there's no one to ask! Can't go to the teacher. Don't dare ask Pa! And being a well brought-up Calvinist Afrikaans boy, you knew this was a sin. It was so nice, it had to be a *moerse* sin! So now you must pray.

'Liewe Jesus, I'm sorry, I won't do it again. I promise I will never again read such a terrible book. Such a communist book. About that hoer Angelique. Lying naked on her bed. Sies!'

But suddenly remorse makes way for interest.

'Lying naked on her bed?'

Interest bans prayer.

'The purple nipples look angry …?'

Demurely folded hands become a clenched fist.

'… lower and lower …?'

And the boy's resolve stiffens once more and adolescent lust leads the way.

More SPLAT! For sex will happen. If you don't know what it is, you've got a lifelong problem wondering if you ever learnt to do it the right way.

Our parents had wonderful friends from all corners of the world, as we knew it – meaning Europe. There was Auntie Erna from Austria and Ernest from Bavaria and other Germans who like Ma had made Cape Town their new home. Then there was Uncle André. He was from Sea Point and was a ballet dancer. Fey sensitive men were not new to me, as many were part of the family circle. One night there was a dinner party at home, with Ma and our maid Sannie in the kitchen cooking Vienna Schnitzel. The dining room table was wedged in an alcove, which meant that up to nine people could sit on the cushioned benches on either side. Tessa and I would squeeze into the corners next to the windows.

Uncle André sat next to me. His leg kept pushing against mine. Rubbing up and down. He was being naughty, but then I think I was always on display, with blond hair, a cupid smile and a fourteen-year-old instinct! Not tonight! I flounced up and pushed passed the guests, and into the kitchen.

'Ma! Uncle André's touching my leg!'

Sannie was dishing up peas and made big eyes. Ma handed me plates.

'What, darling?' she said in her slightly accented English.

'Uncle André! He's rubbing his leg against mine!' I said, sensing a victory.

'Well, if you don't like it, sit somewhere else. Take this plate through?'

That cured me forever. Gay was never an issue. I once asked Pa what a homosexual was, and, perhaps because we were on our way to church, he said something about them being disgusting and unnatural and *sies*!

My sexual education eventually came on a daily basis. I found 'dirty' books in the cupboard behind the boxes of photo albums of us as babies! One was a thick volume by Krafft-Ebbing that documented famous cases of sexual deviation. So there at a young age I was trying to make sense of men who fucked their dogs, women who played with bananas, and ordinary nice people who had fetishes about shoes, gloves, umbrellas and moustaches! Anyone wearing boots made my eyebrows rise! Then there was another book, of Victorian nudes, mostly drawn and probably quite charming. So in one sitting I would confront virginal sex, anal intercourse, wanking in a boot, dillying a goat and erotic poses in a nun's habit! Everything was a sin, so no matter how nice it was; there was constant remorse and fear of being discovered. I locked the door to my bedroom whenever I went in. I think we were all very private, to the point of ridiculousness.

I look back now and laugh at all that confusion. Then one realises how deep into the minefield we've trekked. Because today, if the kids don't know exactly what sex is, it will kill them! We had crabs and clap and drips and drabs, and for each there was a pill or a powder. Not any more. Sex kills without a cure.

So, if there is anything good coming out of this present horror tale of AIDS, it is that the children out there can no longer grow up in this cave of terror and fear as far as sex is concerned. Like so many of us did. They must know all about sex now. Don't wait until tomorrow, because there's always tonight.

I can't lock doors any more as I did then. For forty years of my life, the fact that I was not heterosexual was a secret that had to be kept at any cost. So I denied and lied and pretended throughout my childhood, into adolescence and youth. Now in middle age that exhausting routine is over, thank God! No more denial!

Yes, I'm older than most world leaders. Yes, I am homosexual. Yes, I am also frightened. Yes, I can become sick too. Yes, I can also die of AIDS.

So why haven't I got AIDS?

Have I been careful, always? Have I not been exposed to it? Do I not have 'live sex' as often as I pretend to? Growing up in Pinelands as a sheltered shy white child was probably the best protection against later infection. I was too scared to do anything! So many times as a randy teenager I waited for something to happen. It was not polite to ask, so I didn't go up and say: 'Can we fuck?'

In my early twenties I'd sit on a bar stool in my new clothes and wait. Everything always a little too tight, because it usually took a year to pluck up the courage to wear something new and fashionable. Tight trousers on a blond boereseun should've worked in a bar full of interested people. Yet it never did. I often ended up on the train going home, wondering: What's wrong? It was many years later that I realised: the picture was wrong! While in my mind I thought I looked like Steve McQueen, in reality all they saw was just a prissy little queen.

'Why do you look so angry?' someone would ask.

'No, I'm fine,' I'd smile, not knowing what they meant. Having been brought up never to look in the mirror, I didn't know my face. Mirrors were vain, wrong, sinful. So my face picture never matched my brain picture. I thought one expression but presented another. So, an active sex life was something other people talked about. For me, back to Krafft-Ebbing and the dog-eared Physical Pictorials in the secret flap behind the door of my wall cupboard! Believe me, if wanking really made boys blind, I would've had a white stick at twenty-five!

When sixties' Flower Power blew across the horizon and over the Grape Curtain into Cape Town, filling our air with Simon and Garfunkel and long hair and beads and bell-bottoms, I sat and waited for someone to hand me The Drugs. And no one did. I was once given some revolting dagga and was sick on someone's bedspread. I was asked to leave and had to pay for the dry-cleaning.

End of drugs.

I waited for those orgies I'd heard about, where boys and boys and girls would be naked and in slow motion would have sex to music that was not Henry Mancini! I once was at such a party and things moved into a bedroom. I followed and saw the expected sex happening. With 'Moon River' playing? I knew, *this was it*. Then someone said: 'Pietertjie, go and get the towels. And while you're about it, find my cigarettes? And just pop down to the shop for some more tonic water?'

End of orgies.

Now I look back and thank God for that hopelessness and helplessness. And an extraordinary imagination that fed daily climaxes with images dredged up from tired old magazines, and once from the pages of *Lady Chatterley's Lover*! If I'd gone down the wide road of sexual freedom, with all it entailed, I would have been one of the first to die of AIDS. There by the grace of a cross little face go I.

Being over fifty is a celebration of life. The audition is over. No more having to prove, just improve. And that is so personal that no one else will see. No one but you.

A long walk to freedom? Probably not different from the journeys of so many others, but somehow in the South Africa of those early years, for Pieter Uys of Pinelands, it was a walk through a minefield.

Like Tasting Chocolate?

Will I go to hell if I have sex with a black?

Of course, no one ever asked that question in those days, because it was obvious. You didn't go to hell. You went to jail! So, we never thought it was an issue. Black people were not objects of sexual lust. Black people worked in the garden and cooked the food. So, when it happened, I was as unprepared for it as I was on the night the Countess Angelique made my peepee-lizard puke.

There is a little peninsula between Clifton Beach and Camps Bay called Bachelor's Cove. Filled with high round rocks and hidden pools, it was just the place to go in my student days for a quick tan. Near enough to town, far away from the crowd. And it was said that you could lie on the rocks naked and not go to prison. Being naked on beaches was also not allowed.

So I went to Bachelor's Cove whenever I could, bunking classes at university and drama school. Covered in baby oil, my hair sprinkled with peroxide, I'd lie on the rock, nude and rude and free. The air was spiced with ozone, shrieking seagulls floated on a breeze, blue sky merged with bluer sea. And as you lay on your back seeped in Johnson's Baby Oil, nature and the breeze combined with thoughts of sixties' screen idol Troy Donahue. Cut to the car chase: your cock would be sucked. If you didn't open your eyes, and pretended to be asleep instead, you wouldn't have to leap up and say: 'Sis man, you moffie! What the hell are you doing!'

You 'slept' through it. And they – whoever they were – played your game and would feast and flee. You'd sometimes have sunburn all over, except for the outline of two ears and a head right over your lower pelvis! Being homosexual in South Africa was also illegal in those days. So was lying naked on a beach and having sex in public – never mind with non-whites! I was in a veritable minefield of danger. Good sex and real danger started holding hands and running the race together. Who would come first? Me? Or the cops?

Then one sunny day I opened my eyes, because the mouth down there on me was so gentle, soft and personal. Who was down there, making me happy? Not blond. Not brunette. Not even white. Coloured! What? Coloured? And probably without teeth! That's why it was so nice! Jesus, coloured! But so nice ...

Close your eyes and wait for it to finish and go away ...

But it didn't go away when I was finished. Arms around me and a soft mouth on mine. Coloured! Gentle and whispering. Caressing fingertips over baby-oiled back. His brown body rubbing against mine. Loving me like a fantasy and going further than anyone had ever dared. Nicer than I had ever thought possible. And when it was over I looked at his face for the first time and saw his eyes were blue. But I knew he had to be coloured, because he sounded coloured! I pushed him away and grabbed my things and ran for my life.

I had broken God's Law! I had broken the Immorality Act! Not to mention the Act Against Sex Between Boys, the Act Against Putting Your Penis Between the Thighs of a Naked Person on a Public Beach! Not to mention the Law Against Loving Across the Railway Line and the Barbed-Wire Fence?

God would punish me!

So, once again, as so often in the past six years, I was on my knees to Jesus. Ever since Countess Angelique had splattered my seed across my heavenly copy-book, I was spending more and more time on my knees saying sorry. This time it was tearful and terrible.

'I won't do it again ... never again!'

Real tears.

'Please forgive me. I didn't know he was coloured, God.'

I was lying to God! I could smell the boy was coloured! His hair smelt of firewood! His family didn't have electricity. They cooked on an open wood stove. His armpits smelt of musty-boy, because he didn't have those fancy sprays that made me smell like a white poodle.

'God, I mean I didn't know what was happening! I promise I won't do it again.'

I scarcely slept that night. Every time I woke I had an erection. I was dreaming about that rock in the sun, breaking God's Law and smelling the hair and the body of a boy who was not white and with whom sex was therefore a crime. I tried to stop those thoughts and think of good things. Like what? I'd cry and pray.

'Please God, help me to stop thinking about it!'

I even thought of killing myself, but then I took myself in hand, and once that splat was over, I wiped my tummy and managed, as always, to fall into a blissful after-action-satisfaction sleep. Even though I knew my cock would fall off the next day! I'd get cancer and die!

I didn't die. My cock didn't fall off either. It stood straight up and sniffed the air. It wanted more. And to cut again to the car chase, within days I was back on that rock waiting for the end of the world to come and come again! That musty boy with the gentle mouth and the blue eyes never came back. Others did. Some didn't smell of wood fires. They smelt of cheap cigarettes and cheaper aftershave, which they shared with me. I started smoking cheap cigarettes and wearing cheap aftershave and started feeling less white, and more real. We talked like all boys do and shared common experiences. Favourite comics? I'd buy them new. They'd have to find them third hand. Movies? I'd seen them in a cool white cinema, they on a flickering 16 mm screen in a township garage. We often talked about the sea around us. One boy's father was a fisherman.

'We have so much in common!' I said. 'My father loves fish!'

'Where does he catch? West Coast?'

'Catch? Oh please, dear. To eat!'

So his brown pa caught the fish that my white pa enjoyed in a five-star restaurant with lemon butter and no garlic.

They had lied to me. In my church and at my school. At home. In the newspapers and on the newsreels. They said:

'Apartheid is a Gift from God!'

'These are God's Laws, and if you break them you die! Love your neighbour, but don't get caught!'

I didn't die in a terrible blow of divine retribution! So where did the truth lie? If the Immorality Act wasn't what they said it was? If the Dutch Reformed Church was only white? Was it because they didn't want the smell of wood fires in the pews? If being human meant finding your own way and following your inner instinct, then being naked on that beach with confidence may have been the first step to being naked in the world with commitment! Stripped of all the deceit and disguise that comes with fear.

If there is nothing to fear, but fear itself, what's the problem?

Crabs!

One morning the itching was too much and I forced myself to look. I hated looking at the equipment, because I didn't think it was all that marvellous. Experience taught me that although medium-sized cars aren't stretch Cadillacs, they can go for a long time without breaking down. But what I saw down there was horrifying. A small flea-like thing with many little white legs was MOVING in my little forest of pubes!

Jesus-shit-whatthefuckisthis?

I'm dying!

Something terrible is happening to me! I've got beetle!

Beetle? No, *crabs*!

The terror. No one had ever told me about these things! That dirty boys have crabs and clean boys pick them up! Like mice in a dusty room, these goggas hop across from certain dusty crevices and corners. Not great news, but all homes have cockroaches if they're not looked after on a daily basis.

I didn't know! Again I wanted to kill myself, but knew they'd find my dead body swarming with feasting beasties! Oh, the shame! Oh, the punishment! Back on the knees ...

'Dear Jesus, I'm sorry, I've got ...'

Can't tell God I've got things that look like crabs. What to do?

Hey, do kids still get crabs today? Do they know what to do? Or is it just part of the modern landscape, like rape and abuse and death? Ignore it and it will go somewhere else? In 1964 it was death! Who could one ask? No one knew I was having sex with boys. I was normal! I could never let on that I was 'one of those'! I was trapped. Maybe I could say I was with a whore? Worse! A toilet seat? The cat?

The chemist.

'Can I help you?'

'I need ... something for a friend ...'

'For a friend?'

This was a chemist far away from home.

'Yes, a friend.'

This was a chemist who knew a crab-covered liar when he saw one.

'Can he come in and see me?'

'No!' the crab-covered liar spluttered.

'He's too ill?'

'Yes.'

The chemist took long pauses. The ticking of the large clock sounded like drumbeats to the gallows.

'What does your friend need?'

'Eh ... well, he's got a sort of ...'

'Fits? Seizures?'

'No.'

'Bleeding?'

'Eh, no ... more of sort of funny-like ... itching.'

It was out!

'Itching?'

'Allergy!' I said.

'Ah.'

Not so bad after all. Why hadn't I thought of allergy before?

'Yes,' I smile with medical confidence. 'Do you have anything …?'

'You mean for crabs?'

I nearly died. Everyone heard. The clock stopped ticking. It giggled!

'Crabs is not the end of the world, you know? Just put this on your genitals and around the testicles. And boil your underwear.'

I took the ticking time bomb from him and walked out trying to smile, probably looking like a guilty serial killer with crabs!

The chemist called after me.

'And Pieter, how's your father? I sing in his choir!'

Death by crabs!

I'm not alone here. I'd say everyone of my generation went through that cave of fear and terror as far as sex was concerned. How to do it? Which way to do it? And what could go wrong and, when it did, how to handle it? And suddenly finding that the smaller brain between the legs is more sensitive and more sensible than the brain-washed mass between the ears? To hell with the Immorality Act! Sex will happen!

Maybe the reason South Africa could so easily slip into a democratic jacket after 27 April 1994 was because we'd been practising for years. Breaking those laws that God himself would reject. Talking to each other in spite of those laws. Eating with each other, drinking with one another, fucking, sucking, licking, coming. And always going in fear of who would find out and what would happen. Many of those people aren't here. They were forced into suicide because of the disgrace and terror. Others carry the wounds of their punishments, now disguised by age. Or, like me, they never forget how our illegal love in those trenches formed the basis for our lives today.

Recently I was doing a new Evita Bezuidenhout show at a Cape Town theatre. There was a knock on the dressing-room door, which is rare. To find backstage is usually quite an achievement. I opened the door to a group of people. Small elegant children excited to be out at night. Little girls with ribbons in their hair, little handbags in gold chains and golden sandals. Twinkling eyes of expectation, and that frozen smile, the fear of meeting someone famous.

She wasn't there, I had to say apologetically.

'Mrs Bezuidenhout has already left,' I said to the smallest girl. Her face fell. 'But can I give her a message?'

'I liked her dress,' she whispered, like so many little girls who believed that the image on the stage was real.

'I'll tell her,' I whispered back, knowing that Evita's dress was hanging behind the door and that the most famous white woman in South Africa was in a box under the dressing table, where mercifully she belonged. I was introduced to the other people. Some women – 'my sister', a mother of the girls, 'my wife', 'her mother', maybe another grandmother.

A young boy stood aside and a man my age came towards me. He shook my hand.

'I'm Robert, Pieter, sorry to intrude. I just had to come and say hello and show you my family.'

I smiled and nodded, wondering who he was. An actor? A politician? The fact that he was coloured was neither here nor there, except more likely him being a politician in today's South Africa. I brought out some postcards of Evita from the dressing room and handed them out. Everyone had something to say and compared the poses: Evita with flowers, Evita with her Living Legacy 2000 award in San Diego USA, Evita with Mandela, Evita with Tutu, Evita with her little black grandchildren.

Then suddenly I knew who the man was. Robert smiled back and shrugged. What could I say? Thirty-five years ago? Then he was coloured and I was white. Now we're both middle-aged. He pulled the young boy nearer.

'He wants to meet you.'

The boy was nervous. His hand was cold.

'You came to his school with your AIDS programme.'

I looked at the boy. He smiled shyly and blushed.

'And how was it?' I asked.

'No. Okay,' the boy stammered. 'We must know about AIDS. It kills.'

He stumbled back into the safety of his family.

'Your son?' I asked Robert.

'Grandson. It's good what you do with the schools about AIDS. It's a terrible thing that's happening to the kids today.'

I nodded.

'I think we at least had an easier time way back then ...' I said.

He looked at me.

'Did we?'

His eyes were still as blue as then, when they reflected the sea and the sky.

Onslaughts Overseas

I lived many lives during the 1960s. The good student, the quiet son, the thinking person, the randy goat, the breaker of God's Laws and the white South African Christian who knew something was wrong but was too scared to ask. Until I found myself in London and watching the BBC.

My parents had rewarded me for a successful first year at university by sending me to Europe by Union Castle liner. It was 1965, and I was studying for a BA at the University of Cape Town; I was going to become a teacher. The trip gave me my first exposure to serious theatre and serious sex. It also showed me my first television, a jumble of images and sounds, from the satire of a post–Christine Keeler Britain to the game shows and variety concerts by the pop stars of the day. Among all this there was a black and white documentary about the latest atrocities committed by the apartheid regime. I wasn't quite sure who they were referring to. I wanted to get back to the theatre and the sex. But I remembered the shots. Of Afrikaans boys like me in a familiar uniform. Under the sacred orange, white and blue flag. With a mountain in the background that meant they were near my home, just across the railway line and beyond the fence. Shooting black people. Incessant screams and shots. Fat white arses in tight khaki pants, wildly beating at some small, thin, crying creature. Masses of abandoned single shoes lying like victims on the shattered tar. When I got back to Cape Town and my second year at UCT, where I abandoned teaching for acting, I mentioned the documentary. I was relieved to be told it was 'cheap communist anti-South African propaganda'!

In 1969 I was back in London to study at the London Film School. I left South Africa the day after Sophia Loren gave birth to her first child. At last she was a mother, and at last I could get on with my life! It was obvious then that in order to get anywhere in theatre, one had to go to London. But once there, it was obvious that they spoke their language better than us from the Cape!

I needed to find a reason to stay, a study permit, whatever would let me live in London. My sister Tessa had already started at the Royal Academy of Music, and when I found the London Film School, it presented the perfect reason to stay.

I went to the theatre all the time. The National was at the Old Vic, and there I would find a discount seat behind a pillar and watch Laurence Olivier, Maggie

Smith, Geraldine McEwan and Robert Stephens do Shaw, Shakespeare, Coward and Wilde. A crash course in Theatre. A quick study in Living.

I wrote my first play. It wasn't meant to be more than a letter in the shape of a drama, but it didn't end after two pages, and soon I had *Faces in the Wall*. Once my two years of study came to an end, with excellent qualifications that would assure me no work whatsoever, I managed to create the job of librarian, and so find the means to stay on at the London Film School for another two years. In fact, I was not going to go home. This was home. My vowels were rounded and my smile tight. I was becoming one of them.

During the long vacation of 1970, I convinced the school to let me use one of the ground-floor cinemas as a theatre and put on my play. I wrote to 140 people and asked them for financial assistance. Two answered with cheques: the Duchess of Bedford and Elizabeth Taylor! With their two hundred quid, I could shop around for second-hand cinema seats. That was the deal: you get us seats, and you can use the space.

The play had a wonderful opening night, with a telegram from Sophia and a letter from Marlene, and an audience of friends and famous people, but no critics. I'd forgotten to invite them, so our second night was empty, bar two people. I went to them before the performance. We were four on stage; they were only two. Would they prefer tickets for the Friday, when hopefully there'd be more of an audience? They were happy to stay, so I suggested that they at least sit together. The man was an American tourist who took us out for hamburgers afterwards, and the woman turned out to be Patricia Macnaughton, who asked me to contact her after the show. She's been my agent and friend ever since. Thank heavens we didn't cancel because of a small house!

This time in London I watched every documentary, although they were all about the same horror: Afrikaans police in blue. Table Mountain. Shots. Screams. And shoes lying on the tar. My people? Doing that to my people?

Why did I not know? Why did I have no answer to the constant question in London?

'What? Don't you know?'

'No. I did not know … don't know … no.'

'But Pieter, you were in the South African Navy in 1964 for a year doing your military service! Surely you knew?'

'No, honestly I didn't know. I broke my arm. I did a radar course. I knew nothing. Nothing.'

I couldn't tell them that all I got in the Navy was sex. In the showers, in the toilets, in the buses, in the dunes, in the jeeps, in the canteen after lights-out. In the bunks.

'Pieter, you then studied drama for four years. Cape Town University. Hotbed of political intrigue against apartheid! You must have known something then?'

'No, I was doing drama. I knew nothing.'

Couldn't tell them that all I got there was sex. In the dressing room, in the loos, in the wardrobe, under the stage, behind the curtains.

'But Pieter, the massacre at Sharpeville?'

'I was still at school then,' I said. 'I didn't know.'

How could I know, hiding under the desk in class, with police surrounding the school, as thousands of blacks marched past along Settler's Way on their long walk to freedom? To go to Parliament and ask for the hated pass laws to be repealed! Some years later I'd meet some people who had marched past us that day, jubilant and excited, hoping to make a difference. Marching and singing past the white Afrikaans school, while we were huddled in the classroom praying to Liewe Jesus!

'Please don't let the kaffirs kill us!'

The fear pumped up into iceberg-size by words: Mau Mau! Massacre! Communist!

In London they asked me about apartheid all the time. Those who came from the bloody streets of Belfast, the bloody ghettos of Lebanon, the bloody day-long wars of Israel, those bloody confrontations in Vietnam, some bloody chaos in a South American jungle, inevitable bloody suppression of Eastern Europe: they devoured my guilt and wiped their slates clean of their sins, while pissing on my picnic.

I could not defend myself or my roots or my friends or my land. Because I knew nothing. So when I said again that I knew nothing, they just threw me out of their favourite pub and called me a fucking Nazi.

I knew then what it felt like to be a fucking Nazi. Because I also knew nothing.

'And so, Pietertjie, you spent four years at the London Film School? What an experience it must have been.'

I know nothing, I should have said, but I lied and pretended to know everything about films and politics and life. Meanwhile I spent my time collecting pictures of Sophia, going to the Salisbury pub and getting picked up, and the rest of the time in the flat I shared with Tessa writing, reading and watching television.

Avoiding those weekly stories about people in the news who all looked like my Afrikaans family. Murderers and killers of children.

'Yes,' I'd say to change the subject, 'I spent all those years in London in the centre of the world, seeing films and theatre and studying.'

Which is true, except for those times that I found a sauna bath in the King's Road and would go and reverse into dark corners and play games in steamy hotboxes. And if there was a rash, there was always something on the National Health to cure it. Every fever had its jab. South Africa became smaller as I got older. The years went by from 1966 to 1972 while I was comparing Losey to Hitchcock and Bergman, Ingrid, to Bergman, Ingmar.

Somewhere in between all that, Helga Bassel died terribly.

Finding the Space

Losing a mother is something we all will go through in our lives. But it was not part of my life. It was my introduction to death. Since that terrible moment, nothing that happens can ever be more terrible. I am numb when it comes to death. I'm sorry when it happens, but someone has just gone through a door never to return? The last time my sister Tessa and I saw Ma was in London a few months before she died on 26 May 1969. She stood outside the Royal Overseas Club where she was staying, wearing her ostrich leather coat and a hat, looking like Ingrid Bergman. Elegant, smart and in control. Then she went home to Cape Town and lost control. She drove from Pinelands, through Newlands and past Kistenbosch, across Constantia Nek and into Hout Bay, not stopping until she reached the highest point on Chapman's Peak. She stopped the car, and left a note and the ostrich leather coat. And jumped onto the rocks below. Suicide is suicide, but looking back now, after thirty years that still feel like a moment, I'm certain the right medical treatment for depression and thyroid disorders would have made her life liveable. In 1969 that wasn't available, so in her worst moment of terror, she went and took our lives with her.

We all had to start again. Strangely, we all became better people through our shared loss and her divided energy filling us all. My father remaining at home with the memories and the guilt torturing him, and yet never imposing it on us. My sister, who through her bonds of music with her mother became a unique performer, with the lethal elixir of pain and passion keeping her at the top of her profession. And me? I started writing. Something my mother said I would do. Something I resented, as I wanted to be an Actor!

'So then, Mr Uys, you left London and went back to South Africa and got into the Struggle?'

I don't know, I should say. Even now, I was never in the Struggle. Certainly not a political one. Maybe always in a struggle to be brave enough to admit to being me. It took more than the four years at the London Film School for that. My attempts at writing for the theatre were giving me another voice. A chorus of voices. All the fantasies that had crowded my imagination for so long could now demand space on paper and a place on stage.

So, with a few plays in my bag and rounded vowels in my bek, I returned to

Cape Town on a wave of homesick sentiment. The first thing I saw from the deck of the liner that brought me home was the sheer cliff from which my mother had leapt. Table Mountain had become her tombstone. It was up to me to rediscover the Mother City in a mother's grave.

It took Mimi Coertse's voice to get me back to Cape Town permanently. A friend sent me a cassette of our great Afrikaner diva singing her famous boereliedjies. He said it would make me laugh. Those songs of the Karoo and the plaas and the Berge so Blou broke my heart. I realised that even though I had a green card and belonged to a union, and had an agent and even spelt my name Peter Ace, as no one could pronounce Uys, I would never be one of them. I was an African! And so I packed up a British life and took the boat back to my Afrikaner roots.

The day I heard about a new theatre opening off Long Street, I knew I wanted to be part of it. The Space Theatre was formed by Brian Astbury, his actress-wife Yvonne Bryceland and playwright Athol Fugard. It was to present non-racial theatre in Cape Town. It was a place where black and white performers could perform together on the same stage, which was illegal in the early 1970s. Blacks and whites sat together in the same audience, which was against the Group Areas Act.

The Space gave me the energy I needed. We did everything on virtually nothing. There was no money, and yet we presented great theatre. No sets, but huge imagination. No costumes, but everyone's borrowed furs. No props except my pa's favourite sofa and cushions.

'Nee, magtig, that's all my stuff!' Pa would boom forth from the front row on an opening night, and it was my fault. I borrowed Pa's things and then only asked if I could once what I'd borrowed was lost.

The Space Theatre was the greatest training in the coming battle for freedom – to work in a place where energy motivated, ideas matured, results mattered, but not in order to get rich. We were the poorest, thinnest fat cats, fed on the adrenaline of success. We wrote plays and directed them, acted in them and printed programmes. We hid blacks when white cops raided. Replaced banned plays within days with new works written within hours. This is where I came face to face with my fear of authority. The terror of 'what they would say and do'! Government censorship.

I wrote a few plays: *Selle Ou Storie* and *Karnaval*. About people I knew. About the people I 'were'. They were banned, not just for obscenity and blasphemy, but because they were in Afrikaans.

'Ons mense is nie so nie.'

Our people are not like that.

It was terrifying! Getting a telegram and a letter telling you to stop your subversive activity, accusing you of being anti-Afrikaans, obscene, blasphemous and 'setting the racial groups in disharmony against each other'. I didn't see that glorious irony at first. It wasn't fashionable being banned in the theatre in 1973. So I was turfed out of my home by a frightened Pa, who saw a cop behind every copse in the garden. I moved into a series of small rooms in Long Street, befriending cockroaches and whores, bergies and kittens, writing constantly. Soon I was the most banned playwright in South Africa, making me feel like Linda Lovelace with lockjaw!

Thanks to the South African government, who were banning my little plays, I eventually saw the light through humour. By inviting prominent Afrikaners to join his Censor Board, the Minister of the Interior, Connie Mulder, gave me my opening to reconcile with an angry Pa! My father loved films with a passion, which rubbed off on me. When I showed him the press cutting about the Censor Board, and he realised that he could see films for free, and uncut too, he was there like a shot. And he was accepted, of course. More prominent than Hannes Uys you couldn't be! What with Dr DF Malan, the first Afrikaner Prime Minister, as a cousin? And other lurking leading political lights as relatives, and some even called Oom!

Within weeks Pa started converting to my contempt for authority. How could I be frightened of the Censor Board? They were all idiots! They were senile old farts who were more interested in their ham sandwiches than looking at the films!

'Make fun of them, Bokkie!' Pa said.

To his credit, the country enjoyed the Mel Brooks classic *Blazing Saddles* with the famous farting scene intact, because this is when Pa arranged for the tea lady to come in noisily with her tray of sandwiches. His fellow censors were so busy sorting ham from pork from cheese, that the furious farts on the screen passed them by.

I learnt to know the oppressive laws better than the oppressors who were supposed to oppress with them. Because the Publications Act that came to be on an April Fools' Day in the early 1970s stated that one anonymous complaint was enough to be acted upon, I would write various anonymous letters of complaint against my own work.

A pink envelope from Mrs Smit of Diep River: 'Sies! It's horrible pornography!'

A white typed Basildon Bond from Dr Barnard of Sea Point: 'Do we need this subversive filth under the mantle of free speech?'

When the Board banned my plays, I could produce the original letters and prove that I had written them myself! What publicity! What fun! What laughter! *Selle Ou Storie* you could see but not read. *Karnaval* you could read but not see! How soon that paralysing fear became invigorating contempt. My fear danced and I laughed! The Publications Control Board became my Public Relations Department, inspiring publicity that money just couldn't buy. But it was too good to last, and eventually they just stopped coming to the shows.

The public, on the other hand, came to look and listen. What was working? Some of my Afrikaans plays were banned, but the English ones survived. *God's Forgotten* reflected a future in South Africa that chilled audiences. *Strike Up the Banned* was my first satirical revue that reflected the enemy in all its stupidity. But success didn't happen overnight.

I left the Space in 1974 and toured the province in a borrowed minibus, with a handful of actors and a stage manager, performing plays in small halls and at festivals. Because one play was allowed to be seen on stage, but not read, we had to do it by memory. But then you could translate *Selle Ou Storie* into English, and the stage manager could run the Afrikaans play on his English text. This was legal, because it was in another language! Eventually the strain of trying to make sense of absurd reality became too expensive.

A few self-produced efforts failed to break even. There was no chance of 'real' work in the theatre for me. The censors had been surpassed by an even more successful ally: self-censorship. The fear of what might happen decided what would happen.

'Write us a play, but nothing challenging or provocative.'

So I stayed without a job. It never crossed my mind to apply to one of the State Arts Councils, or the SABC. The trenches felt like home. An assistant editor on a Sunday paper gave me a weekly column. It went on for four years and helped me sharpen my pen on the weekly news. Like a Sunday cartoon, I would write about the absurd crap that was politics and the criminal shits who regarded it as democratic. With humour and a tongue firmly in the reader's cheek. It gave me the discipline of preparing a topical broadside within minutes. It also gave birth to the woman who still calls me a third-rate comedian with no imagination.

But at least Pieter-Dirk Uys has good legs!

Don't Cry for Me

Evita Bezuidenhout was just meant to be an Afrikaner woman at a Broederbond party in Pretoria. Once a month a column would swirl round her perfumed intrigue as she whispered the latest political gossip into my ear. It was at the height of the Information Scandal. State money was being stolen and a Prime Minister was kicked up into the Presidency to protect him from arrest. So many of the weekly goodies begging to be reported in the newspaper were not covered, simply because of the threat of censorship or being closed down. But somehow this woman in my column could say the unsayable, with a hint of innuendo and hammer blow of subtlety, and get away with it. After a year, someone called her 'the Evita of Pretoria'. A quick glimpse into a biography of Argentina's Mrs Peron gave me the ideal blueprint on which my Evita's life could be traced.

Ambitious small-town girl moves to city.

Becomes an overnight star in a state-subsidised film industry.

Meets a powerful up-and-coming politician.

Marries him and becomes his biggest asset.

That's where the musical parts from the soap opera. While a singing Madame Peron asks Argentina not to cry for her, Mrs Bezuidenhout becomes the South African ambassador to the fictitious black homeland republic of Bapetikosweti, infecting the precious seed of homeland development with crass humour and absurd truths.

The laughter that welcomed us into the laager of 1981 was shocking. We expected to be arrested. Instead we were sold out! It must have come at the right time. The people needed the relief of humour to counter the burden of fear. Drag was the cherry on the koek! All an Afrikaans man has to do to drive his peers crazy is put on a dress. They all scream 'moffie!', but in the dark everyone has a good time. In the theatre no one can see you laugh. Some came to laugh at themselves. Others were relieved to spurt forth the contempt they felt for their leaders. Even some of the leaders themselves were seen to laugh and applaud. Maybe it proved that, when all was said and done, there really wasn't anybody out there who blindly believed that apartheid was a sacred gift from God.

As part of PW Botha's 'reforms', the major theatres were eventually declared open to all races. The simple reason was that they were already illegally open, without permission. So blacks could come and laugh with whites, and often at whites!

Slowly the monoliths of fear dissolved into candyfloss, and people watched me do PW Botha. We remembered how he promised reform and got rid of the Immorality Act, the Mixed Marriages Act and the pass laws. Evita reminded them that he kept the Group Areas Act, so if whites and blacks got married, they couldn't live together legally! The madder and badder the real PW Botha became, railing at the world on television, the more the people remembered how they'd laughed at the joke. His days were numbered. Apartheid was dying. I was also laughing, all the way to the bank! It didn't happen overnight, but the cheque had grown from R20,50 a week to R15 000!

I'd hurtled from poor struggling performer to wealthy unemployed pariah, and since then I've been without a 'real' job. Unless you call being in charge of your own destiny and life a job? No boss, no contract, no small print, no meetings, no meetings about meetings, no permission sought, no permission refused, no ties, no suits, no bonuses, no salary, no intrigue, no bitterness. No fear.

If I do nothing, nothing will happen. If I do something, anything is possible!

The 1980s were so full of action and reaction that when I look back now it all feels like one long year, not a decade. Starting with the first one-man show *Adapt or Dye*, inspired by daily political see-saws and roundabouts, I then travelled the country with *Total Onslaught* and *Beyond the Rubicon*. Touring meant booking a theatre, sending out posters and publicity, driving the blue Volkswagen with the boxes on the back seat, finding a cheap meal, doing the show, getting out of the theatre as quickly as possible and disappearing into the safety of a Holiday Inn room. No parties. No after-show dinners. No dressing-room fan-fun. You just never knew who was there with a grudge and the law on their side. Criticising the government was one thing our 'free speech' allowed within reason, but making fun of them was something else.

Helen Suzman used to invite me to lunch in Parliament. I'd sit in the visitors' gallery looking down on PW Botha writing his notes, licking his lips, signing the death warrants. He once looked up at me, fixing me with that lizard's glare, and I nearly peed my pants! Those were the days when Helen was alone on the benches of blood, the small Madwoman of Houghton, 'Helen of Goy', railing with contempt against the bastards who couldn't get rid of her. She saved countless lives and protected millions of hopes. And all she said was: 'Free Mandela and end apartheid!' When portraits of former apartheid leaders were thrown out of

Parliament, even her picture ended up on the heap with Verwoerd and Vorster. Hopefully that has been remedied. Without Helen Suzman, there would be no rainbow, just many black sashes!

Using words like 'poep' and 'kak' was taboo. 'God' was a no-no. Not to mention 'democracy', 'one man, one vote' or 'majority rule'. Instinctively one used the banned ANC colours somewhere in the show, not always together, or at the same time. When possible, a quote from the banned biography of one of the Mandelas, his or hers, was woven into the rough fabric of satire. I call it 'satire' because there is no space here to try to analyse what it really was. The bitter black humour of our 1980s comedy was not satire. In the 1960s 'satire' described the brittle and brave attacks on what was cancerous in a relatively normal society. Look at America's Lenny Bruce and South Africa's Adam Leslie. In those days the clown had purple hair and a green nose, because the world was normal. But already in the eighties men were putting bombs in prams and women were smuggling drugs in their children's toys. Lockerbie disappeared under the debris of an exploded airliner. Hijackers broke the rules and often got away with murder. There were very few bitter jokes about those things. The classic definition was tragedy + time = satire. But the existence of apartheid in South Africa, where a skin that was white made kings, and a black hue created underdogs, was tragic and absurd. A pencil through the hair of a black person could determine his racial classification! There was no time for repose here. We had to scream our outrage from the stages of the nation. Rail at our accepted way of life. And so my comedy had to be real to reflect the green hair and the purple nose of a crazy world outside.

Evita went from cult to classic, appearing on the front pages with her glib admiration for PW Botha and her secret passion for Pik Botha, and condemning them all with her gushing praise. I could not appear on SATV for obvious reasons, but Evita Bezuidenhout was constantly invited and seen live on TV by a nation, still wondering who this woman was! Why did she make them feel so strange?

Her family also gave me the chance to reflect the contrasts in the Afrikaner. Her husband Oom Hasie was a former cabinet minister in the government of HF Verwoerd. He had two portfolios: Minister of Black Housing and Minister of Water Affairs. And he combined his two portfolios by building a black township in a dam! He was then found on the backseat of his Ford Fairlane in 1959 in the parking area of the Grand Hotel in Laagerfontein, having sex with a black woman! Sies!

Evita's daughter Billie-Jeanne was a go-go dancer at the Bapetikosweti casino, who fell in love with the son of the President of the homeland. She eventually married Le Roy Makoeloeli and gave Evita three black grandchildren! Evita's twin sons were two sides of an Afrikaner coin. De Kock was gay and Izan a neo-Nazi. I performed them all at some stage, especially in the play *Farce About Uys* and the film *Skating on Thin Uys*. Somehow they reflected many sides of me – Evita the actress, Oom Hasie the conservative, Billie-Jeanne the kaffirboetie, De Kock the moffie and Izan the fascist!

An Afrikaans journalist fired the feared gay question at me in Bloemfontein. 'So tell me, are you queer?'

Being queer in 1983 would have suited everyone. Put Pieter-Dirk Uys in the pink corner and blame that for everything. So I gave a cryptic reply.

'I'm queer on Monday and Friday, heterosexual on Tuesdays and Thursdays. Wednesday I'm bi, Saturday I do it myself and Sunday I rest!'

Ironically, no journalist ever asked Evita such pertinent questions. She wouldn't have understood anyway. To her gay means happy.

Evita doesn't use bad language, nor does she blaspheme. That is her only strength, and the reason she is the Queen Mum to so many families today is probably due to that. The fact that she tells the truth is okay. We don't mind someone telling us that people were killed by our policy. It's the words 'poep', 'kak' and 'God' that we won't tolerate!

Maybe she also saved my life? Who knows if an Afrikaans actor dressed up in drag and making campy comments about those in power would enrage them to take up arms? The phone at home was tapped, but that became a status symbol and a good punchline! Can anyone phone a number, be held up by a message and wait for the bleep, and then issue a death threat? They tampered with my car once by taking the four bolts out of the left back wheel. The hubcap fell off as I started to drive. I saw the empty screws and remembered what Doris Day did in one of her movies. So I took one bolt from the other three wheels, and could travel with three bolts on each of the four wheels and live. Poisoned meat thrown over the wall for my cats? They were vegetarian. I only knew about the poison when the gardener had a sore tummy after finding and eating the gift!

After a show at the State Theatre in Pretoria in 1984, I was stopped in the parking garage by three very large Afrikaner policemen. This was it! They were enraged.

'Pieter-Dirk Uys, now you go too far! You mess around with the Afrikaans language! You bugger around with the Afrikaans culture! You make us Afrikaners look like Nazis, but, hell, you've got nice legs!' They left with autographs!

Ten years passed like a year, doing that singular tango in front of a firing squad. It was Theatre. It was Comedy. It was easy to move quickly because I was alone. I was also a white Afrikaner. If I'd been black? They asked me that in Australia on my first trip outside the laager in the late 1980s.

'Pieter Dyk-Ars, you're a white Afrikaner making fun of apartheid. If you were black, what would you be doing?'

No one had ever asked me a question like that before! On South African TV it was always only about Evita's dresses and Pik Botha's fan mail. This was live and in the Real World! I couldn't say what I usually did: I don't know. I had to find an opinion.

'If I was black ... I'd be in Lusaka making bombs!'

That was my answer, and I didn't sleep for a month in case anyone had heard and told someone back home. The braver I thought I was, the more pressure was put on Pa. By now the political relatives were already ganging up on their cousin and threatening him with financial demands on his loans and mortgages 'if your son does not start behaving as we expect him to'. Fortunately I was earning more than Pa could lose. There was a good cheque each month that allowed him to travel and relax.

'But if you argue with me about politics,' I warned him, 'I'll stop the cheque and you'll be poor!'

It worked, and even though it must have riled him to be controlled, Pa knew that my politics were not for turning. His criticism of my work was invaluable. Pa was a very good average member of my audience. He hated me swearing on stage. I'd call it effective comedy and a wake-up call, but maybe he was right.

'Bokkie, why do you always have to use those words in the first ten minutes? I hate hearing those words, vieslike woorde! They make me go deaf and blind and I want to leave. You put your finger in my eye! If you want me to listen, why don't you tickle me behind my ear so I giggle, and when I turn to see what's happening, my eye will find your finger?'

Starting with *Adapt or Dye*, the stage shows were put on video – back in the days when video was a novelty and no one thought anyone would see it. At least I'd have a video to send to my great love and inspiration, Sophia Loren. So, in 1982, *Adapt or Dye* went into the video rental shops and to everyone's amazement broke all records. The Censor Board were forced to react. They put a 2–21 age restriction on that video and all subsequent videos of mine. What a gift! As a result everyone over two and under twenty-one watched those shows, and within seven years I had an audience of a few million in South Africa, filtering their political fears through the web of political comedy.

There was no light at the end of the political tunnel. We lurched from one law to another edict, from states of emergency to states of terror. Sanctions and boycotts isolated the country. The spectre of a final bloodbath to finish off apartheid loomed on the horizon. The humour became more brutal, less funny, often surreal. One started moving away from punchlines and jokes and towards sketches of people trapped in the quicksand of evil and fear. I did a sketch of a political wife trapped in her addiction to pills and booze. A chilling indictment. Then the Pretoria arms merchant with a paralysed son fighting a pointless war on the border. Nothing funny there. The coloured boy remembering his proud grandmother and her decline into illness and death because of the Group Areas Act.

Some people reacted with annoyance.

'You can't do this! We don't want to feel those emotions! Make us laugh!'

Evita made us laugh. She reminded us that a future without democracy was impossible, and prepared for the worst, trying to make friends with blacks and attempting to pronounce the names of her kitchen maids and gardeners, whom she now called 'pastural plurals'. PW Botha became more bizarre by the day and my impersonation of him became more like a Muppet on speed. I even did his voice on stage for the Spitting Image puppet at the 'Two Dogs and Freedom' concert in London in the late 1980s.

Then suddenly it all changed gear. PW Botha fell off his plinth and was wheeled to the Wilderness, where he belongs. FW de Klerk took over as leader of the National Party and as President of the country. While he looked like PW with his bald head and glasses, that is where the similarity ended. De Klerk gave us pretoriastroika, and our walls fell as they did in Berlin. Suddenly it was legal to be illegal! The black political parties were unbanned. The ANC showed a real face and a smile. The feared Communist Party had to step out of rumour into life, and was much smaller than we were led to believe. And Nelson Mandela was released from prison.

Born in the New SA

If I were to write the story of my life, it would start: 'On 11 February 1990 I was released from life imprisonment in a Whites Only jail.'

I remember lying on my bed in my Melville cottage on that afternoon, watching the release of Nelson Mandela on TV. The day before, a newspaper had printed the first picture to be seen of this man since his imprisonment twenty-seven years before. This man, who in the nearly three decades of my existence had been portrayed by propaganda as the most dangerous enemy of the South African state. The word 'murderer' was usually added by those in power, who in turn murdered in the name of their security and no one's freedom.

The world had to wait to see its most famous political prisoner. Nelson Mandela was late for those last few steps on his long walk to freedom. It is said that Winnie held up the proceedings in true superstar style. Anything is possible. When he appeared at her side, tall and smiling that miraculous sunrise, the world changed from static to fast forward. Everyone has their own story of that moment.

Evita Bezuidenhout was also watching television in her Embassy in Bapetikosweti. She remembers:

> Actually it was in the kitchen, because our main TV set had been stolen the week before. I was there with all my staff. I didn't realise how many of them spoke Xhosa. We watched the scene at the Victor Verster Prison. A nice Boland day. Boring television commentary about leaking taps and cows, probably to fill the time. I looked from one black face to another. So many and they all looked alike?
>
> Who was Nelson Mandela? I pointed at a man.
>
> 'There he is!' I said.
>
> My staff laughed.
>
> 'No, madam, that's Peter Magubane from the *Star*.'
>
> 'There's Mandela!'
>
> 'No, madam, that's a garden boy ...'
>
> 'How will I know when Nelson Mandela appears?' I asked in desperation.
>
> 'The man whose hand Winnie is holding will be Nelson Mandela,'
> said the cook.

'Not necessarily ...' I breathed softly.

And then I saw him.

The man who could have spoken like Robert Mugabe.

The man who could have said: 'Take the farms and kill the whites!'

And they would have killed every white in South Africa and no one in the world or on CNN would have even looked in our direction.

But he didn't say that.

He spoke Afrikaans. He formed a government with the party that had imprisoned him. He wore the No. 6 Springbok rugby jersey. He had tea with Mrs Verwoerd.

Nelson Mandela came out of jail a reformed member of the National Party!

Suddenly the white tribe was faced with the reality of the old enemy. We looked. We listened. We tried to remember what we were looking for. What sign of hatred and revenge? We only found compassion and a smile. Our fear was suddenly less fearful. We fell in love with this guardian angel, who reconciled with humour and healed with tact. The enemy was gone.

Whom do we fear now?

Our own images in the mirror filled that space. We were now free to think and have opinions. We could change those opinions if they were wrong. We could be smacked if they were offensive.

Those all-powerful signs on the beaches and the public parks were going fast. Soon, former political prisoners were buying old WHITES ONLY and NO DOGS OR NATIVES ALLOWED boards and mounting them on their lounge walls in their new Houghton homes as trophies from a bygone barbarian age. Apartheid was in a terminal coma. We could gather round its deathbed and look at it properly for the first time. Not a giant in invincible armour, but a tall thin skinny blind and deaf mute that had flailed out wildly at anyone and anything for forty years with a bloody sledgehammer to destroy everything in its path. Now suddenly we all knew it was a failure. Now we all felt part of the Struggle to end it. Supporters of apartheid were as rare as original jokes. Democracy flooded the land and all was well with South Africa.

While Mandela was the spiritual Father of my Nation, my real Pa died in 1990. Again the freeway of my life suddenly ended on a bridge that led to nothing, poised in the sky like the famous no-go bridges on the Cape Town Foreshore.

The last of my fences was gone. I was now on the edge of the cliff, with no parent to protect me from falling. My vertigo prevented me from ever looking down, but I know it is high and it's far to fall. The winds up here are pulling and tugging, but one somehow learns to lean into the gusts and balance on a hair.

Now there was no one to protect me against anger. I found out how, throughout the eighties, Pa had been a soft target for those bastards in high places. Ironically, they were often second cousins, and they made his life hell with their insinuations and snide remarks about his communist, obscene, blasphemous son! He never let me down, or tried to steer me towards the safe correct shores of collaboration. Pa hung in there with me, and even in his moment of death showed me energy in dying. He was on his way somewhere else. There was no time to linger. He went into another room, and I felt him take my love with him to light up the way. Whatever happened at that moment, it turned my page for me. I had turned fifty and now I was my own father. I was also my own mother. I had become grown up.

Pieter-Dirk Uys, two years old, in his slippers, dressing gown, bib, and grandma's hat – 1947

Helga Bassel, Pieter's mother

Ma, Pieter, Pa and Tessa. Chapman's Peak – 1949/1950

Pieter and Tessa playing in the garden of their Pinelands home – 1949

Ready for a fancy dress party – May 1954

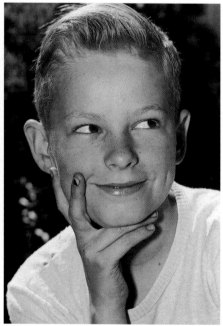

Pieter – 1958

Pieter, Ma, Tessa and Pa at *Sonskyn*, Pinelands –1957

Presenting flowers to Marlene Dietrich on her last performance
at the Alhambra Theatre, Cape Town – April 1966

Going on tour with *Adapt or Dye* – 1981/82

With Tessa – 1987

Evita Bezuidenhout

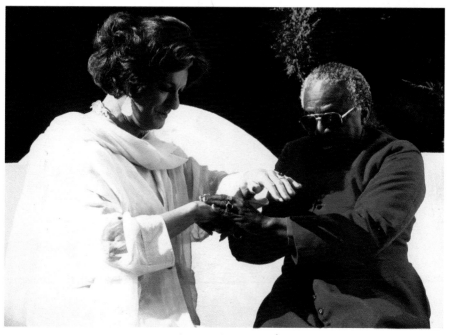

Evita and Desmond Tutu compare rings

Ouma Ossewania Poggenpoel and her daughters: Evita Bezuidenhout and Bambi Kellermann

Evita's son De Kock Bezuidenhout, dressed up as Queen Elizabeth II,
at the V & A Waterfront, with fellow queens, welcoming the arrival of the
royal yacht *Brittania* and the Queen, on her visit to South Africa – 1995

Semen, Blood and Urban Legends

While South Africa had been struggling against apartheid, the rest of the world had been battling for fifteen years against a similar giant. This one they could not see. HIV/AIDS had become the number one killer in Third World countries, and took as its First World rewards Rock Hudson and Freddy Mercury, as well as countless ordinary victims of a plague that had no cure. With apartheid on our plate, there could be no other issues on the menu that demanded attention. Locals saw the AIDS epidemic as something far away, in a hemisphere across the globe. Because most of our television originated in Britain or the USA, the red ribbons on the dress suits and designer fluff of superstars and icons constantly reminded us of their public commitment to make the world aware of this new terror. But most South Africans, white and black, weren't that concerned.

It was a gay disease, and most of us weren't gay. Certainly not blacks, according to Winnie Mandela, who made it her personal crusade and defence against a kidnapping charge.

'Blacks are not homosexual!'

That was quite funny at the time, coming from one of the biggest fag hags in politics. Those who did not laugh just went deeper into their township closets. No one knew anyone suffering from AIDS. It was always someone else. Always somewhere far away. We all felt sad when reading about the losses in other lands, but didn't linger on that press report. It was something we didn't want to think about. Glossy new South Africans seldom saw the obituaries clustered in alternative American newspapers. *Variety* was reflecting the fact that the theatre was losing its memory. Stage managers and dancers, chorus boys and props people were dying of AIDS, or 'pneumonia' as it tended to be noted even there, and there was no one to fill the gap. The officer class of culture was dying, and the foot soldiers were at a loss how to replace that experience with mere talent.

I had already brushed up against the reality of AIDS, and the incident had left me paralysed with fear. In 1981, on a visit to the city that never sleeps, I heard about something horrible breeding in the dark chambers of Manhattan's sauna baths. I loved the excitement of those sex-seeped dungeons of lower Greenwich Village, where you could spend naked nights prowling around dimly lit passages, peering into dark rooms and watching other people do things you'd not yet managed to work out for yourself. By now I was so pissed off with being primly on the shelf, I was determined to dive into the deep end and see what happened. Maybe in the dark no one would notice the off-putting details of a balding, overweight, beaky-nosed blob, and give their all? It hadn't yet got that far, but the time was close. Poppers made the surrender so much more comfortable – inhibitions flew away and the animal took over. Happily my small pet was still sleeping with only one eye open, not yet roused to roar.

I shared a cab with a couple I'd met at a party. We were all going down to the Village, they to their apartment and I to a night at the Baths.

'Where can we drop you off?' they asked.

'Just down on the corner of ...' I mumbled, not wanting to be specific.

'You're not going to the Baths?' she said, disturbed.

'No, I'm meeting a cousin at the bookshop.'

She sighed with relief. Or did the outrageous lie make the smirk sound like a sigh?

'Good. My dad's a medical consultant around here. They've found a killer bug in the Baths.'

My heart stopped.

'Oh? Really?'

'Something seems to be thriving in the damp darkness, and the queens are dying,' she went on.

'Come on,' growled her boyfriend with his big hands and large shoes. 'It's some virus that the queers are passing on through anal sex.'

'Oh?'

I saw my dreams of being impaled by Vlad the Impudent fade to nothing.

She looked at me with a frown.

'Haven't you heard about this gay sickness?'

I gulped.

'No, I'm from South Africa.'

'I know,' she purred, 'but you are gay?'

'No,' I shot back as the cock crowed thrice.

They dropped me at the corner. I waited till their cab disappeared up the street, then walked across to the heavy wooden door of hell. I stood for some time, thinking. The small brain between the legs was naturally shouting encouragement in Afrikaans!

'Rubbish, man, you won't pick up that sort of thing. Just go in and look! Just think: Gang bangs! Big cocks! Porno movies! This is New York, not Newtown, Joburg!'

The other brain, between the ears, was panicked into its usual terror mode.

'Yes, but what happens if something happens?'

'Nothing happens, man!' screamed the small brain. 'You're you! Fat, boring and on the shelf! Give me a break. I need to go!'

I went home and strangled my desire! There were no other bodily fluids, and I survived another day without the gay plague.

In 1984, again in New York, I visited a friend who took me to see a friend of his. A photographer famous for his pictures of New York men: muscular, naked, provocative, sexy. I'd memorised a few in past moments of self-abuse and was keen to meet this person. He had AIDS. Suddenly there I was, face to face with someone out of Auschwitz. He looked ancient. He had lesions on his face. He was sweating. The table was covered in a Manhattan skyline of bottles full of various herbal remedies. He coughed and struggled for breath. There were two other people with him, a man and a woman. And my friend embraced him and they held each other and laughed about something. They laughed a lot.

Laughter with all that fear? Did no one see what I saw? How could anyone laugh? It all sounded as if it was happening under water a million miles away. All I could think of behind my frozen smile of hello was: Must I touch him? Will I get it from his sweat? Don't have anything to drink out of his glasses! Or eat! Or use the toilet! Dear God, never the toilet! And must I breathe here?

Then this dying old man, who was my age, turned to me and put out his hand. His smile was still dazzling, his eyes were bright and filled with laughter.

'And you're the one who is this Evita, this Paulette Goddard of the Great Trek? I've got some of the postcards! Pity I'm a bit off colour today. We could have done a photo session.'

What? Mrs Bezuidenhout with a black dildo up her arse? Handcuffed and in a sling, dressed in leather? I heard myself laugh politely and say: 'That would be fab!'

I went closer to him in a trance. I took his hand. It was cold. I felt the bones in his fingers. He pulled me towards him. I had no strength to pull away. I saw his pale lips crinkle into a bunch of dead roses, and he kissed me. Not on my cheek. On my lips!

'Welcome to New York, darling,' he rasped.

The rest of the visit was drowned out by the Funeral March booming in my head. I'd been infected! No doubt about it. I was going to die of AIDS. I saw myself sit there in that elegant apartment and laugh when they laughed and nod agreement and shake my head and coo delight and look sad. I was being so me, so unaffected. So calm. Acting normal while screaming for help inside.

We eventually left and walked down the beautiful New York streets as the autumn sun winked through the trees.

'He's looking much better,' said my friend.

I just nodded. I'd seen death. No, actually I'd seen an ill man on a particularly bad day. He lived for another two years, cared for by his friends who loved him and laughed with him. And loudly too, when remembering that silly little queen from South Africa who looked as if she'd seen a ghost. She had.

So, by the time the 1990s happened and Mandela had freed me from the jail of being white, I knew there was something out there that had my name on it. This was now ten years after the last orgy in a dark room of a New York brothel. Ten years of watching every pimple, worrying about every bump, panicking about every pain. The worst that happened was hay fever, but then in my family everything tended to be hay fever. Even as my father was suffering from a heart problem that eventually killed him, it was just 'damn hay fever'! But AIDS was still the gay disease, and it was usually in those secret circles where the subject came up. More of us were talking about it in Cape Town. South Africa didn't seem so far away from the rest of the world any more.

Black and White in Drag

In the past, most black politicians were banned, and those who were visible were so unfamiliar that impersonation was difficult. We'd see that meddlesome priest Desmond Tutu for twenty seconds on the eight o'clock news, as he was taking in a breath to forgive the world. All we saw was a mad little black goblin spreading his talons to tear at the fabric of our fragile Christian boer-democracy. He was the first to ask me: Why didn't I do blacks in my show? It had never occurred to me that I could. After all, I was white.

'Is there apartheid in your chorusline, Pieter-Dirk Uys?'

And so I did my impersonation of Archbishop Desmond Tutu. He came to see the show and said: 'You're so naughty, it's nice. But you still don't have enough rings on your fingers!'

Within days, a little box of theatrical signet rings to grace the fingers of a Dame Edna arrived!

Another significant gift from a potential target was a colour photo of Winnie Mandela, taken during the eighties at the height of her political purity. Turbaned, beaded, coppered and draped in her magnificent ethnic beauty, with the words: 'Dear Mr Uys, the day you do me, please look like this. We admire you – Winnie Mandela'.

It was like having contact with a divine superstar! Remember, then she was the cousin of the real madonna! Blameless, pure and passionate. Ironically, when I now do Winnie Mandela on stage, I do look like that photograph. I have added the tyre bangles and matchbox earrings and the vibrant madness that has made her our black cat with more than nine lives.

Targets for black comedy in the 1994/95 honeymoon were focuses of admiration and joy. Desmond Tutu, Nobel Prize winner, but always pretending to be no more than Madiba's stand-in, kept the wheels of the media churning. Winnie was tumbling off her pedestal on a weekly basis. Behind the scenes she was directing her private war against a local media that was driving her out of focus, no doubt helped by her own carelessness and impending madness.

Cape coloured characters never felt 'black' to me, as they were so much a part of my heritage and affections. Always remembering those illegal liaisons on the salty rocks of the past, I happily researched and found a seventeenth-century matriarch of the Uys clan, called Wilhelmiena Opklim – which could only mean she was coloured and traded as a whore between the Cape and Stellenbosch. While it drove Pa to apoplexy, it made me feel like I belonged as an Honorary Coloured. Indian accents always made me feel like Peter Sellers. I was more at home in my own skin: Afrikaans spoken as English with guttural gasps and nasal snorts.

My tribe was still in charge. While calmly opening the front door to the former enemy, and with reconciliation as the catchphrase, we were all poised to run to the hills with the family jewels once the temple columns collapsed. But they didn't even wobble! With uncomfortable ease, the former mortal foes shed their bush camouflage and settled down to the best wine and finest food, and talked for a year. The National Party and the African National Congress shared a common bond and a rare treasure: South Africa. But, more than anything else, they had two leaders who had nothing to lose. Nelson Mandela had lost everything for twenty-seven years and knew he would be given anything he asked for. FW de Klerk had had everything for a lifetime, and knew he would get history on his side by giving it away.

Did I still have a job? The bad guys were going so fast, who could replace them? Would I find myself without a target once apartheid was gone? And when would my honeymoon with the new democracy end and the rainbow marriage begin? Which meant: get a decent job because the battle has been won? Get back on stage and test the waters with your tongue!

When I did my election show *One Man One Volt* at the Market Theatre in Johannesburg in April 1994 as we were sailing into the new sunrise of freedom, there was violence in the streets. The audience had seen their destination on the evening news. They were coming to the lower part of Bree Street, while three blocks up, all hell was breaking loose! They were going to the Market Theatre to be entertained. So, after having kissed their children and belongings goodbye, they loaded the Rottweiler into their Mercedes cars, cocked their pistols and ran the gauntlet of red traffic lights to get to the Newtown Precinct, hoping they lived to tell the tale.

Urban legends resurfaced and raced into headlines. People were scared to come to the theatre, because of impending violence! They were scared their cars would be stolen! They feared an empty house on returning home! These things happened to a few people, but not to many. In fact, during my season of *One Man One Volt* at the Market, the few car windows broken were because the Rottweilers couldn't get fresh air!

The SABC filmed my show to present to the nation on the night of the election, but banned it because of political pressures! So much for a change! It was a strange and wonderful experience, preparing a satirical portrait of the past, present and future. To look back, hopefully not in anger, but acceptance and hope for tomorrow.

The unbearable tensions leading up to the first election created a powder keg of emotions. Some South Africans were desperate to get out. Foreign cameramen were desperate to get in. Everyone needed a passport to vote, and votes were needed so passports were easily available. Even German tourists who went into shops for change came out as new citizens. Chaos ensued with a smile and a dance. We voted over four days. Millions of South Africans queueing up all over the land, waiting to make their mark. Having waited for centuries under the worst conditions of prejudice and fear, they could now happily wait through nights and days, rain and sunshine, to be free.

The world watched their television sets that morning of 27 April 1994. Most wanted things to work; some were hoping to sip health coffee over a new bloodbath. No one liked white South Africa for what it had done. Few wanted us to get away with it. Then they saw the queues. Miles of men and women and young people, snaking across fields and squares, over hills and dried riverbeds. Curled in a circle within a square to make place for everyone.

Everybody voted! Some people voted more than once! It didn't matter, because on every level it was free and fair! The world rediscovered what democracy meant to everyone on those magical days. How personal democracy is. How sacred it should be and how imperative that everyone use their right to vote.

Nelson Rolihlahla Mandela was sworn in before the world on 10 May 1994. It didn't happen in Soweto, or Alexandra township, in Sharpeville or the Transkei. The inauguration of the first black democratically elected President took place in the embrace of the Union Buildings in Pretoria, overlooking the Jacaranda City towards the Voortrekker Monument. Virtually on the spot where the murdered architect of apartheid, Hendrik Frensch Verwoerd, was buried in 1966.

President Nelson Mandela said the words: 'Never, never and never again shall it be that this beautiful land will again experience the oppression of one by another.'

I knew he was right. As long as we are still alive and sane enough to remember how terrible the fear was, it can never happen again! I was wrong. It has happened again! Today the fear is worse than in those terrible days. Whereas apartheid became the banner to rally the people, AIDS is the shame to scatter the community. As Nelson was blessing us, the new black plague was getting closer.

While we celebrated our freedoms and some took advantage of the lack of control, the virus came closer. The trucks roared across borders like stampeding rhino, from Zaire through Harare into the Northern Province on their way to Durban. Each time they stopped, the exhausted drivers joined in the celebration of the new freedom. It was all love and no wars. Just whores and easy sex without condoms, because up to now there was no problem. This was not Uganda! Let us love and celebrate! So, with each unprotected physical climax the freeways for the HI-virus widened. If only this was more like Uganda! There would have been a large billboard with the face of the President saying: Protect yourself against AIDS!

President Mandela was busy reconciling a divided nation. Zulu and Xhosa had to be appeased. White and black had to respect each other's baggage. Bushmen and traditional leaders had to get letterheads. Everyone wanted cellphones and gold-rimmed spectacles!

Auditioning for Amandla

Meanwhile, I was trying to find my way along these newly lit boulevards of free speech, the little yellow beam of my ancient torch neutralised by the glare of openness and transparency. My battle with censorship and the Oom-sindroom was over. Apartheid was gone. We'd won. I'd written myself out of a job! No more bread and botha. Where to now?

Within months of the election I had completed shooting a television chat-show series called *Funigalore*, in which Mrs Bezuidenhout interviewed the new leaders and old enemies. I had sent a fax to all the most prominent members of the political spectrum, from Nelson Mandela to Freedom Front leader Constand Viljoen. Mandela said yes; Viljoen said no. It was an extraordinary experience, detailed in the book *Funigalore*, which describes the scenes behind the show. A middle-aged man dressed as the most famous white woman interviews some of the most important leaders of the new democracy. And they all treated her like a lady!

The Speaker of Parliament, Dr Frene Ginwala, dressed her in a sari in the staid dining room in Parliament. Minister without Portfolio and guru of the RDP, Jay Naidoo, danced the tango with her. Roelf Meyer took her to a game park. Mac Maharaj, Minister of Transport, took her to Robben Island and showed her his cell. Nelson Mandela beamed and said: 'Ah, Evita, you look very beautiful!'

And the crown prince of the movement, Secretary-General of the ANC and former trade union leader Cyril Ramaphosa, took her trout fishing! It was during that bizarrely wonderful afternoon, standing waist-deep in a lake, wearing huge rubber dungarees and waving around fishing rods, that he asked if I would do the cabaret for the ANC Congress in December, which was then some months away. Obviously the answer was yes. I didn't think he would remember.

Cyril did not forget.

And so it came to pass that I arrived in Bloemfontein for my big audition for the ANC government.

It was 16 December 1994. We Afrikaners knew it as Dingaan's Day, the Day of the Vow, Blood River Day or Geloftedag. The ANC remembered that date for other reasons. It was the birthday of the liberation movement! And so the Congress was being held in this bastion of Afrikaner Nationalism for many reasons. Bloemfontein is in the centre of the country and where the ANC was originally formed. There was enough space to house all the delegates in hotels, and throw the party for the Party on the campus of the University of the Orange Free State! A bit like doing *Fiddler on the Roof* in Nuremberg!

I got there early enough to see that the stage was too high, the lights too small, the microphone too weak, the venue too large. It was like an aircraft hangar. Empty, it looked like a small town. Full, it was surely not big enough to hold all the guests? Two thousand executive comrades were expected. And there was no dressing room! They found a ladies' toilet outside and put a sign on the door: No Entry. Inside I found a glorious performer I'd known since early Market Theatre days. She was going to sing for Mandela! She was furious.

'When will they wake up that we artists are not animals?' she spat. 'Look at this crap! A lavatory!'

We both rolled red onto our pursed lips.

'And if I am to be the Streisand singing for my Clinton, why do they make me feel like rubbish?'

She borrowed my eyeliner. I used some of her powder.

'And you, darling? What is Evita going to wear?'

I showed her what was in the carrier bag. A kaftan of sequins in the design and colour of the new Y-front flag. A Chris Levin original.

'God, it's not fair. They'll see you on the moon! With that crap lighting I'll merge with all the black curtains!'

It was not a large ladies' toilet. So she and I could not comfortably stand together in front of her small hand-mirror. I said I'd wait outside for her to finish, as she was on first. A crowd of waiters and waitresses with trays of glasses, bottles and beers raced by. Few noticed the white man sitting on a box wearing false eyelashes and a gash-red mouth. That was minor in comparison to what they were experiencing. They were the white Afrikaans students of the university! They were serving those who now governed, but who used to serve them. I savoured the moment and saluted their style. They were charming and friendly, and not a k-word passed their lips.

In our ladies' toilet it was different!

'Shit! I voted for this party and now they treat me like a kaffir!' my co-star wailed.

A bang on the door alerted us to the fact that the sign had fallen off. There stood a cluster of comradiennes, dressed to kill and dying to wee.

'Sorry, this is not a toilet,' I red-lipped. 'It's a dressing room.'

They were not impressed.

'It says Toilet!' one important lady articulated carefully.

A torrent of Xhosa from within the small space put her in the picture.

'What now?' she said, exasperated with the strain of being in power with a full bladder! I pointed to the row of portable toilets on one side of the building. The ladies looked at them. Then coldly at me.

'Did I fight the Struggle to go to a Zozo hut?'

And they surged off to their respective limousines and were driven back to their hotels to pee! Long live the Struggle! I was told to have Evita ready by eight. In my cabaret I would start as Mevrou, then strip her off to reveal PW and Pik Botha, then Desmond Tutu, and possibly Margaret Thatcher. Nelson Mandela I'd keep for last. Winnie Mandela was in the bag, just coming along for the ride. I would not be doing her here! Nelson Mandela didn't need to be reminded of that woman! We waited and re-rolled red on our lips, powdered our noses and fluffed our hair. African Time took over, and soon it was past nine and the President had not even made his speech. He was to be followed by a massed women's choir, but because of the lateness of the proceedings I was told: Be ready to go on after Madiba!

So, in the sequinned kaftan in the colours of the new flag, the carrier bag full of props and costumes for the chorusline, I went nearer to the doors and waited. This was a hangar, so the doors were really slabs of steel, each the size of a small parking lot. The evening was warm. Stars twinkled in the heavens. Outside on the tarmac stood the whole South African Cabinet, smoking and drinking, talking and laughing, while inside, on a faulty sound system, the most famous South African was making his speech. His Donald Duck tones came and went as the speaker faded and surged:

'We in the ANC ... a collective leadership ... however as we ... reconciliation ... the past ... the present ... the future ...'

A minister waved at Evita and she waved back. Word had got round that she was there. More ministers waved. One came right up and peered first-hand at this most famous white Afrikaans woman.

'I'm sorry, Madam, I don't know who you are,' he twinkled.

'Don't worry, I don't know who you are either,' Evita trilled.

A bodyguard was close at hand, staring unamused at this spectacle. Who was this white woman? Why had he not been briefed? And what was in her bag? A bomb?

I was aware of his hostile stare and tried to avoid eye contact, which in Evita-guise is difficult. The guard fingered his holster. That was definitely a gun in his pocket! He wasn't just pleased to see me! A senior Minister waddled over and kissed Evita's cheek. The guard was guarded. The Minister smiled at him and waved him away. Eventually the guard reversed, filled with justified suspicion.

'Darling Evita,' the Minister gushed.

'Darling Comrade,' the tannie retorted, not having a clue who he was.

Applause and whistles from within. Mandela had finished his speech. It was my moment. I wished for a spacecraft to abduct me!

But it was not to be. The women's choir surged onto the stage. No one was going to stop them from singing to their hero, not after four centuries of rehearsal! They sang. And sang. And sang! Madiba swayed and clapped. And I desperately wanted to pee!

Eventually, led by the choirs in rhythmical salute, the President was led out of the hangar to his official car. My heart sank. He wasn't going to stay for me? I couldn't believe this turn of events. After all, he was the only person there, as far as I was concerned. I pressed Evita back against the steel doors and tried to look inconspicuous.

The ululating mass appeared, swaying and singing with a jiving Madiba beaming in their midst. Some were carrying a large chandelier, which they'd presented to him as a gift. Borrowed from the foyer of their hotel, I computed, as I sorted pertinent material in my head for what lay ahead.

'No,' I hissed to myself, 'stop this! No jokes here. Don't lose concentration! This is an audition, stupid!'

The armed guard heard the hisses and was still checking me out. The ANC's toyi-toyi machoute shuffled out into the night air. Comrades applauded. Mandela stood tall and laughing, the shepherd amid his milling, bleating sheep. I merged further into the shadows. Then a sudden swirl of movement in my direction. Mandela had espied the entertainer in the wings. He broke away from his bodyguard and walked towards me, his arms outstretched.

'Evita, my dear, you look so beautiful.'

We embraced. The watching masses applauded. A cameraman appeared. There had been strict instructions that no flashes would be used, because of the sensitivity of President Mandela's eyes after recent surgery. This was why he was not staying for the rest of the evening. He pacified his minders.

'I want a picture with Evita!' he said, and the photo was taken. Later I found out that while he was President, he had a picture on his desk of himself with Mrs Bezuidenhout at an ANC rally before the election! Or was it this one? There we stood like Liz Taylor and Sydney Poitier, his hand in hers. In my heels and hair, Evita was as tall as he. We conversed sotto voce, out of the side of smiling mouths.

'President Mandela, we can't go on meeting like this. Every time you see me I'm wearing a dress!'

'Don't worry, Pieter, I know you're inside!'

Then he was gone. I was ready to meet the lions in the den.

The band played 'Sarie Marais' and Evita made her entrance along the gauntlet of former warriors and lawbreakers, now fashion icons and lawmakers. She started her address to her new government with 'Amandla!' and the audience roared 'Awethu!' They knew this woman. Some had watched her on video in exile. Others on stage in London. Even in jail on a Friday night, when the Botha regime thought a comedy show by a man in a dress was as harmless as a tasteless tacky joke, they'd watched *Adapt or Dye*. The comedy reflected not just the madness, but also the state of a nation in turmoil, and those locked away from it saw the way the wind was blowing.

'The wind of change has blown the ANC into Bloemfontein!' Evita marvelled. 'At first I didn't know where to come tonight, but when I saw all the new Mercedes cars, I knew where you were.'

They rattled their car keys in delight. She pointed to her full carrier bag.

'I also knew it would be foolish to leave my groceries in the car ...'

And so Evita eventually made way for PW Botha, known to all in exile as the big crocodile. The house came down. They'd all been at the sticky end of his wagging finger. Then came Pik Botha, the 'big rhinoceros', still a farce to be reckoned with. Then Margaret Thatcher, horrified to notice that, like the IRA, the ANC was not just a terrorist organisation, but a reality and, in our case, even a government!

Then I saw her, sitting like an empress, while all round her were standing. Surrounded by her bodyguard-cum-football team, her personal Xhosa Nostra in matching leather coats and Ray Ban glasses. The Mother of the Nation. Estranged wife of the Leader, soon to be a rebel without her Xhosa! Winnie Mandela. And I had her in the bag! There was no choice. I had to do her here and now.

Once my Tutu had danced off into a punchline and applause, there was a moment of expectation. Who would come out of the bag now? An ethnic print kaftan. Nice. A knitted wig. Nice. Turban to match. Fine. Huge matchbox earrings. Oh? Bangles of small rubber tyres. Hello? Gold-rimmed spectacles encrusted with jewels. Oh shit! Winnie Mandela was there, not only in the audience, but also on stage!

'I am so sick and tired of contradicting my husband! No one can keep me down! I am back! One day I'm up; next day I'm down. I'm sick of those bastards who keep calling me a murderer. If you don't stop, I'll kill you …'

Suicide. So it went on, me tightening the noose around my neck. The reaction from the floor sounded like either 'Kiss the Boer' or 'Kill the Boer'. Meanwhile Cyril Ramaphosa, the Crown Prince, and Thabo Mbeki, the Dark One, were behind a potted palm tree to the side of the stage, like two schoolboys who'd planned a practical joke, laughing at me, wagging their fingers and drawing them across their throats! Had the audition now become a death sentence?

Suddenly it was over! I bowed and grabbed the bag to run for my life. Then out of the smiling milling crowd they appeared, Winnie's Boys, sunglasses reflecting my pale face in their lensed mirrors.

'Hey, Dirk Uys, that was good, man!' they raved like fans.

'Yes?' I gulped.

'Ja, man! We know you do Winnie in your show. So we all took a bet that you would not have the guts to do her. And you have the guts!'

'Do I keep the guts?'

'It was great!' they chorused.

'And what did she say?' I muttered with a dry mouth and failing heart.

'No, Mama loved it.'

'But … I make her out to be a murderer!' I whispered.

They whispered back.

'Ja, everybody makes her out to be a murderer! But you make her out to be a beautiful murderer!'

I'd passed the audition!

Celebrating the Rainbow

The New South Africa's liberation party carried on for four years – four glorious years – of Madiba Magic. Our President became the world's number one guest. At every opening of any parliament he was there, smiling that smile, shuffling those steps and focusing the world's attention on our second chance. The American President zipped up his trousers and depended on the support of the South African President. The British Prime Minister waited on hold, while the Russian President tried to send a fax. The fax machine had been stolen!

And so the world came to us. From all over, the most brutal and bloodied leaders purred like kittens while posing for their portrait of acceptance. Standing with the world's moral leader, even a Yasser Arafat, a Fidel Castro, a Muammar Gaddafi and all the Spice Girls could claim a shared legitimacy. A democratic halo of reflected greatness.

Madiba dazzled with his inventive diplomacy. Who could have thought it up round the tables of the public relations consultants? Having the former first ladies to tea in Pretoria? The glorious vision of a Mrs JG Strijdom, a Mrs BJ Vorster and a voluptuous Mrs PW Botha sitting around the stinkwood table in Libertas, sipping rooibos tea poured by the ex-convict, and nibbling koeksisters while the old angel just sat and beamed.

Mrs HF Verwoerd was 'too frail' to attend. So President Nelson Mandela went to her, flying off to the white enclave of Oranje! The fascinated world watched the most famous former political prisoner lean over the stooped shoulders of the small widow of his former jailer and steady her shaking old hands as she read a message of welcome in Afrikaans. Then Mandela went up on the hill behind the house where the only known statue of Hendrik Verwoerd is in existence. Because of a lack of funds among right-wing residents of Oranje, the statue was not life-size. All Nelson Mandela did was to stoop down and peer into the piggy-like features and quack: 'Ahhh? I didn't know he was so small!' Thus putting down the great white helmsman as a small footnote to a minor historical era. And how would that read for the generation of today, when they ask: 'Who was this Verwoerd? There are still so many streets, suburbs, buildings and boulevards named after him!'

Could we allow ourselves to answer them with a straight face?

'Hendrik Verwoerd? He was a white Christian Dutchman who ruled South Africa briefly. He was responsible for imprisoning Nelson Mandela and making him immortal.'

Satire in a democracy can be a disaster. All the targets had a sense of humour! The black leadership now revelled in being teased. They didn't mind, because they didn't have to prove anything. They'd certainly passed their audition. They'd been in jail for life. They'd been punished without major cause, tortured, beaten, humiliated and exiled for their beliefs. They had won. Small pinpricks from an irrelevant white comedian in a dress were not going to make the slightest dent in their armour. My career as a South African satirist was in severe trouble. I was thrilled.

Politics in South Africa no longer killed. It just irritated. In those early years of our fragile Rainbow Miracle, the last thing I wanted to do was criticise a politician who'd misread a rule or overstepped the mark. Compared to where we'd come from, this was definitely going to be a far better place, come hell and/or corruption. Both would fill the space left by the Bothas and their segregation in due course, but who could predict that then? Having voted for a black majority, I was not going to stab them in the back. So I put my little dagger away and did other things.

I created and fleshed out Evita Bezuidenhout's sister, Bambi Kellermann. Also born in Bethlehem in the Orange Free State of the late 1930s, she eventually became a grand horizontal of urban legend. Bambi with her blonde Dietrich hairstyle and Marlene voice. Madame Bambi and her German accent overlaying the dulcet tones of a boeremeisie from Bethlehem! Having married a Bavarian Nazi in the 1950s, she had to get a job to earn money to hide him from the Nazi hunters. He had a style to which he was accustomed. So, Bambi became a stripper and a whore. Eventually her husband fell among old friends in Paraguay, and reinvented himself as Minister of War in the government of that country's President Stroessner.

Now, in 1994, General Joachim von Kellermann was long dead. Bambi was back in South Africa with her husband's ashes in an urn on the piano. She came at the right time. By weaving the style of Kurt Weill into the FAK songs of my youth, one could reflect the horror of a Nazi past in denial along with the present convenient amnesia of our Afrikaner heritage. Bambi was dangerous and made many enemies. A sure sign of pertinence and good investment in South African entertainment.

During my year of abstinence, I also gave birth to the spectre of Evita's ancient mother, Ouma Ossewania Kakebenia Poggenpoel. Born in 1900 in the British concentration camp of Heldersonop during the Boer War, her hatred of the English and her disgust at having sacrificed a life – believing the lie that apartheid was a gift from God – made her as dangerous and even more reactionary than any Afrikaans character I had ever attempted. Evita was fast becoming politically bland and Disney-like in her appeal.

I took a show called *Negerküsse* on an extended tour of Germany in 1993, at the same time that, like black and white South Africa, the east and west of Germany were reconciling and uniting. That meant seventy performances in forty cities, including some in Austria and Switzerland. With some text in German, but mainly in English, satire in Deutschland proved to be quite a task. A German joke is no laughing matter! The show was named after a chocolate filled with white marzipan. Its politically incorrect title created enough discomfort to make it all worthwhile. Small reward, as three months later the German tour ended with the producer pleading bankruptcy!

I'd also started an annual visit to the Tricycle Theatre in London NW6. It's there that I made my first venture into the outside world with *Adapt or Dye* as a late-night show in the autumn of 1985. Now it was different. They had celebrated our democratic renewal, and Nelson Mandela was everyone's Madiba. The problem was not who to blame, but where did one point a finger? Apartheid was dead; what was the point of a satirical show about South Africa if everything had been solved?

Towards the middle and end of the 1990s, South Africa had slipped from page one of the world media to a small mention in the supplement on Third World issues.

Nelson Mandela was in charge, and so all was well. The exploding bubble of violence and the loud cacophony of suburban burglar alarms and barking Rottweilers became part of the soundtrack in our African democracy. So, taking a South African political revue out of its environment and into a foreign political cauldron meant doing my homework about where I was to anchor my material. I researched the political reality of a United Kingdom with its 1990s closet racism, illegal immigration, class deconstruction, bonking Royals and Toryfied Labour. Within a *Guardian*, a *Daily Telegraph* and a *Sun*, as well as a *Hello!*, I soon found perfectly fertile ground into which to sow universal issues. I was on a moral high ground, feeling pretty fine on the newly hewed political and social plusses that the Rainbow Nation offered me. No longer would an array of stamping feet in gumboots from Soweto, sweating armpits from KwaZulu-Natal and a cacophony of clicks and grunts from the Market Theatre be hailed as art of the highest order.

I hit the jugular of what was hot, fashionable and 'in'! No one wanted to sit through a well-made foreign play about South African emotions, especially by a white South African writer, as they had during those struggle years. The critics would now easily tut-tut the depth of a new Fugard play and even suggest a little humour. The tables were not turned, just stacked. At my Kilburn venue, *You ANC Nothing Yet* was followed by *Truth Omissions*. Then came *Europeans Only*, followed the next year by *Dekaffirnated*. The political jokes were no longer enough. Audiences wanted opinions on the substance of survival and the reflection of international pain. Fear was again the target, but in preparation for this new century, this old solution called fear was becoming a marketable way of life.

I visited New York, as part of the Brooklyn Academy of Music Theatre Festival, taking *You ANC Nothing Yet* through the murky shallow waters of Clinton's pre-Monica American wet dream.

A detailed review in the *New York Times* of 20 November 1997 by Lawrence van Gelder, a critic who had reviewed the likes of Lenny Bruce, Mort Sahl, Whoopi Goldberg and other comedic icons, gave me great inspiration and support with his positive comments:

Humor, like wine, often travels poorly. So it is a pleasure to report that the volatile cargo of satire packed by South Africa's comic conscience, Pieter-Dirk Uys, has arrived in the United States in most savory form.

Brimming with irreverence, Mr Uys's work is a refreshing jolt to the senses of Americans dulled by sitcom humour and inhibited by the bland norms of correctness in a nation afflicted with political apathy. It is also a showcase for a fine actor, gifted political humorist and courageous humanitarian ...

As advertised, Mr Uys is a national treasure, and in *You ANC Nothing Yet*, he stimulates the mind and invigorates the conscience, while tickling the funny bone.

Now I had been given small stars of excellence by critics in the world's major cities, from Sydney to Berlin, Amsterdam to London, and New York to San Francisco. It didn't matter any longer if my local critics in Cape Town ignored any development, or just giggled at the length of Evita's dresses and her legs.

I'd also moved from the Mother City to the country, driving out to Darling on the West Coast one day for no real reason and buying a derelict old Victorian house. At the time I was in a relationship which had been pending for twelve years. Now for the first time, this 'affair' gave me a 'companion for life'. That life had two more years of hell to go before it evaporated. Meanwhile, we renovated the old house in Station Street and moved in, with the seven dogs, four cats and hundreds of CDs and videos and crap.

Three months later, the old Darling railway station, no longer in use by Spoornet and having found a new life as a studio for the local carpenter, was suddenly empty. The words 'Evita se Perron' floated into mind. Not only a nod at the real Mrs Peron, but in Afrikaans 'Perron' also means 'station platform'. So, for a year we leased the small building as a cabaret theatre, serving boerekos out of the smallest closet-kitchen, to a maximum of fifty people. Suddenly I had my own theatre!

The venue was an instant success and has been a work in progress ever since. The 'companion for life' soon flew away via page three of the *Sunday Times*, bleating ill-treatment and affront, losing a court case for 'support', and his name now escapes me. I bought the Darling station and the adjoining land, and today it stands proud with two cabaret theatres, a kitchen and bar, and an arts and craft section, with its art gallery, art school for the community children and a

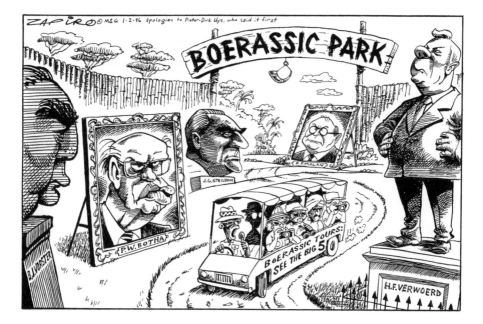

piano school. And cats who are the pride of the Perron. They'll kill me if I don't mention their names: Marilyn, Moggie, Die Koei, Ginger Rodgered, Boesman, 2K, Windgat and Elsie-Balt.

The lavish garden, called Boerassic Park, is full of statues of former political farts. It reflects the absurd reality of being in the premier wildflower area of the world while filling the empty spaces with plastic flowers! Against the walls of the original station building is the greatest collection of Afrikaner political kitsch in the world, from the Battle of Blood River and the Voortrekker Monument, to Whites Only signs and posters of Hendrik Verwoerd and White Supremacy. Underlining my belief that to hide the past is to give it unwelcome power, the whole pink corrugated-iron empire, with its politically incorrect symbols of the past and celebration of National Party bad taste, creates instant laughter and smiles. Elderly Afrikaners recognise their past with tears. Their children put that past into perspective with loud laughter. Then blacks pose in front of them with enjoyment of the battles won. The cats complete the unique picture.

Evita Bezuidenhout performs two matinée shows each Saturday and Sunday, while Saturday night allows for my new work.

Since the start of the Perron, all my new work has been tried and tested there for months, and then, once perfected, has been taken across the world. It all started here on a Saturday night! Every week I can try out new ways of pushing the elastic of the jockstrap!

The 1999 General Election gave me the perfect erection!

PART II

ELECTIONS

Second Time Around

The election of 2 June 1999 would wave goodbye to Nelson Mandela as our President. Breaking with African tradition whereby one usually has to shoot the incumbent to get rid of him after twenty years, our remarkable Madiba stepped down after a mere four years. If he'd stayed on for another term, would it have made a difference to where we are today? Too late. We had to prepare to welcome Thabo Mbeki as his successor by the end of June 1999.

Elections have always been the most wonderful motivation to roll out a new political revue. Minor issues would suddenly become major and all problems seemed unsolvable. Politicians used their art of bitchery and intrigue to trap former colleagues and best friends. They all showed their true colours of hypocrisy and corruption. Instead of having them committed, we'd vote them into positions of power. We voters should all have our heads read! Suddenly everyone who seemed not to care showed an interest in the news, as well as the soaps. Politics had become a firm rival to the best operatic melodrama.

In the old South Africa, apartheid elections happened occasionally and among the chosen few. The choices were never representative, and so the satirical material was obvious and bland: from Minister Piet Koornhof waggling his Disney ears to PW Botha wagging that finger. From our stages we were performing to the converted.

Before the 1994 election, my revue *One Man One Volt* played to full houses, but the audience probably represented 0,005 per cent of the population. That election – 27 April – was a huge milestone, but the second election of 2 June was more dangerous. How could I take the entertainment out of the theatre to the people in the real world, who didn't ever go to the theatre – the other 99,99 per cent? Voter education through entertainment?

So the Great Election Trek was conceived. A journey around South Africa with a show, starring the most famous white woman in South Africa. An entertainment that would underline the importance of the second election, and the sacred gift of democracy. A way to celebrate with humour the need to commit ourselves each day to the defence of our freedoms.

I've always been fascinated by trains, and enthralled by the way politicians have used them to spread their political manifesto. I remember newsreels and movies reflecting the American campaigns of a Roosevelt or a Kennedy, standing on the open platform of the last coach, bedecked with flags and bunting and waving hope to the enraptured crowds. Argentina's Evita Peron, waving from her train, was glamorous and dramatic. Images of the famous White Train taking the Royal Family through South Africa in 1947 are still vivid. The fact that the Communist Party of the Soviet Union used trains to take their dogma across vast Russia after the 1917 Revolution did it for me. We would get a train! Evita Bezuidenhout's Election Train. The Amachoochoo!

We'd call ourselves Evita's People's Party and start in Darling at Evita se Perron. With Nelson Mandela waving us goodbye, we would set off on a nationwide rail tour, stopping at designated towns and cities and presenting Election Indabas in town halls and large local venues. We would have a press coach with Internet facilities. We would have a lecture coach, and take schoolkids from one stop to the next, exciting them about their impending voting age. Tannie Evita would kiss babies and sign bare flesh from the southern tip of the Cape to the northern extreme of the beloved country. And it would all be free! To the public, that is!

Lynne Maree joined me. She and I had originally met at the Space Theatre when she'd just left school. She is an actress, director, writer, cabaret artist and one of the few people in the theatre whom I trust with Theatre. It is her passion. Like me, Lynne is serving a theatrical life imprisonment without trial. We are doing time together, and she was the obvious person to ask to produce this next saga with me.

To put a long story in a paragraph: we sourced venues and towns on the logical rail routes through the country and measured how far a day's travel would take us. We structured drawings of the train, diagrams of the designs on the coaches and the colours of the bunting. We planned everything, from the toilet paper to what staff we would need, from a medical presence to the legal reps. Evita's dresses, hats, gloves and shoes had to be planned and found. Plus, I was then in the fat size. I would probably lose weight during the exercise, so I would need fat sizes and thin sizes! Bedding and cooking and cellphones and condoms had to be sourced and budgeted for.

I went to the Spoornet offices in Johannesburg and met an enthusiastic supporter in the charming head of Passenger Services, and his associates. They all loved trains as much as I did. He was also a fan from the Struggle days, and so we wholeheartedly started planning the reality of the Amachoochoo. At the time I didn't know that the plans of our ambitious project had not been shared with the upper management of Spoornet, which ran the rail system, or in the boardrooms of Transnet, which oversaw transport nationally, simply because it was still in a theoretical stage. This was a fatal mistake.

Lynne and I started a series of meetings about meetings, sitting round smaller tables that became larger tables, changing shape from square to round to oblong to homeland-size! As the news of the project seeped up the corporate ladder, we would meet more important people, who wanted to get onto the train too! It was my first brush with the new generation of ama-Boss: the young upwardly mobile African with gold-rimmed glasses and manicured nails, expensive taste and excellent accessories, but no sense of humour at all! Having shared the gift of humour with the old warriors of the Struggle throughout the 1990s, laughing with ministers and presidents on television and at the Bloemfontein audition, I sat in the icy atmosphere and realised that the party was over.

Most of these Very Important People were returned exiles – 'Retexes' – who had spent most of the Struggle safely sipping whisky in Swedish or Danish or Dutch or British hotels, expecting the anti-apartheid movements to foot the bills (which they did), while moving onto another subsidised college degree. They were back in South Africa with their Eurocentric accents. They wanted money and power.

'Who is this Afrikaans woman, that she demands a whole train to herself?' asked one gloriously arrogant woman in A Position of Power. 'Whites mustn't think they can demand as in the past!'

'Demand' was her favourite swear word.

I glanced at Lynne. Her lips were pursed, her face white with fury. We were also losing it, meeting by meeting. Many of the important comrades round the table did not realise that this 'Afrikaans woman' didn't exist! When I mentioned this, as charmingly as I could, another glorious woman in A Position of Power at the SABC snarled: 'We don't believe in encouraging homosexuality among our youth.'

By now our original pals at Spoornet had been bypassed. We never saw them again, except to communicate by e-mail and fax. The project had become a Management Issue. It also took on more noughts than anyone could imagine. We had by now linked up with a PR company run by an extraordinary energy. She never stopped talking and listened to nothing. Whereas our first meetings with her started enthusiastically round a big corporate table, within weeks Lynne and I were drinking cooldrink out of a shared paper cup in the passage. By then no one was coming to the meetings any more.

We killed a lot of corporate enthusiasm when we announced that, while a business mind could plan for a profit margin of a few million, we were not in this Election Trek for the money.

'But sweetie darling, everybody's making money! This is a potential gold mine!'

We were on our own in a crowd, and that's where we had to go back to! Being on our own! When a Transnet budget was structured round a table the size of Swaziland, and we saw that our little train would cost the taxpayer over two million rand, Lynne and I stood up and shook hands with a smile.

'Thank you, comrades,' we purred. 'We'll be in touch.'

We were back to square one. What was our original motivation? Voter education through entertainment! Not, who will play host to the Minister and his entourage when they get on the train for two days? And as for the money? Our Amachoochoo would become another gravy train. While there were millions of rands available for voter education in preparation for the June election, that money usually came with an agenda. We'd also had enough of the gold-rimmed spectacles and careful Retex vowels. I did not want to fall out of love with my audience. These Very Important Comrades did not represent South Africa!

No one owed us anything. Let the state look after itself. We decided not to expect or 'demand' money from anyone. I contacted my friends and agents in the United Kingdom and Europe, and set up a fund-raising junket starring Evita Bezuidenhout. In a series of shows in London, Paris, Amsterdam and Copenhagen, Tannie insulted, encouraged, offended, embarrassed and energised her audience into putting pounds, francs, guilders and kroner into her cocked hat. With a good exchange rate, it gave us R125 000. Not quite two million, but Lynne and I had experience of making small magic out of no money.

We packed away the designs of the seven-coach train and borrowed a minibus from Tempest Car Hire. Evita and her fat/thin wardrobe fitted in the boot. We employed two stage managers, who also did it for love and cooldrink money. A Dutch theatre friend accompanied us for support. We also managed to attract the attention of a few television crews, from networks in Denmark, Holland, Australia and eventually the mighty BBC. A young French filmmaker followed us with his three-man crew to make their version of *In Bed with Evita*.

While big business peered at us with suspicious eyes, the people rallied. Throughout our Trek, when we were ready to pay for our bed and breakfast, it was donated by the proprietor. We were given food and drinks, boxes of apples and packets of biltong. MTN gave us support with cellphones and a phone-in line. The SABC sent a TV crew to make a series of short takes. SAfm radio gave us a five-minute morning slot before the seven o'clock news, to report to the nation from the front line!

I told the team: This is uncharted territory. It can become a technicolour dream! Or it could become a black and white Mad Max nightmare! We are going into 'the most dangerous country in the world'! Rape, murder, hijacking, theft and assault are rife. Fear keeps everyone indoors. We'll be travelling through war zones. We'll be performing in townships where the blood is still wet on the tar. But we will have no guns. Guns attract other guns. We'll have everything else: dried mangoes, biltong, droëwors, cellphones and condoms, but no guns!

So we set out gunless and determined. We never needed a gun anywhere along that 10 000 kilometre route through nine provinces. Having performed the sixty free shows in townships, ghettos, cities and locations, we all lived to tell the tale, and it included not one incidence of violence. There were close shaves, but usually because we expected the worst.

I never keep a diary, but as we started this strange expedition, something had to be put down, if only to be sure it happened. Looking back now, all I remember is being forever on the road, standing forever on a stage, sweating forever in the heat, driving forever in darkness, surrounded by roars of laughter and delight. I look at the notes now and realise that the Election Trek did take place.

Before we set out, something extraordinary happened. Evita Bezuidenhout took her Election Indaba to the South African Parliament! I'd written some letters to see what the reaction would be. One to Nelson Mandela inviting him to join our launch, another to Deputy President Thabo Mbeki asking him to come and have some fun with us.

'You will have the nicest time of your life! And don't worry about being made fun of: I still find it impossible to "do" you on stage! Can't you wear a funny hat? The pipe doesn't give me a PW finger or a Madiba shirt! Please, Comrade le Roi, don't make life so difficult for moi!'

There was no reply from Thabo Mbeki. But the Speaker of Parliament, Dr Frene Ginwala, did reply. I had asked her: Doesn't voter education start at home? And wasn't Parliament the home of democracy?

Her staff reacted quickly and invited me to address the members of Parliament ten days before our Trek started. They'd made the old House of Assembly available during lunchtime on 10 February. Would I need a dressing room for Mrs Bezuidenhout and parking place for me? Yes to both.

Lynne and I arrived early enough to make sure that this was not an illusion. No, everyone was expecting us, and I was ushered into the private bathroom of a senior parliamentarian. He arrived in his office as Tannie Evita stepped out of his bathroom. The man nearly had a heart attack. He stuttered and blushed and begged for autographs. She could have declared war on Lesotho and he would've agreed!

In the hallowed hall, still only half-full at one o'clock, I took stock. Here I was in Parliament, by invitation, and in drag! Mrs Bezuidenhout was dressed in her newly discovered ethnic finery, an explosion of bold oranges, browns and yellows. Her long skirt had a slit up to the knee. Puffed sleeves on a matching top. The huge turban was of the same material and self-folded to complete the picture of what Winnie Mandela wanted me to look like. In the chamber, on the place where the sacred mace had once stood, towered Evita's large, round, green cactus.

The performance was based on the Perron show *Tannie Evita Praat Kaktus*, in which Evita uses the cactus as a symbol for the survival spirit of the Afrikaner. It takes us through a revisionist version of Afrikaner history. The symbols are exposed as lies and the victories as propaganda.

'Jan van Riebeeck did not bring civilisation to South Africa! Now we know the truth. He was an escaped Dutch convict who came to steal chickens from the Bushmen!'

Doing it here in the House of Assembly, where the apartheid era was born and ended, was perfect. Here in the sacred place of former enemies, I was crapping on their carpet and asking for toilet paper! It was outrageous!

By the time the presentation started, the chamber was full. The upper echelon weren't there. It is said they all watched on in-house TV from the safety of their offices. Most of the rest were present.

The former Ambassador to Bapetikosweti acted as if she owned the place, and then said so. 'I was here, while most of you were either in jail or in exile!'

She then proceeded to tango where angels fear to waltz. The SABC filmed the entire experience, and for the next ten days extracts were shown on every newscast. The nation watched in amazement as Tannie Evita commanded the attention of those who ruled, managing to dissolve them in hysterics. Everyone laughed at everyone else. ANC at PAC, PAC at NP, NP at PFP. Evita was saying things that

the man in the street wouldn't even dare think, and yet her powerful targets fell about applauding. It was the ultimate celebration of freedom of speech. No one had asked me for a text. No one had looked in my bag. No one had made a single demand. Can't see this happening in London, Washington, Paris or Rome?

When I eventually toured my show *Dekaffirnated*, which was based on the need to demystify words like 'kaffir' and 'nigger', and fight racism with humour, I took it to London and eventually New York. I had to stop the show at that moment and explain: 'Evita Bezuidenhout was in the South African Parliament …'

'But she doesn't exist?' the Brits bleated.

So I tried to localise it to make things simpler for them.

'Imagine Dame Edna Everage in the House of Commons?'

'Oh? Isn't she there already?'

It was easier in the United States of Bill Clinton's Cockupracy.

'Evita Bezuidenhout was in our Parliament,' I'd crow. 'Monica Lewinsky didn't even get as far as the Senate! Monica Lewinsky only came as far as the Oval Office!'

The South African press splashed Evita's invasion of Parliament over the front pages. The daily television exposure gave her gravitas. The nation now knew who she was and awaited her with bated breath. A daily personal election e-mail from her to various political personalities appeared on the front pages of some newspapers, preparing the voters for what could become a bumpy ride!

e-vita's e-lection e-mail to:
Dr Frene Ginwala

Frene, my skat! What an impressive five years of parliamentary democracy you have had! You, a woman of style, substance and superb irony, to be stranded amid the debris of a multiracial non-racial non-sexual political miracle?

Sies, how frightening! And yet you carried it off superbly. No, let me rephrase that: 'they' carried it off superbly. Because we know, Parliament is moving. Day by day. Bit by bit. On Monday the fax machine, on Tuesday the computers, on Wednesday the carpets.

I think Parliament should be moved. But not back to ou Pretoria, which is too full of consultants at R6000 a week. It should be moved to a place where Parliament can get on with its job of governing without distraction. No perks. No diversions. So? Bloemfontein! I know of an old Sanlam building that's been empty for years. Parliament could be on the bottom four floors and the Freedom Front's white homeland on the top five.

And now, with our pending election, you sit with another horror story? After five years of trying to teach the terrorists and communists and racists and fascists and convicts how to behave in Parliament? They'll all leave for big business and then you'll be stuck with a new lot. Raw recruits who know nothing about anything, let alone democracy! You will have to give them the same pep talk: no toyi-toying, no spraying graffiti on walls, no stick-ups. No pickpocketing, no easy hijacking cars from the government garage, no free food for exhausted families from your township communities and no squatting or dumping.

One thing I have encouraged voters to do, is to make their cross for every politician we don't trust and get them into Parliament! It only takes 500 000-plus votes to put Louis Luyt's FA, the Freedom Front, the ANC (especially Winnie), PAC, DP, ACDP, IFP, NNP etc. into your hands. Sterkte suster!

P.S. As Pik used to say: Rather have them inside spitting out, than outside spitting in!

Where Angels Fear to Tread

Last-minute panic about what will fit into the Kombi and what into the Daewoo. Tannie Evita starts at her Perron, kissing the brown babies and hugging the locals, while her choir sings 'Nkosi Sikelel' iAfrika' and her staff wave farewell, some dressed as Jan van Riebeeck, Sarel Cilliers, Paul Kruger and other obscure national figures from the white history books. Evita is on her Great Election Trek, bringing relief to the drudge of politics and the urgency of voter registration, with hearty laughter and a healthy dose of politically incorrect comment.

Starting in Belville's Civic Centre during the lunch hour, we virtually dress-rehearse to an empty hall. Two middle-aged civil servants eat their sandwiches in the front row, while the back seats fill up with brown faces and most of the street people. It is important to get our technical structure sorted out. Evita needs a lapel-mike and so does Basil Appollis, who is joining her to give another side to the story. His comments as a coloured man in a multicultured democracy highlight the fears and prejudices of a non-white community. In the Cape he brings the house down with his references to local politics, using the colourful vernacular of the Cape coloured. When Tannie leaves the stage to change into her special outfits, he can make fun of her new-found designer democracy.

That evening we flood the Paarl Town Hall with energy and a good house full of local inhabitants. I still see the old photographs of my pa and his sisters on that very stage when they were children at the end of the first decade of the previous century, performing in the patriotic tableaux organised by their mother, Ouma Gertie Uys. Is she watching now as we perform in this derelict space, only used on occasions and falling to pieces because of lack of funds?

Evita enthuses old white tannies and ooms, coloured mothers and their men, brown schoolkids and black comrades with the same message: 'Your vote is sacred. Your vote is secret. Your vote is your power to build a greater future for yourselves and your families. Get the right ID documents! Register! And smile!'

TUESDAY 23 FEBRUARY

We leave the familiar green winelands of the Boland and snake up the ravines towards the arid Karoo with its midday heat for the lunchtime Indaba in Laingsburg. When God was making that specific hill outside Laingsburg, her cellphone suddenly rang and she was diverted. So God never got to putting in the trees and the streams and the soft soil. She just left the barren rock and ashen dust where the coloured people eventually made their homes, far away from the soft shade of the pepper trees next to the gentle river where white people live.

It all changed in the 1980s, when a terrible flash-flood forced itself through the town. Like so many cars and trucks and buses before it, a wall of muddy water raced through the streets without stopping, dragging life and limb with it. Even today Laingsburg carries the byline: people died here, mainly white people, because the brown people were safe up on their horrible hot hill where no water could reach!

As we pass the Grand Hotel, still snug against the railway line next to the station, I can recall those nights here in the 1950s, on the way to Johannesburg to visit the Afrikaans cousins in the small Austin A40 with Ma and Pa and sister Tessa, hearing the steam engines huff and puff and hiss just a windowpane away. There are no more steam locomotives in Laingsburg, and very few passenger trains even stop here now. But there are still lots of little barefoot boys coming out of the local school into the hot sun, finished with their day's slog.

The little boys saunter past the community centre on this hot Tuesday. High noon in Laingsburg, forty degrees in the shade of the tired trees. The activity in the building attracts their attention. There among the colourful Christmas decorations still hanging from the peeling ceiling is the banner announcing EVITA'S PEOPLES PARTY. Other posters say VOTE in eleven languages, while some just shout REGISTER!

There are local white people sitting in rows, with some familiar brown parents, the schoolteacher and even the fat traffic cop. The centre of their attention is a middle-aged white woman in a bright coloured kaftan with lots of jewellery and make-up, speaking fancy words that can scarcely fit into an open mouth!

The little boys crowd round the open door and stare. This is the woman they've seen on television! In Parliament! This is the woman who speaks to the politicians! Yes, they might not have shoes or warm clothes or cooldrinks or schoolbooks, but nearly everyone on the dusty hill has a television set. While the world has forgotten about them, they know what is happening outside the Karoo and know nothing has anything to do with them!

The teacher sees the children peer in and shoos them away. They are too small to come into this important Election Indaba. And like so many other teachers communicating with his class, he hisses: 'Hey? Djulle? Fok off!'

Tannie Evita blanches but recovers.

'No, you can't chase them away!' she trills. 'These are the voters of tomorrow. They must come and join my Indaba! Kom kindertjies!'

And so the hundred barefoot kiddies crowd into the small hall and sit cross-legged on the floor, hearing maybe for the first time that the future belongs to them too. One day they will also have this thing called The Vote. And this election in June should be understood by everyone, even those under the voting age, as an investment in their future.

'Learn what to do now, so you will do it properly when you have to!'

Evita Bezuidenhout ends her Indaba with a fist held high to the call: 'Amandla/Vrystaat!'

The children yell their delight. And when her election song, composed and sung by Lionel Bastos and Yvonne Chaka Chaka, booms forth across the snoozing dorp, the children join her in an impromptu jive.

'Mrs Bezuidenhout?' asks one little boy with sparkling eyes, his coloured accent giving each sound charm and a smile. 'Can I ask you a question?'

Evita nods grandly.

'Are you a man?'

I stop dancing and narrow Evita's eyes. The other little boys hold their breath.

'Do I look like a man?' Evita purrs dangerously.

'No!' The boy blushes browner. 'But this thing you do? Is it like on the teevee?'

The cluster of wise little faces nod gravely.

'Like on the teevee?' Tannie asks.

'Ja, like acting,' the boy ventures. 'Is what you do like acting?'

'Yes,' winks Tannie Evita. 'It's acting!'

The boy gives a thumbs-up to his pals.

'Sien, ek't gesê dis mos 'n fokkin man!' And then humbly to the woman herself: 'But don't worry Mrs Bezuidenhout, we won't tell anyone!'

My secret is safe in Laingsburg!

'You must come and meet our ma's,' they say, and lead the Ballot Bus up the gravel road towards the distant township on the hill. And so, on this very hot day in this exceptionally hot place somewhere on the dark side of the new moon of our democracy, a white man dragged up in a bright dress meets the black mothers and brown fathers of her new little boy friends and is treated like a queen.

'What shall I tell them in Parliament?' Evita eventually asks.

The unemployed people think for a moment. There is much they need. Then a mother of four wearing a small green hat speaks.

'Mrs Bezuidenhout, just remind them that they promised us jobs. We can't eat a vote!'

WEDNESDAY 24 FEBRUARY

After a night in Beaufort West, we start early for the heart of the Karoo: De Aar. It is here where all the railway lines seem to meet in a spaghetti junction. It was once the steam-train heart of the country. We find the Town Hall, which is unprepared for an audience. No, they have not received our posters. Ah, the address was wrong. We'd sent it to someone who was not on our side and he destroyed all the information. What are we to do?

'Never mind!' says the brown man in charge. 'Evita doesn't come to us every day. Leave it to me!'

He rolls up a cardboard A4 folder and starts down the main street, becoming a town crier and announcing our presence, urging the people to come and celebrate. Within an hour the hall is full to bursting. The town crier turns out to be the Mayor, who then puts on his tie and welcomes us warmly, leading his community in laughter at the expense of politicians and gravy train corruption.

I pen a note to Lynne: 'Imagine the chaos if we had a train!'

We've invited all the political parties to send their representatives to the Indabas so that they can promote their party line and take questions from the floor. The ANC and the New National Party take us up at most stops, with an occasional Democratic Party member. We have as part of our caravan Judy Sole, the founder of the proposed Green Party, as well as a religious nut we call God, who would bring the roof down with his fire and brimstone crap. He stays for all sixty shows, sleeping in his car. We never heard from him again in life or in politics!

Here in De Aar a woman stands up and announces that she will not vote again, to spite the government! Another woman gets up and pleads: 'Evita, how can we vote for you?'

The Independent Electoral Commission (IEC) in Pretoria had originally made loud and important noise in their support for us, assuring us that they would publicise our visits through their communication networks in the

various communities. The only time this is taken up is in Kimberley. The local IEC go out of their way. Kimberley is the capital of the Northern Cape and home to the legend of diamonds. Drum majorettes lead Evita in a procession through the streets to the historic Town Hall, where members of the provincial government and up to 1000 people welcome 'the woman that Nelson Mandela admires'. Many political parties are present and Evita's People's Party comes into its own, especially when the election song booms forth. Tannie joins the citizens of Kimberley on the Town Hall floor for a jive!

THURSDAY 25 FEBRUARY

A long dreary drive brings us into old conservative territory: Potchefstroom. In contrast with the Kimberley party, the dour Potchefstroom Town Hall, a great example of neo-Nazi Boere-baroque, still echoes with the sinister political intrigues of the past. There are only twelve miffed whites sitting like a small island of pollution amid the empty seats. The furious Afrikaans caretaker bangs doors and slams windows. The adjoining banqueting hall is host to the local government and town council in another meeting of import. Our Indaba creaks towards an empty climax.

Suddenly there is a commotion outside in the streets! The buses from the townships have arrived. The kids knew we were coming and had signalled their support, but the township is far from town, a result of some clever Broederbond planning. At last here they are, and the Potchefstroom Reichstag is filled with 800 young black kids.

All the comrades want to ask questions of this woman on stage.

'Madam!'

'Evita?'

'Wena!'

And there we are, celebrating democracy as the only answer to any political question, when a young man gets up. He is eighteen years old. He is going to vote for the first time. He is so excited and so proud. And so angry! And he says to Evita Bezuidenhout, this woman on stage who doesn't even exist: 'Madam, we fought for freedom! All we got was democracy!'

It now stands as an obituary to the twentieth century.

How many millions fought for their freedom, only to be satisfied in a new designer cage that only made the neighbours jealous? How long did it take me to find out I was not in a democracy? My late twenties, when I was turfed out of an Islington pub and called a fucking Nazi boer? If I was never free till 1994, was I free now? Yes, but only until I stop fighting to stay free! Maybe people are not born equal; maybe they are born free to fight for the right to be equal.

This young man from the Potch township has no illusions. He will vote on 2 June. He will watch his heroes get richer and fatter. He won't find a job, just a task that scarcely pays. He will probably find an easier way to earn a living by selling drugs. He may get drunk and have sex carelessly. He might get a virus and die unknown and unremembered. And I don't even know his name, this young man who said those unforgettable words on that night in Potchefstroom! But I see his face and his anger and I will never forget!

FRIDAY 26 FEBRUARY

Now we can base ourselves in Johannesburg in familiar terrain with friends and family, and travel out to the final Indaba of the first week. In the township of Actonville outside Benoni.

The community hall of Actonville is surrounded by mosques and the shrill sunset calls from the minarets, reminding us that we've come at the wrong time. People are on their knees at prayer. Bad planning. So we wait and, lo and behold, once the spirit has been fed, the people stream towards us, still wearing their mosque Gucci and chewing hastily grabbed morsels for supper. Our audience here is mainly Muslim and Indian, and, never having heard of Salman Rushdie, Mrs Bezuidenhout does not watch her tongue. She skates on thin ice and is received with hilarity and applause.

A potential voter gets up and asks an often repeated question. Because of the system of proportional representation, he wants to know why he must bother to vote for a party 'if they've already prepared their lists'. He wants the choice of personality above party dogma. The delegate from the ANC finds his party accused of having made mistakes during their last four years of government.

He smiles.

'A lazy party doesn't make mistakes,' he says, hinting at the other political parties who haven't bothered to turn up.

We leave with gifts of samoosas and cooldrinks.

SATURDAY 27 FEBRUARY

Lynne and I spend the day sprawled on the carpet studying maps and checking our budgets. We fear we'll run out of money before the end of the Trek.

'Never mind,' shrugs Lynne, 'something will happen!'

It took only one week to fully realise the enormity of this project. We can never cover all the bases. There are too few of us and too many venues that want the Ballot Bus to visit. Our budget doesn't allow for that. We are, in fact, producing a R5 million voter education project on less than R200 000! So we spend the weekend in Johannesburg trying to find the missing links, mainly jacking up the promotion of the Indabas and how to awaken the interest of the main political parties, who have up to date been mainly absent!

The IEC has been supportive, but their communications from head office in Pretoria to provincial and municipal levels is poor. Wrong information is faxed; dates are wrong. Expectations are often anchored in what fees will be handed out at the venues. Pay first, help later? We have to reclaim the ground we gave over to others, thinking that this was the best way to reach as many people as possible. Bottom line? Do it yourself!

SUNDAY 28 FEBRUARY

Our day of rest, and I've never worked so hard phoning, faxing, thinking, wondering, worrying, planning and not sleeping!

e-vita's e-lection e-mail to the IEC

Let me start by saying how nice you IEC people all look when we see you on television. Those lovely expensive tailored suits and imported outfits. And the ladies with sculpted hair and Michael Jackson noses. And, ja, those Gucci cellphone covers. No, I'm sure yours is a very difficult job. Or should I say, it was simple until you people made it so hard. You have to create something to do!

And now you have a full-time job, working out ways of confusing us so much that on 2 June no one will bother to vote. And so you won't have to spend any money at all!

I only found out yesterday: you IEC people are responsible for what will happen on election day! Siestog! You have to organise everything, prepare everything and make everything work smoothly. And here I was thinking all you had to do was hand out dated T-shirts to small children and deliver the sausage rolls for mayoral receptions!

Now that I know, I feel so much better. Because now I am sure that the fact that South Africans outside the country can't vote – but criminals in jail can – is just a silly bureaucratic bungle. The fact that there are people on the party lists who are not registered on the voter's role is just a slip-up. The fact that if you are not where you are registered, even with a bar-coded ID on 2 June, you lose your vote, is just a little mistake. That the 20% of eligible voters out there who can't vote because they don't have the right piece of paper is just an oversight.

Please tell me I'm right. Because, dear IEC-people, if all this confusion has been planned and organised, then I'm afraid you have constructed the most sinister and successful coup d'etat that this country has ever experienced. No, I think I'm right. After all, this is only the second free and fair democratic, non-racial, non-sexist, nonsensical election. Practice makes perfect.

P.S. See you in 2004?

Practice Makes Perfect

The Ballot Bus drives onto the campus of the University of the Witwatersrand. There we play the Great Hall, a massive, sprawling Weimar-type auditorium, which seats 1200. Though we start with only about 300, by the end we are 75 per cent full. A startling mix of youth, black, brown and white, all here to be entertained by Evita. This is an audience, we assume, with more of the political facts and background at their disposal than those on the Trek last week. We are wrong; they know as little about voting structures and have even less interest in the political circus. Evita teases them for being eternal students, on an extended vacation with someone else's money, and catches some out for not having ID books.

The ANC rep is an older white woman in brogues and tartan skirt. She strides up to the mike with the confidence of an old anti-apartheid warrior and, fist in air, shouts: 'Amandla Comrades! Aluta Continua!'

She is greeted with a bemused silence. Oh, for the good old days when she was one of the students here at Wits, behind the barricades, fighting a just fight worth dying for and not just waiting for the next subsidy cheque? Now rally cries to Continua the Aluta just sound behind the times and silly.

From chalk to cheese, we leave the centre of Braamfontein and travel the long Ontdekkers Road towards Roodepoort on the West Rand. The Roodepoort Theatre has a pristine auditorium, lots of lights on stage and mirrors in the dressing rooms, which are used to the yodelling of choirs and the temperament of local Wagnerian mezzos. A white middle-aged audience look like dusty refugees from a seventies disaster movie! A party of people with Down's syndrome fills two rows. They are automatically invited to attend anything that performs in this theatre, but before 8 pm they all file out to go and eat dinner at their establishment, leaving us slightly perplexed. Not knowing who they are, it makes us wonder if we are facing a staged walk-out. When we find out the details, we feel sorry not to have met them and made them feel more at home.

Meanwhile our resident paparazzi, the French team and the SABC cabal, film for Africa. They have been encouraged to move about freely, and they do.

Interestingly, it seems to add more substance to the occasion, for audiences are used to seeing this happen on television newscasts. If we didn't have the real crews, we would've hired actors with cardboard cameras to give that substance!

TUESDAY 2 MARCH

Lynne and I have a face-to-face meeting with the IEC. They are situated in an elegant building among jacaranda trees, and peopled with attractive comrades with manicured nails and plaited hair. We breeze through security, who are otherwise engaged, and meet up with our contact. Soon we are in the conference room, surrounded by posters and diagrams and impressive proof of planning on a national scale. No one can explain exactly what they represent, but the colours are divine.

We share with them what we have experienced during our first ten days of field work, and try to encourage them to communicate with their communication experts to communicate! It seems nothing on our behalf has yet been done! Everyone promises passionately to communicate with 'the ground', and we have tea.

The evening performance at the State Opera in the centre of the capital is like an out-take from a Leni Riefenstahl film of the Third Reich. The whole complex still has so many ghosts and spooks of the former regime and culture, that the mere fact of Evita Bezuidenhout being there seems to underline the change that has taken place. I meet some backstage workers who remember my visit to that very place in 1984 with *Total Onslaught.*

While most of us working at the Market Theatre had supported a ban on working at the State Theatre, I had explained that if I was going to have any effect on the standing of the national symbols of state, I had to make fun of them in their own backyard. In this case, in their hallowed hall of Kultuur! The huge auditorium seats over 2000 and was full on that night in 1984. Prime Minister PW Botha was up the road, apartheid was in full swing and 95 per cent of the white audience supported it to the hilt. They were shocked and horrified and peed in their pants! Equal opportunity satire had never been more relevant than on that night: everyone got a swipe! The future tricameral parliament that would give representation to coloureds and Indians in separate parliaments was a gift from the gods, and those civil servants in the audience could never take it seriously again. The revue ended with Evita announcing that she's leaving to go 'up the road' to PW Botha, 'but come out and wave me goodbye?'

And so she stepped off the stage, Danielle into the Lions' Cage, in her fur coat and emeralds, leading her fawning fans, my enemies, into the foyer and outside to the waiting car. It was a white 1967 Cadillac de Ville convertible with leopard-skin seats and Wagner booming forth from the hi-fi. The driver was a sexy young man clad in leather from head to toe, looking menacing and just up every old queen's street. Evita took her place in her car and the huge mass of people crowded round. This was Elizabeth Taylor at the Oscars! They clapped and laughed and waved and came for autographs. Even hunky boys in police uniforms shuffled forward and asked 'Tannie' to please write a message for their girlfriends!

That experience in 1984 was the first time I'd taken Evita and her baroque reality out of the safety of the theatre and into the world. She definitely helped me to hide myself in her camouflage and damage the status quo from within her demure familiar conservatism.

I was back there fifteen years later, in front of a good mixed audience of local Pretoria folk, black and white. The blacks exuded wealth and prosperity. They enjoyed laughing at the image of themselves as seen through Evita's designer-democratic eyes. The whites seemed constantly amazed and shocked at the ease with which blacks enjoyed the fun. It was now pretty obvious that whites would always be in the minority at our Indabas. Logical too, if you know that we are a big black majority with a small white lining. A free show was something even blacks found suspicious.

'What's wrong with it?' many asked, 'Can we come? What's the catch?'

White people phoned first.

'Can we pay?'

I'd say it was free.

'No, we'd rather pay! Then at least we can reserve a nice seat?'

I'd say it was first come, first served.

'That's the problem,' they'd sigh. 'We're a bit nervous about the sort of element you might attract!'

The only element I seem to attract are jealous drag queens!

Why is it always the white liberals who seem to be so concerned about what blacks will think?

'You mustn't make fun of blacks!' they would hiss. 'The blacks won't like it!'

Don't worry, I'd say, it's a democracy. The blacks can now tell me.

'You mustn't criticise blacks!' they'd cringe. 'They won't understand!'

Don't worry, I'd say, this is now a democracy. The blacks can tell me. It's now so easy for blacks to communicate with whites. Bang!

'Yes, but you must be careful!' they'd warn. 'The blacks won't think it's funny. The blacks won't laugh!'

The blacks won't laugh? I think blacks have been laughing at us whites for the last 350 years. We all thought they were saying 'Yes Baas' in Zulu or Xhosa. In fact they were hooting: 'Whitey? You poephol!'

Today Pretoria presents us with representatives from most parties, and a few interesting questions are levelled at the NP, the DP and the ANC. Our friends from the IEC Ivory Tower give us an expensive party in one of the concrete mausoleum-rooms, and we meet them all in a flurry of our tired denims and sandals and their Gucci and Pucci! We just have enough time to bite into a sausage roll and swallow soda water before it's all in plastic doggy bags on the way to the disadvantaged.

WEDNESDAY 3 MARCH

A quick morning visit to our public relations people, who are all away at 'meetings', which means: don't call us, we'll call you. By mid-afternoon we are wending our way back to Pretoria again. This time we take a right turn off the freeway into the township of Mamelodi. This booking has been sitting in the schedule like a visit to a blind dentist! While black audiences in the city, or even in rural communities, have proved to be accessible and friendly, Mamelodi is by reputation neither. Recently in the news again for the hijacking of tourists, one is constantly remembering the many reports of violence and crime and blood-letting in this huge sprawling African city, lying cheek to jowl with Ou Pretoria! The reaction of people to the fact that we would perform in Mamelodi is all gloom and doom, ironically mostly from blacks who live in former white Pretoria itself.

'Darling, you'll be murdered and eaten for dinner!' a Whitney Houston clone had whispered over her Campari at the party the night before. And so with our map carefully stuck to the dashboard, our cellphones and earrings hidden and cars locked from within, we very white doves drive into the black belly of the Third World beast!

We are met by our hosts at the gates, where the tarred road becomes pock-marked and gravely. Township taxis edge the road like beads. Huge billboards announce their wares. There are people everywhere.

'It's OK, people!' laughs the young black man in a T-shirt that says 'Free Mandela'. 'You'll be fine. Just follow us.'

We follow so close we could've been in his boot!

The community centre is surrounded by the standard razor-wire fencing, and we find safe parking behind the building amid high grass and high hopes. It is still late afternoon and the sun is shining on us all. At the front is parked a battered single-decker bus without windows, from which a man is handing out IEC T-shirts and using his mike to inform the crowd of our visit. There are hordes of kids milling around. As the SABC team want Evita interacting with the crowd, I quickly put her together in the dressing room. Within minutes, Mrs Bezuidenhout appears in her leopard-skin dress and gets into the bus, helping to hand out T-shirts. The force with which they are ripped from our hands makes me grateful for the safety of the battered old vehicle.

It has now become clear, through experiences like this, that the IEC see a successful registration-education campaign as simply the handing out of T-shirts. Most kids are under eighteen, and voting is the last thing on their minds. They want a free wardrobe!

Eventually a cluster of large black ladies approach the bus and ask Evita to come and shake their hands. Hell, if Anwar Sadat can fly to Jerusalem, what's the problem here? There is no problem, of course. The ladies want to finger the material of Madam's dress and look at her rings! Girls will be girls! They also show Evita their ID books, all bar-coded. Evita congratulates them. Not enough! They want T-shirts! Knowing how few are left in the bus, Evita throws all caution to the wind and starts mingling with the huge crowd. The loud music from the bus hi-fi sets everyone dancing, and the genuine feeling of fun and party dispels all fears of expected massacres and muggings. In fact, throughout our visit to Mamelodi we feel welcome, safe and pleasantly entertained by the warmth and interest of the people.

The audience in the hall starts small, but grows and grows as the Indaba progresses, and most of the seats are taken by the end of the evening. Again the laughter is loud and specific, although much of the historical farce aimed at white fears goes unnoticed. A small handful of whites have made the effort to come to Mamelodi. Some had been in the State Theatre the night before, and their presence is visibly appreciated. There is a lot of hugging going on.

I do notice a black woman in the middle block listening to Evita's chat with a frown. She is not impressed by this loud Afrikaans woman being so racist, so superior and so warmly received by the other black people. What is wrong here? She obviously doesn't know the secret! Eventually her companion laughingly whispers it into her ear. Evita's critic dissolves into chuckles and becomes a fan. Once they know that this woman up there is actually a man, Evita can say anything! It is commedia dell'arte, the circus is in town!

Sadly no political party thought it safe to venture into Mamelodi. So, after the Indaba, with Evita safely packed away in her box, we spend time with some young people and encourage their questions. They are all eager to punt the election. They are ready to add their passion to the process, but no one seems to ask them to help. I wonder if anyone eventually used them? Or instead just gave them a T-shirt and moved on?

Then, like all normal white South Africans, we pack up, lock our car doors from the inside, hide our cellphones and earrings, and to the accompanying laughter of our bemused hosts and with collective knuckles showing white with tension, we leave the Third World in convoy with the other whites, to join the First World a mere ten minutes away.

THURSDAY 4 MARCH

We are now in the last three days of voter registration, and so Evita's motivation is clear and urgent. We leave Joburg early, getting back on the N1, and pass Pretoria to sweep up the freeway to reach Nylstroom by eleven. This Indaba is a low point. The people who come to the lunchtime show, a few whites and a cluster of black kids in IEC T-shirts – a real rent-a-crowd – are sullen and determined not to be moved. It is hot and sticky. The few party reps can't get a rise out of the potential voters, and there are no questions from the floor. Emergency Drill 13a! Evita cuts to the car chase and ends it all sooner rather than later. It's like being back in the seventies. Tight-lipped Afrikaners and thick-lipped Africans sharing the same space, but separated by an aisle and a lifetime of prejudice and segregation. Had no one heard of the rainbow nation? At least the droëwors we bought at the local butcher was nice!

Chalk again becomes cheese with our evening Indaba in the City of Pietersburg, capital of the Northern Province. The massive Jan Botes Hall is like a huge aeroplane hangar; the foyer just a smaller version. M-Net have prepared a live link-up for their 7 pm programme *Front Row*, and so our audience are informed that they will be part of a satellite link with the world! They give Evita twenty minutes on the programme and the questions are bright and funny. Our audience react with delight and applause. Hopefully the world out there also has a chance to smile, because the news is getting worse on a daily basis. Violence and crime have become an obsession, and there seems to be no let-up on tensions leading up to the election, which is still three months away!

The Mayor of Pietersburg makes a welcoming speech, filled with humour and the occasional barb at Evita's supposed platonic friendship with Pik Botha. The tone is set, and one of the more successful Indabas blossoms to the delight of a good representation of the racial and cultural mix of Pietersburg. For the first time we have a Freedom Front politician. To put him at ease, Evita says she recognises him from her school days. He is appalled.

'Nooit!' he stammers.

'Ja! You took me out one night and I had to even pay for the cooldrinks! Sies!'

He loses the battle and takes it with a laugh and a bow to Mevrou. The audience also sidetracks their prejudice against his conservative all-white programme and gives him a round of applause. Humour is helping here too.

After the Indaba a group of Venda musicians and dancers explode the huge foyer into a colourful eerie traditional dance space, with music made by blowing a note through a reed, or piece of bamboo or seaweed. A North African echo lives in these haunting sounds. Evita stands in her glittering gold and black gown and watches while holding hands with eager young black men and being hugged by eager older black men and women. The media snaps and films away.

The Mayor and local IEC take us to dinner at the Holiday Inn. There we meet up with the Freedom Front man and members of his radical party. This could be a bloodbath! But again we are struck, as so often during this Trek, how friendly and familiar representatives of parties are to each other, no matter what their policies might be. With whites making up only 4 per cent of the population in the Northern Province, they cannot afford to be white and racist and typical, but the blacks tease them more about their good manners and everyone laughs. What does the T-shirt say: Love your enemy – it will ruin his reputation!?

FRIDAY 5 MARCH

We spend five hours driving from Pietersburg down to Nelspruit in Mpumalanga. We take the scenic route via Tzaneen, but in the rain and mist it becomes quite a strain. Lush tropical vegetation, wild St Joseph lilies and mango trees give this world a different texture. We drive, in the soft sticky humid rain, to Komatipoort, the border town with Mozambique and Swaziland.

Faced with a cluster of young white parents, each with four or five children in tow, Evita asks: 'All those children? Don't you have TV here?'

No laughter at anything. Either she frightens them to death because she reminds them of a hated mother-in-law or teacher, or they are waiting for the real comic to come on stage once this tannie is finished. Eventually some leave, offended during the Blood River part of Evita's rewrite of history.

'We Afrikaners believed we won the Battle of Blood River against the Zulus because God was on our side. We were wrong. Now in our democracy we realise the truth. The only reason the Voortrekkers won that battle is because they made the Zulus drunk and pushed them into the river!'

Others just sit and stare at the black mayoress in her red polka-dot dress, rocking with laughter while her friends rock with her. But we are all dripping with sweat and Evita's eyelashes hang by a thread. The local IEC official waits for us outside as we pack up, and smothers us with sarcasm about playing a traditional white venue.

'Why should blacks bother to come?' he sneers.

Well, it seems whites didn't bother to come either. We can't wait to leave this border town and head back to 1999.

SATURDAY 6 MARCH

Today I have to deliver an Evita cabaret at noon to the Nelspruit Chamber of Commerce. This is a long-standing engagement that happily results in a cheque that helps to pay for our petrol! Then we prepare for the evening Indaba at the Bergvlam High School Hall, a modern building up on the hill among flaming red-bloom trees and purple shrubs. The IEC have been registering voters there on this last day of registration, and we meet up with the small sarcastic IEC man again. He has changed his tune and is now glowing with compliments, disguising his contempt. He even offers us all a party after the Indaba, which, when the time comes two hours later, has happily suddenly been cancelled!

Even though it is as hot and sticky as Komatipoort, there is an enthusiastic selection of Nelspruit citizens present: black, white, Indian, Afrikaans, English and even the odd Mozambican illegal! The Premier of Mpumalanga, Mathews Phosa, arrives with his entourage. He is still on crutches from a recent leg operation, but when Evita invites him to address his subjects, he takes to the stage. The Premier gives us a glowing welcome and warmly underlines how important and successful our Great Election Trek is regarded by his people. Who are 'his people'? The ANC? The government? The blacks? Never mind, he is generous and funny, and this is a delightful end to the second week. Back at our hotel, all five of us in Evita's People's Party sit round a large table and eat and drink and laugh about our lives till we cry!

SUNDAY 7 MARCH

Today has been kept free to travel, and a long way we have to go too! We start at sunrise so we can be back in Johannesburg on familiar turf early enough to relax, wash our smalls and Evita's pantyhose, fit in a movie, a meal and an early night. It happens as planned!

e-vita's e-lection e-mail to the leader of the New National Party, Marthinus van Schalkwyk

Marthinus Skattie, Tannie gaan in Engels skryf sodat jy jou Ingels kan oefen.

I am so glad to see you up on so many poles throughout the country. High enough for the dogs not to be able to reach! You look sweet and much older than we thought we could make you. Those funny glasses give you a hint of brain and the haircut hides your funny ears. I know you wanted us to show you wearing your new langbroek, but you wore them back to front! The zip was at the back! Practise!

I know it is difficult to make people remember that the word 'New' in front of National Party means the old days are gone. You give the NNP credibility, because you're too young to remember anything! I remember the first time we met, at one of Oom Pik's lekker parties. I think you were eleven! Far too young to be out so late, but you are a determined person. Siestog, and then you ate so many jelly babies, you were sick all over Oom Pik's new shoes! Definitely the most passion you have shown to date.

As the most senior member of the National Party – the others are either in the Wildernis, in Greece, in jail or insane – I can only give you advice on what not to do: don't be kragdadig, don't be arrogant, don't be glib. Leave that to the ANC. You must be sweet and dierbaar to everyone and you can promise them anything! Because God forbid that you will ever be in a position of power and so have to deliver on promises?

Your posters are a bit confusing. 'Let's get South Africa working' – a contradiction in terms? – on one pole, and then: 'We will bring back the death penalty' on the next. What does this mean? Get them working and then kill them? Nonsense! Leave all that death talk to Oom Louis and his FA. All you can do with the National Party is to lead it gently into that area of history where it will be remembered only for ending apartheid and freeing Oom Nelson.

Ja, thank heavens for a nation's short memory. To think that only 10 years ago the ANC was still banned and no one knew what Tata Nelson looked like! If we'd known what fun being in opposition was, we'd have done this long ago!

P.S. And wash your knees! You've been playing in the garden with your Dinky Toys again!

Barefoot over the Drakensberg

A day of madness as we try to tie down those who promised us help and have disappeared off the face of the earth, and find those who should've returned our calls last week! IEC confusion about where we're going this week. Every time we phone them, we seem to speak to a new voice in an old job! Tonight we're in Johannesburg's City Hall, so we have time during the day to have our two vehicles checked. The team from BCC *Newsnight* join us in the afternoon to film us leaving Lynne's house in Melville and setting up in the City Hall.

We have all been to something special in what was once Johannesburg's great municipal culture palace: symphony concerts, political meetings, arty events. Today the City Hall stands somewhat forlorn in the centre of a deserted African metropolis, a relic from colonial days and times of urban care and pride. The city centre of Joburg has already moved to the City of Sandton. Although not quite decrepit, this old heartbeat of golden Egoli feels sad and neglected. There is no caretaker present. The floor is covered in dust and bird shit. IEC people are whistling while they work, putting up their posters while wearing their IEC peak caps and T-shirts. The venue has a fierce echo and we have to test sound, not only for the audience, but also for the cluster of television cameras belonging to the SABC, the French boys, the BBC and the local press.

Actress Janet Suzman has flown in from London to join us for the week as an observer and kindred spirit. A friend and inspiration since the seventies, when I would send her cards of South African vistas with a bold 'I love you, Vrystaat!' scribbled on the back, she still has copies of all my work written during the apartheid years, kept safely in a box in the garage just in case they end up as the only copies in existence. Truly, my samizdat-comrade in the UK!

The BBC are a bit miffed that other television cameras are present, and that Janet is to write an article about her experience for a British newspaper. The BBC demands exclusivity. It is gently pointed out that we are in the public domain, and that anyone who has the interest could come along for the experience. The fact that there are only three other cameras shows how huge the interest is!

We eventually attract enough people to the Indaba to make the vast floor of Joburg City Hall look populated. Twenty blacks to each white. Some famous Gauteng legislators have popped in on their way to a reception, including the Minister of Education, Mary Metcalfe. Evita teases her: 'How drab you look, my dear! You must be an honest politician to dress so cheaply!'

Comrade Mary was seen to show Mevrou Bezuidenhout a subtle finger-up!

Another in a series of IEC cocktail parties after our Indabas makes us aware of the danger of being hijacked by the IEC. Some people are suspicious that we are sponsored by the government, or the ANC. But we are independent. We are paying for the Trek ourselves. We are not on the road because anyone sent us. This has become our greatest strength. No one can phone up and demand we move left or right. The moral of the story? There can only be freedom of expression if no one else pays! If you are employed to reflect an official line, who cares? That has created the biggest surprise among our audiences to date: that this is voluntary and free!

TUESDAY 9 MARCH

I travel with the BBC in their Kombi for interviews on the road by reporter Jane Stanley, watched over by producer Sanjay Singhal, who is not shy to suggest retakes on the interview to get the answers he wants. One doesn't want to go as far as to suggest any slanted material, but it is a new experience for me.
'Why do you want to do it again? Wasn't I clear?' I'd say.

'Yes, but we thought it was a little vague on the violence and crime aspect.'

'But there is no violence and crime aspect,' I'd smile. 'We don't have guns. We don't need guns.'

'No, we feel your optimism about the election is out of step with the reality.'

'We are optimistic,' I'd purr.

The election was going to be a disaster, they'd decided, and my bushy-tailed hope wasn't helping the story. So I fluff the retakes with great apology, blaming exhaustion and artistic weakness. They are stuck with the original replies!

Newcastle is in KwaZulu-Natal, on the route to Durban from Gauteng. The Town Hall is a pretty Victorian gem, and when we arrive we find a cluster of old ladies patiently waiting to get to the front-row seats. The Pietermaritzburg newspaper *Natal Witness* has Evita on their front page in colour, with a detailed programme of our KwaZulu-Natal trek. If only the press in the other provinces had bothered to do this! The hall is full with a mixed crowd, again reminding one of a bygone era with all the whites downstairs and all the blacks upstairs! There are no questions for the few reps on stage.

The Deputy Mayor invites us for another cocktail party, and we find ourselves showing symptoms of sausage roll fatigue. After lunch I join the French team in their Kombi on the road to our next stop, which is Pietermaritzburg. Their questions are completely different to the previous session with the BBC. They are upbeat and optimistic, maybe because they've been with us since the beginning.

Meanwhile, travelling in my car, Lynne and Janet are so deep in conversation about theatre and the world out there, that they pass Pietermaritzburg and have to turn back. When they arrive, we realise they'd taken the road to Swaziland!

The Pietermaritzburg City Hall is probably one of our treasured examples of colonial gothic. It looks like a movie set and has been carefully restored and cared for. The air is hot and muggy and Mrs Bezuidenhout is forced to sweat like a real person. She is backed on stage by one of the biggest organs in the country, and says as much without innuendo. That's the problem with Evita: she has no sense of humour or irony. Maybe that's why she has survived for so long. She doesn't make the joke; she is the joke.

There is a very substantial audience filling the downstairs area, as well as the gallery that sweeps round the auditorium. Also, for once, many political parties have taken to the stage: the ANC, the DP, our constant Green Party woman and the ever-present surly presence of the leader and singular member of God's People's Party!

The BBC want to take Evita out 'to a student pub'. They want interaction with 'The People'. I don't usually take her into places like that, as it is virtually impossible to keep up a performance that requires total concentration. Then Evita becomes a drag queen and sometimes meets up with other drag queens, and our make-up runs! But giving them the benefit of the doubt, I shave my chest and put Tannie into a cocktail frock and off we go. It's not a pub; it's an upmarket restaurant. A few members of our audience are there and delighted to see Mrs Bezuidenhout there as well.

The BBC team have sourced a couple on the patio. They want Evita to talk to them on camera. It seems that the man said he was not going to vote! They are a white couple, he older than his companion and Afrikaans. The camera glares at us. He looks nervous. Evita sits next to them. The producer hisses instructions, but Evita ignores him.

After some small talk, Evita asks: 'Are you going to vote, Herman?'

'No,' Herman says. 'I don't have time.'

The BBC lick their lips and come in for a close-up.

Evita trots out her propaganda and wags a finger in closing.

'… and just think how many of our people have died so that you can vote?'

'I've always voted, Evita,' he smiles. 'Look, like you I'm white.'

He puts his arm around his companion.

'The election is in three months,' he says in a soft voice. 'I am waiting for a heart transplant and I don't think I'll get it in time. So really, there are some more important things for me to do in the next ninety days, you understand?'

I am dying inside. But the camera smells real blood and noses closer. The producer hisses.

'Tell him he's got to say why he's not voting!'

Herman hears the hiss.

'Well, if you really want to know: my wife and two children were murdered three months ago by a gang of blacks and I don't feel very comfortable supporting their democracy at present, you understand?' Then he takes his hand and places it across the lens. 'And stop this filming please …'

I take off Evita's hair. One way to wreck a shot. The camera crew scuttle off to find some other target.

I apologise to Herman and his lady. He looks drained. She asks for Evita's autograph. I put on the hair again and sign their menu. So much for the mighty BBC's research and homework. Our relationship takes a cool turn, and when they leave us at the end of the week, we're all glad. I stay nervous until the extract is aired on *Newsnight*, fronted by Jeremy Paxton. It is brilliantly edited and presented and his support for us is appreciated.

I go back to the hotel and have dinner. Janet Suzman provides a valuable outsider's eye on the politics – the clarity of intention and opinion of someone who comes from such a solid, predictable European liberalism. And yet she is putting her British solutions for African realities on hold. Janet is also learning, just as we are. There is no blueprint here. We all realise how fragile our little rainbow nation is, scarcely four years into its first democracy!

WEDNESDAY 10 MARCH

Richmond is a part of KwaZulu-Natal that has constantly been featured in world news alongside Beirut, Belfast and Bosnia. Massacres, murders and obviously politically motivated killings are a regular horror from the Richmond area, and when the violence blew up again just before we left on the Trek, people said, 'Lucky you're not going to Richmond.'

So we phoned Richmond.

'Can we come to you?'

'But haven't you seen the news?' they asked, surprised.

'Yes. We want to come!'

And so Evita's People's Party went to Richmond. After all, people are also living there!

The drive showed us a beautiful green gentle countryside, like so many other places that hide pain and hurt. The village is like any English village in a sixties film. The Memorial Hall could have been the set for an episode of *Murder She Wrote*. Most of the tall gangly white ladies with handbags and brilliantly guarded smiles even look like Angela Lansbury! But that's where the similarity ends.

In the street stand a cluster of the unwieldly police vehicles called Hippos. Uniformed men armed with huge guns loiter on the sidewalk. Camouflage outfits can be seen moving in the grounds under the trees, behind the trees, in the trees, even as trees! And in the middle is the Mayor of Richmond, living in the shadow of protective steel to insure his oft-threatened life. We are in a war zone, like minstrels of old coming to play our tunes of hope and harmony as bloodstained fingers tighten on triggers.

The Memorial Hall is not big. In fact, it's so small and cramped that there are people everywhere: on chairs, on the floor, standing at the back, outside the open windows and on the stoep to the side. Besides the predictable paisley and puritan locals, there are small Zulu schoolboys in white shirts and grey shorts, sitting cross-legged among the rifle butts. There are various political strongmen present, not wanting to miss seeing the former Ambassador to Bapetikosweti, eyeing each other over pink carnations in lapels and shaking hands just a trifle too long.

The Mayor sits within shouting distance of his bodyguard and within shooting distance from anyone who so wishes. And the media? Where did they suddenly come from? What was happening in Richmond to attract so many from so far? Was there going to be a massacre before tea? The Norwegians are there, zoom lenses erect. Some Dutch. Germans. The British press clustered between our

French boys and the SABC-ouks. A local TV cameraman seems to be resting his equipment on the knee of a seated policeman!

It's a difficult Indaba: how to refer to the reality of recent violence and fear without creating violence and fear? Reminding ourselves what this is, a voter education through entertainment diversion: some theatre, some fun, a bit of relaxation and hopefully a sight of the wood in spite of the trees?

Evita, of course, calls a spade a spade and doesn't compromise for the sake of local tensions. The result is the laughter of recognition and relief. The Mayor and his bodyguard are compared to PW Botha going to Soweto: '... except His Worship here has more guns!'

All the warring parties are represented: the Inkatha Freedom Party, the ANC, the United Democratic Movement and the DP. That poor white sucker ironically got all the flack: 'What did you do during the Struggle to justify demanding to be the Opposition to a black majority government?'

The IFP rep, an elderly elegant aristocrat, speaks only in Zulu. Some questions are in Zulu. Evita smiles and pretends to understand, nodding in the right places and adding agreement and applause where needed. The Zulus are duly impressed, and so am I!

It all lasts ninety minutes, with questions from the floor about political violence and rampant crime. Some politicians want to see them as the same issue, others separate them into political and civic matters.

Evita wags her finger at them all and takes no prisoners.

'You must stop behaving like greedy politicians and start thinking like statesmen and leaders! Anyone can kill! It takes a great person to keep people alive!'

Personally I would have thrown a jam tart at the old bitch, but somehow it is the right candyfloss at the right time.

After all is said and done, the Mayor and his Council give us a party! More sausage rolls! It all takes place in a quaint cottage next to the hall, hemmed in by the police Hippos and a crowd of black councillors. Their white colleagues are inside, laying tables and rearranging the cocktail snacks. No one is let in, including the Mayor, until Evita arrives. When I apologise that she had to leave to see to issues of state, everyone applauds. Not everyone links me with her! Then the doors open and we can enter the party parlour.

We leave Richmond and the razor-wire, relieved and slightly high on an overdose of adrenaline. And alive! Poor media. They came for a massacre and all they got was a sausage roll!

Uvongo is way down the KwaZulu-Natal South Coast from Durban, near Port Shepstone. The Town Hall could have been Brighton! As a result the full house of 600 is filled with white colonial refugees from their suburban fortresses with their seven-foot-high security walls and armed patrols! Ten black faces maybe, including the Mayor of the town, who obediently stays on one side. This old-school stiff-upper-lip racism brings out the worst in me. Luckily Evita has a chance to congratulate the audience.

'We know you here in Uvongo were the most rabidly anti-apartheid community on the South Coast. Thanks to your sense of humanity and your unprejudiced attitude to your black brothers and sisters, apartheid was eventually slain! Amandla!'

The audience applauds until the irony sinks in, and they never quite recover their original smile of contented superiority.

Afterwards, while we are talking to the Mayor and his few black colleagues, a white woman comes up and says: 'But isn't your show geared for us whites? I don't see how our blacks would understand what you're on about.'

She then smiles at the blacks listening to her. One of them replies with a matching smile.

'Funny, we were just saying: it had to be geared to black democrats, because none of you whites seemed to get it!'

THURSDAY 11 MARCH

Next on our schedule is the University of Durban-Westville, which was created in the old South Africa as a place for Indians to study. Set up on the rolling hills overlooking Durban, it has lately also been shaken by student riots and internal dissent. Just the place for Tannie Evita to go and do her tango in front of their firing squad.

We're in an 800-seater hall, which is soon well filled. There is muted reaction from the students, mainly because the bad acoustics seem to kill all sound. Some very good questions enliven the audience's interest.

'If I'm registered where I live and where I have to vote, that means I can't vote on 2 June because I can't leave my studies here and go home where I'm registered!'

The DP rep had an answer: 'Go to your local IEC office and fill in a change of address form.'

We had never heard this information before, either from candidates or the IEC itself.

'Is it true that if you don't vote, your support will automatically go to the majority party?' was another question. We immediately contact editors in Gauteng and Durban and ask them to check this out and dispel the rumours, or underline solutions with facts. The ignorance among the youth is frightening. No one really seems to know, or care, what happens.

The University of Natal, up on another hill of Durban, has allowed us to have our Indaba in their Jubilee Hall, as all other venues are full of sports activities. When we get to the hall, we find a gym class in full swing. No one knows we're coming. There are only fifty chairs available, and our friends, the IEC, have been busy reserving them all for their 'VIPs and guests'.

Lynne gently commandeers the IEC people to find chairs in basements and rooms and fill up the hall. She has a wonderful icy Meryl Streep Executive Expression #5, and God help anyone who pulls rank! Tables and rostra are mobilised. Of course the IEC guests don't bother to pitch, so all seats can be used by the public and the few students. Former Minister of Correctional Services, Sipho Mzimela, is the UDM rep, after being thrown out of the IFP. He is funny and to the point and has a wonderful time reacting to all the libellous detail in Evita's political gossip. The DP rep from the noon session is with us again, articulate and funny, sounding a bit like Evita when he says: 'Last week I was offered an NP puppy. I said no. This week I was offered a DP puppy. I said: it's the same puppy! They said: yes, but now its eyes are open!'

Once again there is no dressing room, and Basil Appollis and I have to change into our various disguises down the road in someone's office with use of an outside toilet, where we disturb a copulating couple! The Indaba takes on a new shape, as we cannot leave the stage area once we're on: we'd literally fall off the cliff into the jungle below! The ad libs and some emergency thinking rejuvenate the whole structure. This is probably the best thing that could happen to us at this stage. Make no mistake, we are getting pretty tired by now!

In the next twenty-four hours we have to travel 650 kilometres to Ladysmith for the noon Indaba, and then on to Welkom for an evening presentation. So we spend some time over a bottle in my suite to plan the madness of the next day.

FRIDAY 12 MARCH

The Ladysmith Town Hall is another architectural gem. Great plans have been faxed to us during the last weeks explaining what Mayor Vilikazi has planned for our welcome. It all happens according to plan. Once Evita has been constructed in a small toilet at the back of the Hall, the Mayor's Mercedes picks her up at the back door and takes her through the town, escorted by the local police car, sirens ablare, until we reach the front of the Mayoral Chambers. A red carpet snakes its way from the kerb, ending abruptly in the middle of the sidewalk. Evita gets out and is embraced by the elegant Mayor, splendid in his chains of office, with a twinkle in his eyes and a laugh in his voice. He escorts us into his offices and into an ante-room, where his Town Council is waiting to greet the former ambassador and her entourage. Already people are thinking Lynne is Evita's daughter and the technical boys her sons! They don't mind and play the parts. Flowers and gifts are presented by his people to her people, and our host has a wonderful time being part of this episode of the local *Dynasty*! A moment is savoured when his hand brushes against Mevrou's august bosom. Black men can blush! Besides, that bosom is alas not soft and warm, but merely balls of knotted pantyhose filled with birdseed!

Things change when we enter the hall itself. As we walk in majestically, Evita on the Mayoral arm, his black councillors stand, but the majority of whites stay pointedly seated. There is no room for the First Citizen of Ladysmith, and so he shrugs and sits alone in an empty row of reserved signs. We sense a situation here. The white audience begrudgingly react to Evita, making us wonder why they came in the first place.

When the local ANC rep stands up to give his allocated three minutes of encouraging propaganda, half the whites get up and walk out. The NNP man speaks next, and very badly too.

'Let's pretend apartheid didn't happen,' he seriously suggests. 'Let's look at the excellent structures of government under the old National Party!'

Evita interrupts.

'You mean, skattie, let's take the water out of the ocean and watch the fish do the tango?'

It seems most of the NP's supporters had already left, so the remaining blacks hoot with laughter.

When the UDM comrade stands up, all the other whites stomp out. This has obviously been prearranged.

Evita watches them waddle out, familiar fat arses in tight floral dresses and men with stomachs hanging over belts.

'Siestog, they're probably going to feed their horses!' she twinkles, and the remaining audience applauds. Throughout all this the Mayor doesn't flinch and plays the perfect host. One Afrikaans woman stays behind and apologises for the bad behaviour of her friends. She promises to vote and we forgive Ladysmith!

We pack quickly and start the four-hour trek across the Free State to Welkom. Luckily we have good weather, cool but not raining, and the traffic seems to be on our side. We drive into Welkom, known for its pastime of watching traffic lights change. This mining town is set in the goldfields, and the barren plains seem to stretch into infinity on all sides. We move into the Ernest Oppenheimer Theatre. This is heaven. Dressing rooms! With hot water! With electric lights! Toilets that flush! Just toilets! The working air-con is just too much of a good thing, and tears of relief flow!

After so-called halls with no dressing rooms, and sometimes no hall, we were being rewarded for our pioneering madness. We feel so secure backstage at the Ernest Oppenheimer, we don't even bother to go out in search of sandwiches. From seven o'clock a collection of community choirs come into the foyer and start singing, attracting people from surrounding areas. It goes without saying that whites stayed away in their droves and the blacks had a wonderful time. More and more we are noticing that our audiences represent the majority and not the moneyed minorities. And those whites who do attend stop being white and become South African and celebrate, not just the humour, but the fact that we can do so together!

Welkom turns out to be one of the best Indabas. There are old and young, returned exiles and struggle veterans, maids and madams, babies with vocabularies and loud shrieks. Evita controls the excitement like an SS puppetmistress! Yet only the African Christian Democratic Party are present and prepared to speak. We find out later that some other parties were there, but stayed hidden from view.

The sausage-roll-out/IEC party that follows repeats a disturbing and irritating pattern. Their VIPs and guests become the elite, and everyone else must stand aside and wait, while the gold-rimmed spectacles peer at the snacks and the manicured nails pick out the morsels. Political rank is used as a class above the masses! Echoes of old Broederbond pomposity and creaky power plays remind us that nothing really changes. But here in the Welkom foyer everyone, including the comrades, is waiting for Evita to arrive.

When I appear in the usual black jacket and pants, they ask: 'Where is Madam?'

I have to explain with a straight face that she has to meet Pik Botha at the Wimpy! Then the kids bunch together and a choir singalong takes place, from 'Sarie Marais' to the 'Click Song'. Ending with 'Nkosi Sikeleli', including the

Afrikaans section of 'Die Stem'. That 'Uit die blou van onse hemel' still gives me the creeps, but if blacks can sing it with such respect, who am I to complain? I join in; at least I know the words!

SATURDAY 13 MARCH

Today is our last Free State call: a noon Indaba in Kroonstad. So we pack and leave the Welkom Holiday Inn and schlep through the ugly flat higgledy-piggledy world of gold mines and discarded equipment, burnt mielielands and tired sunflower plantations. Lynne and I take bets: is Kroonstad waiting for us with banners flying? Are there millions of people waiting to see this caravan of comedy and concern?

Yes and no.

The Town Hall is deserted. We find the manager, who is expecting us. He is not concerned that everything is so quiet. He is proud of this building, a reminder of the worst of the communist rococo of 1950s East Berlin! Eventually a Kroonstad township choir arrives, and the sixty young people stand on the steps of the Town Hall and start singing magically. Then eighty young girls appear from nowhere, drum majorettes in their purple and gold, dancing and twirling and smiling. The choir and the crowd they attract all seem to have cellphones, and after twenty minutes the friends they have phoned arrive in taxis and cars. The Indaba swings from the start, with dancers in the aisles and singers in the gallery. Tannie Evita is welcomed like the Queen of Sheba!

Once all the blacks are already seated, the whites arrive. This time they got the timing wrong, and Evita points it out to the delight of the kids. By the end of the presentation the hall is full, with young whites trying out new toyi-toyi steps and blacks dancing with Evita on the stage! Once we're packed, the drummies mob our little two-vehicle convoy and demand goodbye hugs from us all. We wave at a big mama in a blue Tswana dress, beaming and swaying to the drums. We found out that she has organised all of this single-handedly from her small township home. When she heard on her portable radio that we were coming, she decided to help. If it wasn't for her energy and care, nothing would've happened in Kroonstad. The story of South Africa: one person can make all the difference!

Which brings us to the global picture. The support of SAfm's radio programme 'AM-Live', which broadcasts Evita's five-minute report-back to the nation every morning before the seven o'clock news, means that South Africans listen during breakfast, or in their cars on the way to work. It has meant that I have to be up and awake by 6.45 every morning, near to a working phone or in an area where the cellphone picks up a signal, with my notes prepared and Tannie's voice ready. But that little window to the world has meant that whoever hears what we're doing can imagine where we are. If we celebrate an audience of 56 people, they see 56 000! When we dance with small schoolboys, they see the swirl of a Hollywood musical. The magic of the imagination is fired by the excitement of eccentricity and made personal by the appeal of this mini-madness. Like the two Disney dogs and one cat in *The Incredible Journey*, Evita's People's Party has grabbed the attention of the people and has made everyone smile just at the thought of it. And that's really what it's all about. We are here to tickle the tummy of the cross beast. And I think the beast is actually smiling!

Saturday night in Bloemfontein!

Bloemfontein is truly the centre of South Africa, a city that knows everything about everyone everywhere because so little happens here! But no, corruption in local government is on everyone's lips, and what could be more pertinent than the Premier of the Free State, Ivy Matsepe-Casaburri, as our VIP guest. The Bloem audience is muted and polite. Most of them seem to be beholden to the guest of honour, and so they all watch her carefully. Their boss is present, and when she occasionally laughs like a blocked drain, the underlings venture a smile. Comrade Ivy has flown back from meetings in Gauteng to be on time for the Indaba. She didn't want to miss meeting Evita Bezuidenhout, and eventually posed for a picture with the Boere Diva.

Evita constantly teases Mama Ivy, suggesting that after she'd run the SABC and now the Free State, what was left that the government wanted destroyed? Ivy shakes with either laughter or apoplexy.

For the duration of our session, people come and go. Afrikaners tend to leave soon after the first dig at our failed 1000 by-law Reich. But it doesn't really matter. The house lights stay on, everyone can be seen. The cameras wander around. No one is tied down to protocol, or even good manners. No one has to pay, or stay, or say anything. Believe what you will! Just sit back and have a party with Tannie Evita. And they do!

SUNDAY 14 MARCH

We all get up early to wave farewell to Janet Suzman, who has to get a 06:30 am plane to Joburg to catch her connection to London. It's been a wonderful week with her. Besides sharing her detailed anecdotes about a full and successful life in the British theatre and films, Janet has been like Chekhov's Masha from *Three Sisters*, sitting in the backseat of the car with a copy of Alan Paton's *Cry, the Beloved Country* as we drive through that very setting, muttering incantations in her flawless English. And then letting rip with a glorious Braamfontein curse when we manage to swerve out of the way of an oncoming truck driving on our side of the road. Janet is the needed affirmation of our theatrical roots, and a constant inspiration to go for the jugular and be braver than the brave. She has also made us feel special by being with the Trek as a virtual stage hand for the last seven days, carrying props and cooldrinks, helping with sound checks, and remarkably sitting though fourteen Indabas. When she published her experiences in a British paper, she remarked how extraordinary it was to see a different energy and approach with each audience. It was also a chance for me to try out different lines on Janet, as poor Lynne knew the repertoire so well she could be my understudy!

As we have no Indabas today, it being Sunday and the Free State, we drive slowly down the map of Africa, passing small dorps and watching people come out of church. It's a beautiful day, and again the vastness of the land never ceases to encourage lumps of bad purple poetry to spout forth between chewing at the biltong and sips of energy drink! We stop in Aliwal North and spend some hours swimming in the hot springs, drinking wine, having a phone interview with the *Chicago Tribune*, befriending a cat and two old dogs, and getting unbelievably pissed!

e-vita's e-lection e-mail to
Mangosuthu Buthelezi

Honourable Minister, Highness and Zulu Warrior Number One! I address you with nervous care and careful detail, as I do not want an angry e-mail in return, nor a twenty-page fax! Not to mention a burnt-down house, or an exit visa to Uzbekistan! You are our Minister of Home Affairs and as an Afrikaans icon I always believe charity begins at home. I'm glad you are against the idea of that bloody Yugoslavian leader coming here to South Africa to seek refuge, once they get him out of Belgrade. But he won't surrender to NATO. I see too much of the bedônnerde ou boer in this President Milosovic!

One hundred years ago it took the entire British Empire to force us boers to our knees, and that was only because they committed ethnic cleansing with our women and children. But if you're so against the Serbian Verwoerd coming to South Africa, how come you're okay with the other people who have done even more to destabilise their communities? And I don't want to point a finger at Libya's Gaddafi, Cuba's Castro, or that short Arab with the Clicks tea towel round his head. We all know they are the great democrats and upholders of human rights. Otherwise we wouldn't allow them to speak in our Parliament, nie waar nie?

I mean, all these people who are just walking into our country from neighbouring basket-case places. People who know that here in South Africa we can offer them a perfect market in which to ply their trade. And their trade is: Crime. Because here in South Africa crime not only pays, it becomes prime investment! So no charity for criminals! I see one political poster after the next up on the poles, promising the return of the death penalty in exchange for a vote. I think the phrase 'death penalty' is misleading. It should not be seen as a 'penalty', but as 'reward!'

And I don't think we should hang criminals either. Rather put them in a nice warm police cell with television and then show them, continuously, twenty-four hours a day, seven days a week, Felicia Mabuza-Suttle shows! Believe me, after a week they will hang themselves!

Some estimates put our illegal immigrants in this country at four million! Liewe aarde! In the old South Africa we had 27 million illegals. But then you knew who they were, because they weren't white!

How will you solve this, Oh Mighty One? Our poor blacks are so unhappy because they are losing their work and often their lives to these ethnic aliens. Maybe it must all wait until you become Deputy President in the new Mbeki Dispensation. And you should, skat, because you passed the audition. Last year when Madiba and Thabo went overseas so often, they left you behind to run South Africa. Gits, we were nervous! But Nelson Mandela is so clever. He only made you Acting President on a Sunday, when no one answers the phones! No, actually he did put you in charge on a Tuesday and then you invaded Lesotho! But he didn't do that again, did he?

I hope you keep your KwaZulu-Natal. It's a good thing for any democracy to have a strong opposition. Let the NNP keep the Western Cape, let the UDM try to refloat the Eastern Cape, give Mpumalanga to the PAC and Free State to the FF. That leaves Robben Island for Louis Luyt's FA and the ANC can manage the rest!

PS. Love your old 1987 picture on the IFP poster. Clever to have airbrushed ou PW Botha out!

And Into
Ye Olde Kaffreria

We prepare ourselves for the Eastern Cape. Out of all the provinces visited, this traditional zone of Xhosa wars and homeland whores is now the butt of jokes and punchlines to lectures on how not to run a province!

'You even steal your own deficit!' Mrs Bezuidenhout coos in the Queenstown Town Hall.

Maybe the people of the Eastern Cape are economically depressed. One is certainly aware of a lack of creative activity in farming and commerce, but spiritually depressed they don't seem to be, as they rock with laughter and roar with delight.

The Mayor of Queenstown gives us a party in his chambers. By now Mrs Bezuidenhout has already changed into her glittering gold and silver evening gown, and when she enters the room, it is electrifying. All the councillors line up like football players to shake the icon's paw! The women study Mevrou's outfit and one lady keeps peering at her chin! A hint of beard to come? I hope not!

The Mayor gives his formal speech of welcome '... we in the collective leadership ...' And then Evita daintily fills her plate, nibbling at a familiar sausage roll, and invites the people to partake. By now she has the routine down to a fine art. After some time there socialising and posing for mantelpiece pics, Evita waves farewell, and five minutes later I arrive in my shorts and flip-flops. It's wonderful to be stared at as if I'd wandered in off the street. Then a rotund councillor roars recognition: the cleft in my chin is like Evita's! It's as if they've discovered that the Easter Bunny is actually Father Christmas in drag! Now they want to study my legs, but cannot find a hint of the famous Bezuidenhout bene. How can they, I ask. 'Evita's not here!'

TUESDAY 16 MARCH

The Great Election Trek enters Stutterheim, an unimpressive convoy consisting of the dusty minibus full of our speakers and equipment, with our three technicians squashed in between boxes and cases, and Lynne and me in the silver Daewoo, with Mrs Bezuidenhout tucked away in the boot. The car is filling up with souvenirs found on the way: a small brown bear with one eye that we spotted staring out from a small bric-a-brac shop somewhere; a faded print of the Battle of Blood River – the usual. Stutterheim was named after a German General who settled here, but that's where the similarity ends. This is Xhosa town, filled with street vendors, each selling what look like the same wares: bags, shoes, clothes and muti-medicine. At the stage door of the small Town Hall we meet the traditional healer with his selection of roots, bark and leaves, some for stomach ailments, some for female pains and a phallic-looking root we refer to as the alternative Viagra!

After the Indaba, Evita is taken by the Mayor to see the local theatre, a venue that would turn Joburg and Cape Town green with envy. A Commonwealth Conference on Small Town Government is to be held here in Stutterheim in a few weeks, and everyone is preparing for it. As Evita walks through the foyer and down the carpeted aisles, local workers watch open-mouthed. They've also seen this woman on television!

We leave the town with a sure feeling that here reconciliation and development are a reality. The SABC cabal and the French boys want Evita somewhere in the veld, so I keep her fresh and eventually we do some shots with her sitting on the white line along a straight stretch of road leading into infinity, doing her make-up.

East London's Orient Theatre is a huge raked hangar with plastic bucket seats fixed to concrete steps and an echo that can be heard from the moon! The air here is again hot and sticky, the sea being just a few meters down behind the stage. The humidity cloys, and sweat slithers down one's neck and ripples along the spine. The ACDP, NNP and ANC are present. So is God's People's Party, our religious nut with stale beer breath and the charm of a bamboo basket.

A question keeps repeating itself in various communities: voters are concerned about not finding their names on the voter's roll. Evita keeps repeating the IEC's tollfree number: 08-00-11-80-00. People have tried that number, but say there is no answer! Does the IEC really exist, or are they just a fashion show in Pretoria and a plate full of sausage rolls in Nelspruit?

In the front row sits a swarthy man with a Viva Zapata moustache. He's also wearing a black shirt with diamond cuffs, rings and a pendant! Evita is worried. Never mind: he is the Mayor of the town and ends up kissing her hand!

WEDNESDAY 17 MARCH

We wave a damp farewell to East London and chug off to King William's Town. There we find no room at the inn: the Town Hall, which was to be our venue, is pointedly unavailable, and all other civic venues are 'being prepared for the election'. As this is still two months away, we wonder if prejudice has won the day here. We are, however, given a space: the War Memorial Hall on the outskirts of the town. It looks like it's been hit by a bomb! There are no chairs except for rows of stacked plastic at the back of the hall, each tower swaying dangerously when you walk past on the creaky wooden floor. Rotten rostra suggest a probable stage, but are not safe. And to crown it all, an impatient local councillor is standing around demanding payment!

But we're getting better at this by the day. No anger, no abuse, no violence, no nothing; just a wave of the cellphone and a call to the Mayor. It seems there is no Mayor available, but the Town Clerk is dying to meet Evita. He doesn't even know we're in town. So we leave the councillor to help the technicians set up a stage and a seating structure, and go and confront the second highest authority in town.

'You already have our R500 deposit,' we say to the lady behind the counter.

'No,' frowns another secretary from behind a typewriter – hey? a typewriter? – and is adamant. 'We must have an additional R400 and then we will refund the said deposit.'

Lynne is now Faye Dunaway, calm but firm.

'That's very thoughtful,' she drawls, 'but here is a better idea: clean the War Memorial Hall, set the chairs out in rows, put paper in the toilets and switch on the electricity! That's what we will pay for, or else we will just move on to the next town via the local newspaper offices and a call to CNN, Reuters and the BBC!' It was the reference to the local newspaper office that did it!

Eventually the Indaba turned out quite well. Eighty per cent of our audience were schoolkids, senior and junior. So the slant of the material was geared towards them and their future as voters in 2004. Kids always give the Indabas a great energy. It underlines the responsibility of us adults to see that 2 June goes well, so that they have a safe democratic future. There are not many questions for our selection of local politicals, who all look relieved at not being exposed as political puppets with no tongues or opinions of their own in front of the children.

Afterwards we go, without Evita, who is hot and bothered, to the Mayor's Chambers. He has returned from wherever he was and is visibly disappointed that the most famous white woman in South Africa is absent. He then presents me with a gift for 'her', then refers to me as 'she' and gets all his tenses and sexes gloriously mixed up. The sausage rolls vie with samoosas for the first bite.

The University of Fort Hare slides by as we bump our way on terrible roads through a town called Alice. We need to get to Fort Beaufort by late afternoon. We were unable to secure a venue at Fort Hare, which is a shame as there is much volatile tension bubbling in that pot of learning.

Fort Beaufort, on the other hand, looks like a Mexican border dorp filled with dark Mexican border types! A funfair has set itself in the middle of a veld, and small children squashed into baskets are whizzing round at the end of rusty chains as the carousel squeaks its way through a dozen revolutions in the dust.

Lynne and I leave the boys to set up in the Town Hall, also a beautiful building obviously cared for with love. We find a coffee shop in a house and meet the owner, a retired ballet dancer who was once on point with Nadia Nerina and Margot Fonteyn! She tells us the whole town knows about the Indaba and everyone will be there!

And they are! The hall is full and the energy is again indicative of the passions out and around in this province. The DP rep comes on stage accompanied by a large white 'Xhosa' praise singer, and proceeds to play the bagpipes. This is the first time a politician has also come with the funny stuff: if only all of them would relax and let it hang out like this. It puts everything so perfectly into perspective. After the session the Mayor's party is upstairs in the foyer. No wonder the place looks like a palace; the prince is in residence! He specially requests Evita to attend, and so eventually Mevrou is seated in a high-backed chair like Grace Kelly in a scene from *High Noon*, surrounded by her excited Gary Coopers. The councillors then produce two SPAR carrier bags and proudly set out, on the Mayor's desk, three bottles each of green and orange cooldrink and Tab. They then shake out of another plastic bag a cluster of Romany Cream biscuits! Here is a party of style and substance with not a sausage roll in sight! And everyone is united by the same language. Whites and blacks chat in animated Xhosa, leaving our Boere Boadicaea high and dry.

We're not sleeping over in Fort Beaufort, because someone said the drive to Grahamstown wasn't long or difficult. That someone is wrong! We creep along a narrow road, notorious for huge panting kudus leaping out of the dark onto motor cars and killing all within. Eventually we arrive at our destination, a town many of us are familiar with. The National Arts Festival in Grahamstown has made this university town an essential stop for us every July. In fact, tonight we all stay with Lynette Marais, who is the director of the festival and an old colleague from the Market Theatre days, when she was theatre manager in 1977 and I was waiting for a police raid because of my new play *Paradise Is Closing Down.* Ignoring the crazy time, we sit round the table in Lynette's kitchen and talk theatre and other normal things till the sun rises. I don't think we ever touch on politics.

THURSDAY 18 MARCH

If it's Thursday it must be Grahamstown. Once the second largest city in South Africa, it has always had an air of superiority and a dusty colonial nostalgia. Our lunchtime Indaba is at the Rhodes Theatre, and we indulge ourselves in the dressing rooms with their lights, mirrors, toilets and running water – hot and cold! The hall is packed with students and lecturers, and Evita has a grand time teasing them about their traditional liberalism and closet racism, and forces them all to vocally commit themselves to vote on 2 June.

Again we have that important question from the floor:

'If I'm registered where I live, can I still vote where I work?'

How come this issue does not get clarified on national level? Evita asks for the IEC presence. He makes himself known, but has no answer to the question. Evita asks the audience to spend time that afternoon phoning newspapers and radio stations and asking them to help clarify the issue with some answers.

The Mayor of Grahamstown, the quaintly named Ms Faku, comes to meet Mrs B, and pictures are taken. The journalism students seem to be everywhere, making journalistic notes, already with that familiar expression of media-madness in their eyes.

Tonight we are just down the road in the Albany Road Recreation Centre. This is in the coloured township, which rubs up against the bigger black township. Again for us a leap into the Third World, with the oxygen of the First still burning in our lungs. Whereas the noon Indaba audience was awash with lighter shades of pale, this township gig is black and brown with pink dots of white faces punctuating here and there. The laughter is easy, thanks to the fact that this hall is also used as a festival venue every July, and many of the neighbours are used to seeing theatre here. A woman is rocking back and forth in her chair with tears running down her cheeks. It seems just the sight of Evita is too much for her, and she's off again even before something is said.

The hall fills rapidly, and by the end there is standing room only. Although there is no sense of embarrassment about whites being part of the audience, the majority of the people are coloured and their quicksilver sense of humour is in sharp contrast to the predictable doughy chuckles of the noonday intellectuals.

We take Lynette to the Cock House for a wonderful tasty dinner, and talk at length about the value of taking theatre out of the safety of the dramatic womb. This is what we are doing, and it has opened up a new avenue for us, so long used to the confines of the theatre's four walls. We toast her and her vision. It is in many ways thanks to the Festival chipping away at the fears of the public that the Albany Road venue could so easily be accessed by whites and blacks tonight.

FRIDAY 19 MARCH

We're off to Port Elizabeth, on that very familiar winding road from Grahamstown that can last forever when you're stuck behind a crawling truck or bus. We go directly to the sprawling University of Port Elizabeth, where the auditorium promises luxuries undreamt of: air-con, acoustics, dressing-room suites, rows of lights just for show and lavatories with showers! And an excellent collection of enthusiastic students and real people. Then Evita changes into a more striking media outfit, a glittering blue knee-length suit, and is driven to the centre of PE to meet the Mayor, another member of the same Faku dynasty. We do photos outside on the town square, much to the fascination of the hawkers, whores, pimps, tourists, pigeons and people. The beauty of the City Hall as a background makes for a good front page picture in the next morning's *Eastern Province Herald*.

We've been on the road for nearly a month – with two shows a day in different towns, travelling between them, getting up early enough to find them, working purely on adrenaline with audiences that vary from community to community. We have had few luxuries, and these include finding the occasional cup of real coffee! And so, when we drive into the grounds of our guest house in the Walmer suburb of PE, I sense a major treat coming. It's a magnificent Victorian mansion fit for a king, and in this case, also a queen.

Our host is Chris Greeff and it's his birthday. So we grab a bite of his verjaarsdagkoek and a hug, and immediately make our way back into town to the Feathermarket Hall for the evening Indaba. This is also in a recently renovated building, which has the feeling of a nineteenth-century wrought-iron railway station. Stylish and charming, but the vocal acoustics are terrible. I believe this is a great hall for music, but the echo of Evita's voice makes it all sound like an argument! The pattern for Larger Cities has also emerged. We end up with a 20 per cent capacity audience, and in this place many brave supporters are swallowed up by rows of empty red stools, looking like survivors from a sunken ship drifting among upside-down deckchairs. Again, the same old story. Whites are scared of being at a free show with drunk blacks who will rob and rape them, and blacks can't believe it's free. And if it is free, what's the catch?

Interesting party reps have emerged out of this tense city. I've always found in past years that a PE audience is acutely aware of political issues. The huge black township of New Brighton has added to this scenario, and many of the leaders of black consciousness movements come from here, or in many cases, were imprisoned here! Tonight we have our new friend, Mayor Faku, representing the ANC.

'Dear Mayor, when I saw a car with number plate F U 1 outside, I knew you were here!' trills Evita. A middle-aged white troubleshooter stands up for the DP; the NNP and ACDP field lacklustre talents, and the Green Party rep is still with us. In spite of having the daily experience of two sessions in the last four weeks, she still submerges the only sensible political message in fuzz and old hippy shit. Why are political reps so untrained and unprepared? I even want to say: unmotivated? They either base their whole argument on statistics, which they either get wrong, misquote or make up. Or they blindly attack a national issue without any alternative solutions. And as for answering questions? During the last forty-eight Indabas no politician has answered a question directly. They waffle, they divert with trivia, they talk crap with not even a hint of humour or substance. They don't listen to what is asked from the floor, but blurt out pre-prepared bla-bla-bla. They keep saying they have all the answers, but then can't remember the question. I don't think they even know what the issues are. Yet the very issues that should drive the wheels of argument at election time are so obvious: education, health, welfare, security and local government. As yet – and this is March 1999 – not one mention has been made of HIV/AIDS.

After this job is done, we all go back to the magic of our guest house, where Chris has prepared a dinner party for us and his birthday, and we can relax in style. Long whiskies on ice. Cold dry Chardonnay. We thank the friends who have made the Eastern Cape possible through their constant networking: PR Michelle Brown in particular has moved mountains for us. Our tired boys fall asleep on mohair blankets, Lynne has a long bath in her four-poster tub and I sit with the whisky bottle for an hour-long live phone interview with Radio 702.

SATURDAY 20 MARCH

Over breakfast we start counting how many strange beds we've slept in since leaving Cape Town all those weeks ago. And how many strange beds before we're back home. Three! Ten more Indabas to go! Five more days! The end beckons like a last-minute repeal of sentence. We cannot only hope that the Cape Town Indabas will be well attended. We must work the cellphones and spread the word. So while I drive along the Garden Route to Knysna, Lynne plays the four cellphones like a brass band!

The road along the coast is clogged with mist and rain and visibility is quite a strain. We do our noon show at the Barnyard Theatre in Knysna, a small venue with a smallish crowd of locals, including the young Mayor who lives in the squatter settlement up on the hillside. Evita wants to know if he comes to work each day on his skateboard. It seems he does! He represents the ANC, and is pleasingly articulate and optimistic about the future. God rambles on and Judy Green goes into dull, vague ecological details. Evita, naughtily, is seen to suppress a yawn. We had warned Judy: jack up your energy, or we'll make real fun of you!

We pack up in the rain and make for Oudtshoorn, winding our way along the broad double carriageway and passing a stone's throw away from the Wilderness, where former President PW Botha still lives. We shout abusive greetings through closed windows, and skirt the town of George to make our ascent up and across the misted mountains and into the Klein Karoo.

Oudtshoorn was once the centre of the ostrich empire, and this is where the Klein Karoo Kunstefees takes place in April. Originally we were hoping to structure our tour to stop here during the festival, but it wasn't to be. Even without a festive commitment during this weekend, we couldn't get a venue in the town for love or money. Eventually we were given the SADF Auditorium on the edge of the town. We felt there was an official dislike of us being in Oudtshoorn, so we were determined to lift our legs against their precious trees and be there, come hell or high water! At least the Army knew we were there, and with thousands of soldiers barracked in the area it could be an interesting Indaba. And with a local community so rich in culture and tuned into comedy, we had high hopes.

But no one turned up! The 800-seater venue stayed deserted. No political rep appeared. Eventually two black soldiers peered in and smiled. We asked them to stay, but they laughed and ran away. Basil Appollis has an uncle in the town, whom he phones. Within minutes the family races in with two small boys still in their pyjamas, but we decide that as God has deserted us – his bakkie is nowhere to be seen! – we have the right to call it a day and go to bed.

We've just done eleven Indabas in six days. We've just travelled from Bloemfontein through three provinces, and tired is not the word. Catatonic, more likely. And so we kiss the sleeping babies, hug the uncle and aunt, wave at the single soldier weeing against an outside wall, and pack the Ballot Bus. Once Tannie is snug in the boot of the car, we go back to our motel, where we can sit calmly and chew our food for a change and not rush out for the next 300 kilometres!

But what does this say about a town on the verge of yet another festival? Maybe Oudtshoorn is deserted because it's a long weekend? Maybe no one read the papers and didn't know we were coming? No one listens to SAfm radio at seven in the morning? Or maybe it's just good old politics! Maybe it's because of a man in a dress? Or maybe just … because!

SUNDAY 21 MARCH

Today is the first day we have off completely. No phone calls, no faxes, no e-mails, no radio chat! It is also exactly one month since we started our Trek at Evita se Perron in Darling. And we are all completely changed by the experience: having been there, seen things, heard, tasted, listened and laughed – and cried – we feel we have earned for ourselves the right to stand on the rooftops and shout to the stars: we are South Africans and we're proud of it!

e-vita's e-lection e-mail to
Pik Botha

Pik? Is jy wakker? Ek wou jou faks, maar ek was bang iemand sou dit sien. Hierdie e-pos is beter. Maar in watter taal? Ek dink Afrikaans is nie 'n goeie idee nie – te veel van 'hulle' verstaan! Dus: vieslike Engels!

Remember when we sat on Milnerton Beach on Mother's Day in 1985, looking out at Robben Island? And I asked you why we kept locking political prisoners up there? Robben Island could have been such a nice place for National Party picnics. No, you said, we must lock up terrorists and communists and democrats! And I said: Why don't we free them all from jail – and put them into Parliament from where they can never escape? And that we eventually did! And here we are now, permanently in opposition, standing at the foot of the moral high ground and watching the ANC besport themselves in the temples of power! Just to come down the foefie-slides of scandal. Hier kom Allan! Daar gaan Bantu! Oppas vir Winnie!

Of course, this election does take my mind back to the days when we also had to stage such diversions. Then only 900 000 out of 27 million voted our government into power. And today? Anyone can vote in theory, according to the Constitution. But in reality? Liewe aarde, Pik, do you realise that if we go over to Europe to see that man in Zurich on 2 June, we can't vote? If we go over to encourage investment in South Africa on 2 June, we lose our chance to make our cross? Because of chaotic ANC bureaucracy!

If we have in our possession a valid passport or driver's licence or that old blue ID-boekie and go to the polls on 2 June, we can also not vote! We must have the green bar-coded ID book! (By the way, you can get one from that Mr Barzah in Milnerton for R150!) We must have that bar-code, because President Mandela is so sentimental. He was behind bars for twenty-seven years; now he wants the bars in our book! But who is going to stop a million young blacks without ID books from voting on 2 June? I now know why Judge Kriegler ran away to hide in Lapland!

And then this registration business? We stood in queues to be registered where we live. We didn't have an election date. It was like being pregnant and not knowing when the baby was due. Now we know 2 June is the day, but most of us are not registered where we work, but where we live. And we won't be where we live on 2 June, so we'll lose our vote! Now they say that in order to be able to vote, we must go back to where we live and find the IEC. (How? Put some cheese on the carpet? Do they exist? Or are they just a R300 million budget?) Deregister with the IEC where you live and re-register where you work, so that on 2 June you can vote! Otherwise, if you don't go back to where you live, you lose your vote! And if you go back to where you live to vote, you lose your job! Have you ever come across such a mess?

Why didn't we think of it? Instead of all those laws to keep whites in power and blacks without a vote? Look at what is happening now so successfully? The disenfranchising of half a nation through pure and utter incompetence!

P.S. Don't phone me before noon, because I don't know what you're saying and you don't know what you mean.

Die Honde Blaf maar die Karavaan Gaan Aan!

MONDAY 22 MARCH

The last week starts with us waking in the Karoo and breathing the perfect air. We hear that a young actor on his way to Oudtshoorn for the festival next week has been killed in a car smash. One's vulnerability on the roads makes for a collective shudder. We've been so lucky so far on our 10 000 kilometre journey.

Various local radio interviews are fitted in before the first Indaba starts in the George Town Hall after noon. We've backtracked from Oudtshoorn to this former bastion of PW Botha power. Our audience is solidly mixed, and it is remarkable how many of his coloured and black subjects are there to greet Evita Bezuidenhout, now the only remaining working dinosaur from the old Boerassic Regime. Whites are few to see. But George is nothing in comparison to that evening's Indaba in the ATKV Hall in Hartenbos, just down the road towards Mossel Bay.

This is the beach resort where for as long as I can remember the most conservative Afrikaans families camped out, braaivleis and bible in hand. As it is school holidays as well as a public holiday today – the Sharpeville massacre remembered as Human Rights Day – the camping sites are overflowing and the potential for an audience is good. Evita gushes forth to the 120 who attend in the 2000-seater, an audience of lobotomised, suspicious and riveted relics. Here is a perfect social specimen for the research fundis: large white men and larger white women with largish blonde sulky children, picking their noses, glancing with undisguised hostility at a handful of laughing non-whites who sit isolated to one side in their small pockets of life.

The saga of Evita's rewrite of Afrikaner history is greeted with stony silence and many walk-outs. We're now all so tired that we are dangerously on the verge of giggles. The racist dislike of what we're doing is so obvious here that it should be taken seriously, but by now we are so sure that there is a healthy human black majority out there, that this petulant display of injured ancient nationalism is funny and silly. If these people don't want to travel this road of reconciliation, to hell with them. An old oom waits for us outside. He saw some Afrikaans kids trying to let the air out of our Ballot Bus tyres, stormed at them with his walking stick and has been standing guard. While we pack up, he charmingly chats to Lynne, who seems to be the only real lady around.

'This was really not my sort of thing, you know, girlie,' he rasps. 'I like more of the traditional concerts: maybe a band or Gé Korsten singing or such, but I must agree with the newspapers: Mrs Bezuidenhout has good legs!'

TUESDAY 23 MARCH

The sunrise sees us closer to home, with only one more strange bed to sleep in and six Indabas left. Droëwors and glucose sweets keep us going, but as we drive through the mist and drizzle into Swellendam, we need some real sustenance. We're early and can go and have a real piece of meat at the local steakhouse! The Town Hall is small and pretty and full, but as we have noticed in a Western Cape province still run by the New National Party, change comes slowly. The blacks and coloureds still stay at the back of the hall, letting master and madam and the Mayor sit in the front.

Yes, the Mayor of Swellendam is a white woman! That's a first for us, and her speech shows that she's a frustrated understudy to Evita Bezuidenhout. She rallies her flock to commit themselves to voting and they nod like Stepford Wives and Mothers.

Travelling through the Overberg and Langkloof mountains on our way to Worcester, we stop at some wine farms to stock up on bottled replenishments. We also realise that we've each lost up to ten kilos in weight on this Trek.

The Worcester Town Hall is a modern structure of the East German School of Hideous Public Buildings erected in the 1960s. We meet the local IEC man, who has just been round the town in his car with a loud hailer, whipping up support. The trouble was, he spoke too close to the mike and all that the people heard was a garbled noise!

The 900-seater hall is eventually full of mainly coloured citizens out on their lunch break. A tea party is arranged for us in the foyer after the event, and there is already a feeling of being on home territory. The Cape dialect is so specific and loaded with innuendo. Much of Basil's Cape coloured detail was lost on the northern populace.

WEDNESDAY 24 MARCH

The weather clears as the Ballot Bus and silver Daewoo emerge from the Du Toit's Kloof Tunnel and we can see Table Mountain! Stellenbosch Town Hall is in the centre of this university mecca, and still reflects much of what it represented for so long. It is here that the hierarchy of the ruling apartheid elite learnt their p's and q's, except for PW Botha, whose schooling didn't qualify him for a university education! And so Evita reminds the full auditorium where the bad smell comes from: the political past!

My past is also footprinted backstage, where as a small boy soprano I would sing Mozart's Laudate Dominum with the Stellenbosch University Choir. I think that was in the late 1950s, maybe just around the time that my chameleon had first vomited on my tummy and I realised what that piepie thing was really intended for!

The Mayor of Stellenbosch glows in his suit and chain, not white except for his perfect teeth that sparkle like in a cartoon, when he laughs like a cartoon. There is a rep from the Freedom Front who is such a twit that Evita intervenes and says: 'Nee man, Wollie, say something substantial! You're talking more rubbish than I thought a Freedom Front person could!'

While the audience enjoys this hugely, Wollie does not improve, having now been reduced to monosyllabic garbage.

The great City Hall in Cape Town is today a mere shadow of what it once was, except for the balcony overlooking the Grand Parade, where Nelson Mandela made his first public utterance after twenty-seven years in prison 'We ... in the ANC ... are a collective leadership ...' Otherwise the great hall is dusty and tatty. Backstage is like a permanent passage with doors that don't close properly and very little around to suggest that it's being used. Again I see the ghosts of my childhood here: this is where my mother and father played double concertii with the orchestra. Tessa joined them at the age of twelve in a Mozart triple concerto. And every time I step onto this stage over the years, mostly as Evita in some or other capacity, I sense that terror of nerves and the celebration of success that accompanied each one of those classical concerts. I would stand on the sidelines and watch.

'And you, Pietertjie? Aren't you also going to be on stage like your parents and your sister?' they would ask me, prodding me with gloved fingers and looking very tall. I would politely stammer and blush and look cute, and they would like that and go away. I knew I would do something one day, something that no one else could do. I didn't know what it was, and I'm still not sure if I'm there yet. But standing on the stage of the City Hall as a woman who doesn't exist, but whose photograph graced Nelson's Mandela desk, doesn't feel that ordinary either!

The SABC cabal have come and gone during the last week. They didn't film any of the Eastern Cape experience, which is a shame, but are determined to film the entire Cape Town Indaba. Among the supporters are eight young gay men from the Mother City Queer Project, each virtually undressed in the colours of the flag! They present Mrs B with a portrait of Madiba in the style of Vincent van Gogh! Evita admires it and refers to a recent PAC statement that they would punish crime by cutting off people's fingers and hands!

'Van Gogh? The first member of the PAC! He cut off his own ear!'

The four young girls from Darling who sent us on our way over four weeks ago with their a cappella rendition of Nkosi Sikeleli are here again, in a box next to the Mayor. They sing for everyone!

THURSDAY 25 MARCH

Our final day, but the energy levels are rock bottom. It's as if the party ended last night. The lunchtime Indaba is at the sprawling Cape Technikon, sitting on the open wounds of District Six like a concrete parasite. It's held outside in the open-air piazza, which no doubt works on a perfect Cape day. But the south-easter starts blowing and threatens to lift Tannie's hair. The cactus flies away in a gust of wind, and getting a response from the vast crowd of students lolling all over the grass is like wading through treacle. As I see the little plastic cactus fly by in yet another direction, I curtail Tannie's history class and we end the Indaba after a mere forty minutes. And yet this is an important venue. The Technikon is being wracked with racism and ignorance. Hopefully someone out there got something out of this, other than just a lunchtime diversion while smoking a cigarette?

Our lows are dispelled by our final Indaba. We are in the Luxurama Theatre, below the railway line in Wynberg, or is it Witteboom? Verging on the war zones of the Cape Flats and reeking of fundamentalist religions and poverty, this grand old palace of movies and djol still sports the golden glowing blue and purple curtains from the sixties. The stage was the first one in the Cape to get a revolving inset and it is still there, though immovable! The seats are broken, the carpets bare, the walls stained. It's like a local version of the Hackney Empire in the East End of London, or a faded Harlem burlesque hall!

The local audience sits close around the stage, a wide first row that probably includes 100 seats. We have a signer on stage for the first time, and a large group of deaf people have joined us. Sharing the stage with his 'twelfth language' is a constant source of amusement, and some of what he signs to reflect Tannie's bland hypocrisy brings tears to seeing eyes. A cluster of Muslim men sit to one side, checking us out. When they realise we're not specifically attacking them, they get up and leave. The Darling Angels sing again, this time joined by the masses. Patricia de Lille arrives to represent her party, the PAC. In the short time since 1994 when she started finding the spotlight, Patricia has stepped far away from the mereness of a minor marginalised party of mixed signals. She has humour and charm, and for the first time we all hear a well thought-through political point of view, without any of the usual finger wagging, finger pointing or finger in the nose. The sixtieth Indaba ends with a huge ovation and a sense of elation.

It's over!

FRIDAY 26 MARCH

A day spent sorting out the petty cash vouchers and doing inventories of our equipment and everything people lent us. Everything is in good condition. We are still alive and well. Our vehicles have not been hijacked. Our wallets and cellphones have not been stolen. Our hair has not been pulled. And our bluff has not been called! Evita Bezuidenhout's Great Election Trek is now history!

e-vita's e-lection e-mail to
Patricia de Lille

When I saw that there were more women voters than men registered for the 2 June election, I suddenly thought of you, Patricia de Lille. If you stood for a political party that made more sense, millions of women would vote for you. I certainly would. Magtig skat, you've shown us all what hard work means. I remember looking at you when you appeared on TV for the first time. I thought: what a fox-terrier! You are one, and so you must be. Blaf en byt! You're not trying to impress me; you're speaking to those people who need leadership.

But I'm sorry, skattie, this PAC of yours just makes me gril. Firstly, I'm worried about your logo: a map of Africa with the sun shining in Ghana? Does this mean you people don't even know where you live? Then this thing you suggest: cutting off the fingers of thieves? And toes? And arms and legs and ander dinge of criminals? Will that help? And what will be left of Allan Boesak? And who will feed those millions of fingerless victims of PAC justice? Ja, maybe that's one way of creating jobs for those who need jobs!

I suppose in a true democracy like ours, any bona fide party registered with the IEC can suggest crazy things and people have the freedom of choice to vote for it. We proved that back in the days of the old National Party. But promise me that if you decide to rename the PAC tomorrow as the Please Amputate Completely Party, you'll be very transparent with your cuts. Live on television, please!

Hijackers can have their trigger fingers cut off live on *People of the South*; convicted rapists can have their right legs amputated on *50/50*. A convicted rapist out on bail with only one leg will never again manage to catch and rape a woman who has two legs!

P.S. I love your new RDP knitted hair!

The Bottom Line

On 30 January 1999 I had sent this letter to the Office of the President.

Dear Jakes Gerwel,

RE EVITA'S VOTER EDUCATION THROUGH ENTERTAINMENT

We are all on track to start as planned on Sunday 21 February from Darling. The only change is, we no longer have a train.

The cost – two million rand – was unrealistic in the light of the hardships suffered by commuters, who have no transport because of financial constraints. It would be wrong to enthuse a nation to vote from a Gravy Train!

So we're travelling in a Kombi! It's back to the old days of the 1970s when we had no money and no luxury, but passion and hope and energy. And I think the people will identify with this aspect of the project.

But the invitation to President Mandela and his party still stands: 12h00 lunch at Evita se Perron in Darling on Sunday 21 February, followed by a fifty-minute performance of her Election Indaba by Mrs Bezuidenhout herself! You shouldn't be back in Cape Town later than 4.30 pm!

I hope this appeals to the President and fits in with his busy schedule. The voter education-through-entertainment project – known as Evita's People's Party – will take in sixty towns and cities, where she will give the public free Indabas on democracy and the Election. Put a smile back on the stressed face of our nation.

We'd love to put a smile on Madiba's face too!

Best regards,
Pieter-Dirk Uys

When I got back to Darling on Friday 14 March in time to shake the dust of the Trek off my feet and get ready for my show at the Perron of *Dekaffirnated*, this letter was waiting in a large official Presidential Envelope:

Dear Pieter,

Thank you for your kind invitation to join you for part of your voter education journey.

Unfortunately, I am unable to accept the invitation due to the heavy demands currently placed on my schedule, but please convey to Mrs Bezuidenhout our sincerest appreciation for her tireless efforts to encourage supporters of all parties to register to vote so that they can make a success of the elections and strengthen our democracy.

I was happy to see that her new programme had already got underway and was proving to be a joyous success which her ventures always turn out to be – whether in service of the Bantustan policy or of our new democracy! And it was a delight to get reports of her appearance in Parliament.

We wish Mrs Bezuidenhout all success and assure her of our full support for this important campaign of voter education.

Yours sincerely,
NR Mandela

It was the only reaction we got to our Election Trek. And without doubt the best!

Looking back now in 2002, it was like a Boere Priscilla with all her rainbow finery trekking through a black and white Mad Max desert. The highs made you feel like the African king of the world; the lows made you look like a colonial Eurocentric left behind by history. The contrasts and diversity of South Africa are so easily forgotten, merging with bland TV images and faded memories of childhood trips to the Kruger National Park. To travel in 1999 and clock up 10 000 kilometres from the southern tip to the northern donga, from the eastern koppie to the western spruit, is to fall in love all over again. It is the most beautiful country in the world and we who live in it are without doubt the craziest, most absurd, most generous and most perplexing people ever plonked together on a rainbow foefie-slide to the future!

'Hell man Tannie, but you make me laugh!' is the greatest compliment we heard – but laugh at what? Considering that everything we touched on was not funny. Poverty still reigns supreme. Thirty per cent of the people we visited still cannot read or write. Over half of them still do not have jobs. The education system is still in that no man's land between a former fascist system and a future democratic structure. Electrification is becoming a visible reality even in the grimmest of squatter camps, but the huts are collapsing and housing is desperately needed everywhere.

'The ANC promised one million houses in five years,' Evita would say. 'Or was it five houses in a million years?'

And yet again, laughing at ourselves always helps lift a head out of the hole and see a sunrise. Thank heavens politicians on the whole take themselves so seriously that they don't realise they've tucked the tip of the toilet roll into their underpants and now walk proudly with a long tail behind them!

'Politicians are like monkeys,' Mevrou carefully explains. 'The higher they climb the pole of ambition, the more of their backsides we can see!' Sadly she cannot get her lips around the word 'arse'.

We exchange final notes, as the six of us – me, Lynne Maree, Basil Appollis, our technicians Bruce Koch, Johnny Barbuzono and Mories Romkins – with the most famous white woman exhausted in the boot, turn our Kombi onto that last stretch of N2 freeway, before we fall off the unfinished bridge onto the Cape Town Foreshore! Performing to a nation in waiting, with 80 per cent of our audience the former disadvantaged masses, we felt we'd rediscovered the magic of theatre and the power of imagination. Here were so-called forgotten communities in mainly rural areas, most of them sharing in such entertainment for the first time, and taking to it like old hands clapping wildly.

The Indabas were free, which led to the question: 'How much are the free tickets?' People are suspicious of things given away, possibly remembering the free gifts and promises of 1994 that didn't materialise, and checked us out with narrowed eyes and a careful, polite smile.

Do we have news for them! There is a sophisticated majority out there. Maybe they can't read or write, but they've brought up some pretty fine kids on nothing other than determination and guts. They are also hungry for entertainment and can enjoy it to the hilt without behaving like white lager louts. What Mrs B's ice-thin racist hypocrisy brought forth were wide toothy smiles to black faces and shocked gasps from whites.

So, what does this small experience say about the state of the nation? The obsession with bad news is overpowering. The violence and the crime, the corruption and the inefficiency, the tensions and fears are magnified daily in print and picture. The trauma level is rising into the red, and soon, in spite of having the finest Constitution in modern times, and a legendary guardian angel at the helm, we will just be mad.

And so I suppose Evita's People's Party had a very simple mission: to leave a smile on the people's faces. Dispel, if only briefly, the deep concern for a future so clouded with the negative, knowing there is so little we can do to change things. Underline with theatrical flourish that there is a way round the roadblock of paralysis: talk to each other and share hopes and fears. Optimism can, with support and enthusiasm, lead to a better country for us all.

This is voter education through entertainment. The education is simple: Vote. It's secret. It will be safe. It is our right and duty. This could not be voluntary and free! Obviously we had to be part of the bigger picture. When we explained that the Trek was self-funded, they found it difficult to believe. It had to be an ANC plot? A government ploy? An IEC play?

No. We are ordinary citizens with a flair for the absurd, who are doing this project without payment or expense accounts. And because it is not *Sarafina 3*, the people out there have embraced the Ballot Bus and its Tannie with gifts of fruit, sweets and support. Ironically and pleasingly, the money we raised through Evita's shows in London, Paris, Copenhagen and Amsterdam in November 1999 were mainly supported by South Africans abroad. While they all remember the passion with which they could support the 1994 election, they will not be able to vote in foreign embassies on 2 June because 'no funds' are available to set up voting stations in other countries! And so, because we were not sponsored financially by any political or commercial interest, we have kept our independence throughout. Thanks to support in kind from Panasonic, MTN, Tempest, Hollard Insurance, Pick 'n Pay, Downtown Studios and Gallo, we have Yvonne Chaka Chaka's theme song, a sound system, cellphones, cellular communication, transport and printed voter information. Accommodation for those forty nights has mainly been donated through the kindness of guest house owners and hotel managers.

Yes, but what does it all say about the state of a nation working up to a second democratic election?

It says a lot for a young democracy, still bleeding from decades of pain, that such crazy nonsense can still take place and be accepted as such by so many people. It is remarkable that in the most volatile areas such as Richmond, where bloody headlines shriek a story of death and fear, we find representatives of opposing factions deferring to 'Comrade Madam' and sharing a stage amid laughter and good-natured teasing. It says something positive about a nation where an old icon of the apartheid years, now the aikôna of a new South Africa, can still make politicians nervous, especially in spite of the fact that she doesn't exist! And yet wherever we went in her shadow, from town to dorp, from township to squatter camp, village to suburb, Evita Bezuidenhout was hailed and thanked as the first politician 'to visit us in four years'!

People are deeply concerned, interested, angry, committed and confused. They are no longer dazzled by slogans and statistics. The glamour of democracy has been demoted from the T-shirts of celebration to the graffiti of complaint. The dramatic queues of the 1994 celebration have become the drudge of long Home Affairs office waits. But Evita's People's Party is based on what works, not what doesn't. And so there are no Bad Guys. There is no overt criticism. Give politicians enough rope with a smile and they'll hang themselves laughing! Positive energy and excitement go hand in hand with the hope that the forty-one parties at present registered to enjoy the election are passionate and committed to a better future.

Proportional representation is not enjoyed by people who want to vote for other people. And they do want to know that the person they trust is the person who has earned a place in the legislature by auditioning for the people. Statistics have taken over from names. Political achievements are read off like a boring shopping list, but no one can answer a woman in the audience who asks for a policy statement from a party representative on abortion after rape!

Confusion has supplanted commitment. People register and then realise they won't be at that place on 2 June. Why can we not vote irrespective of where we're registered? If we are bar-coded, surely it should be possible? No one seems to know!

Some say: 'There is no money to allow a foreign-based vote, although if you're in the UK on government business, you can use the Embassy as a polling station!'

Others warn: 'If you leave South Africa, you lose your right to be involved with our democracy!'

Rubbish. You can take a South African out of South Africa, but you can't take South Africa out of a South African! Do we now disenfranchise through bureaucracy? This is as stupid as saying whites can vote and blacks can't. It's all too complicated! The 1994 election was about freedom, and everyone was free to vote and many did many times! But while the 1999 election is being more carefully structured with documents and disciplines, it is also an election about freedom. Too many people say: 'We voted in 1994! Why must we do it again?'

So, what does this experience of borrowing from Priscilla Queen of the Desert and presenting Evita Empress of the Veld say about the state of the nation in March 1999? It says: don't underestimate the passion out there. Don't imagine that people view politicians as anything other than servants of the voters. And don't think they will vote out of habit, or fear. They will vote because they want to!

I look back at the events of Tuesday 8 June 1999. The election is over, and a week later the counting is complete. It was calm and free and fair. The ANC win was expected, but the DP wiped the opposition floor with the fading NNP. An Inkatha vs ANC civil war scenario made way for an alliance of powerful opposites. No massacres, no riggings, no moaning. In fact, the second election has gone as smoothly as any election would in an established democracy. We've grown up fast.

Lynne and I watch the final results on television. She is in Johannesburg and I in Darling. The TV cameras pick up all the beaming political faces: Buthelezi, Tony Leon, Nelson Mandela.

And the new emperor, Thabo Mbeki.

He embraces the head of the IEC, Bragalia Bam, and shakes hands with the other gold-rimmed spectacled faces with manicured hands and knitted hair. It is a celebration of a successful election campaign and they are all there to be thanked. No one is missed out!

I phone Lynne.

'Are you watching?' I ask.

'Fabulous new gold-rimmed glasses on our old friends,' she laughs.

'And how are you feeling?' I ask.

'Gloriously redundant,' she says.

'And deeply grateful?' I ask.

'Yes, darling!' she says with a shriek. 'Thank God there was no Train!'

As I put down the phone, Thabo Mbeki was making a victory speech. I focused on the small badge against his left lapel. It is the red AIDS ribbon.

PART III

ERECTIONS

A Clean Slate

When Thabo Mbeki became the second president of a democratic South Africa, there was no reason to be on our guard. The man had proved to be an excellent administrator and career politician. While Madiba spread his wings and soared through international skies, Thabo burnt the midnight oil and started structuring a government that would get down to the business of governing.

There was talk of a sinister blueprint to empty the decks of the old warriors and fill the bridge of the liner with exile-comrades. The Age of the Retex Regime had dawned with the return of the exiles who had spent most of their lives outside South Africa, planning for the day when they could come back.

So the aluta continueth. Thabo took up the reins in Tuynhuis, stepping gingerly into the footprints left by the feet of the Old One. Never did Thabo seek Mandela's shadow in which to wipe the sweat from his brow. He stood in the sun from the first day, a new man, not a clone of the old warrior. It all went well. The media liked him. He spoke with wit and knowledge. He looked great, with his twinkling eyes and his carefully ratted beard. He smoked his pipe in public with the flair of a Clinton playing the sax, until his stern Minister of Health zuma'd in and stopped that. He was approachable and had opinions worth listening to.

The state dinner celebrating the opening of Thabo Mbeki's first parliament in 1999 was held at Fairview, the Parliamentary club next to Kirstenbosch, in Cape Town. I was asked to bring Evita to do a turn. What did they want? I was thrilled to be able to dance for the new boss.

Because of the tight security, we had to be there four hours ahead of time. I had Tannie in a plastic bag, and when they saw her name on my invitation, the guards weren't quite sure what they were looking at.

'What's in that bag?'

'Evita Bezuidenhout,' I replied.

Then one of them got it and giggled.

'Naked?' he winked.

I winked back.

I was the only non-black entertainer, other than legend Nico Carstens, who remembered my parents from the old days. Everyone else was from the New Wave.

The artists' compound was very impressive, with some small cubicles for changing in, each with mirrors and lights. This was no repeat of the shared ladies' toilet at the Bloemfontein Indaba in 94! The general area round the food and drinks soon filled with groups of hip-hop boytjies with knitted muddied hair and rings in ears, noses and nipples. I walked in and said hello. They didn't react. I went into my cubicle, which said 'Tannie Evita', settled down and read a book. Getting into Mrs B only takes fifteen minutes.

Some hours later Evita Bezuidenhout came out in her evening dress and glittering jewels. The comrades went mad with excitement. This woman they knew! They hugged and kissed her and I managed to rub her hand across some really fine taut butts.

Then the announcement from the banquet stage: 'Mr President, Comrades of the Cabinet, members of the Diplomatic Corps, ladies and gentlemen – please rise for Mrs Evita Bezuidenhout!'

What? The President doesn't stand for Evita! Yet they all did. The former darling of the National Party entered and did her piece without hesitation. Again the extraordinary experience of playing with the 'former enemy' like a cat with a mouse who is in charge of the cat food! Everyone got a smack: the ANC, the PAC, the IFP, the NNP, the DP and representatives of so-called democracies and emerging kakocracies. It was a night to remember.

Darling was far away, so when Tannie finished, I peeled her off behind a curtain and put her back in the plastic bag. I wended my way back to my car, past the hip-hop fans who went blank at the sight of me as a man, and heard ministers asking: 'Where is Madam?' I giggled all the way to the Swartland.

'God, I love this land!' I shouted at the cows.

The next day I heard that Thabo hadn't been there. He'd only arrived later that night. I hope affairs of state kept him busy, and not just a bimbo or a bottle! I would have enjoyed hearing his reaction to Tannie Evita's finger wag.

During the seventies and eighties, when Pa was alive, his opinion of my writing and performances was always the most constant. It wasn't always what I wanted to hear, but at least it was there and that meant the work was there too! My family was steeped in literature, mainly of the Afrikaans kind. Anna M Louw married my mother's brother and is regarded as one of the doyennes of Afrikaans Literature, writing novels annually and winning all the right prizes. She'd have a fixed smile on her face when briefly discussing my latest opus and damning me with her faint acid praise. My other aunt, Pa's sister, also an Anna, loved the language and lectured Afrikaans at Stellenbosch University. How difficult it must have been for her to try to smile at my attempts to communicate in her lingua boeraea, unable to spell and making up words as I went along. She was kinder and said even less. But at least I had some reaction from them. Most of the time Pa would say: 'Bokkie, I read that thing you wrote.' That meant it existed. Otherwise, nothing. The big black hole of no feedback. It was upsetting, and finding a reaction became something of an obsession! Any reaction! In those days it was usually negative. Theatre reviews tended to be dismissive, although in fairness the few who knew what they were doing gave me great help and constructive criticism.

Now in our democratic honeymoon, the sounding boards were even more porous. Pa was dead. So the only way to build on each attempt at reinventing one's alphabet with which to entertain was to pretend and hope that many out there have noticed it, but few will react. While we have the greatest creative freedom in the world, there's no one out there to tell you! Having been among friends in the business of entertainment in the UK and the USA, one is constantly inspired by the way we can write, sing, move mountains and make magic here. We manage to deliver more product in a year than those overseas do in a lifetime. Maybe because so few people care, we have the freedom to do so. There are also so few of us doing it, there's a lot of space between the shoulders. Not like in the First World, where artists are crammed in queues, waiting for attention, commissions or jobs. So, do what you instinctively know must be attempted. Don't ever expect the echo of even a noise!

Writing plays has by now taken a backseat. It's too expensive even to consider producing a modest four-hander. Even when performing my one-man shows – and those are legendary for having virtually no set, props or costumes – it takes a sold-out season to even break even. What with the enormous theatre rentals, booking percentages, taxes and 14 per cent VAT demands. An Arts Council subsidy is available on a small scale, but I remain healthily allergic to state help, as I was in the past. Theatre should not depend on the kindness of strangers. It should live by the income generated by the interest of an audience. Let the theatre buildings be subsidised, so at least they are safe, clean and technically excellent.

After the Election Trek, the drama of Drama had left my stage and played itself out on the tarmacs of parking areas. A tired refrain bemoans the 'death' of the business of good theatre. Theatre has never died; just those of us who don't keep up are left behind. There is still an active generation in local South African theatre that has been brought up in the comfortable clutches of government-sponsored arts councils and contracted to repeat without question much of the propaganda they were told. Now everyone sits without an Orwellian master and wants a time-share down here in the trenches.

Don't bother! Just stand up on a box somewhere and tell a story. There's your first act!

Sitting on the rocks, Bloubergstrand

With Sophia Loren in Hollywood

At Evita se Perron, Darling

Pieter with Violet Smoorvis, the mother and grandmother to most of his cats in Darling

Evita in the old House of Assembly, standing in the place
where the apartheid speaker used to sit – February 1999

Holding the Cactus of Democracy in Parliament.
In front is the Cactus of Separate Development – February 1999

On the road – outside Stutterheim on the Great Election Trek – 1999

Evita with her grandchildren – Winnie-Jeanne, Nelson-Ignatius and La Toya Ossewania – December 2001

Bambi Kellermann showing us the difference between a man and a monkey

On the road with the AIDS-awareness show at a school in Port Elizabeth

'If it's not on, it's not in!'

'Why is the the black one smaller than the white one?'

A few of the 400 000 who laughed at their fear

For Facts Sake

It was theatre that attracted the world's attention to AIDS in South Africa. Within weeks of restructuring the Cabinet in his image, President Mbeki's dour Minister of Health, Dr Nkosazana Zuma, commissioned a musical from playwright Mbongeni Ngema to enlighten audiences about HIV/AIDS. The show was called *Sarafina 2*, inspired by the success of *Sarafina*, Ngema's township musical about schoolkids in Soweto and the release of Mandela, which had dazzled the First World on a tour of major European and American cities.

The idea was brilliant: using music and dance to educate the youth. Then the plan went wrong. Zuma paid R14 million for the musical out of the Department of Health budget. Since when did Health have to subsidise Theatre, the people demanded? It then came to be known that no tenders had been called for. No other interested theatrical parties had been invited to feast at the trough! Huge ripples of discontent and jealousy roused the profession and raised many dormant eyebrows.

'Darling! For fourteen million rand I can write ten musicals and have change left!'

A huge *Sarafina 2* roadshow was announced. It performed with spectacular dullness for a few audiences in fewer places and then stopped dead in its tracks. That was the return on quite a large investment.

Scandal! To this day the inquiry has not yet come to a comprehensible conclusion. Outcry followed accusation. The theatre is still suffering from comments from angry people who see the sick suffering because their budget was spent on our entertainment. And, yes, they're right. But what a great idea it was, and what a tragedy that greed and corruption tripped it up.

I, too, started thinking about performing theatre about AIDS. After offering Evita Bezuidenhout free of charge to the Cape Town City Council for voter education in the lead-up to a municipal election in mid-2000, and getting no reply other than 'We are considering your offer,' I had to rethink. Democracy was no longer the issue. Yes, it was always an important area for constant reminder and celebration, but politics was no longer responsible for death. That minefield had moved to sex. I knew that's where I had to go too. And, unbelievably, the government was writing me new material by the day. In a shocking and ludicrous announcement, President Thabo Mbeki started questioning the link between HIV and AIDS! This was not a new angle. Many dissidents worldwide had made themselves the butt of stand-up jokes by insisting that HIV didn't exist. So far not one of them has had the balls to inject themselves with the virus to prove their point. But now the new President of a baby democracy that was dying on its feet of a virus that had no cure was denying the very basis for action.

The press reaction was swift and sharp, but Thabo didn't flinch. He appointed an advisory body, balancing those who believed him and those who didn't. South African AIDS activists came face to face with HIV dissidents who crawled out of the woodwork of Funny Farm USA, with the South African President's approval stamped on their CVs. This is surely the stuff that satire is made of? Surely he needs to be laughed at and made to look as ridiculous as he sounds? The snag was that Thabo doesn't always talk rubbish. His sharp intelligence manages to focus on important points that he can explain clearly, but too easily he falls into babbly-bla-bla and loses credibility by embracing eccentric views. His pig-headedness doesn't allow for compromise either.

'AIDS is not a disease, it's a syndrome.'

Yes, it's an umbrella for any germ that can penetrate a destroyed immune system and create havoc with health. But when a hurricane hits your home, do you analyse if it's a upperstrata phenomenon or a mere prairie pooper? As your

PRES. MBEKI'S SELECT
ADVISORY PANEL OF
INTERNATIONAL AIDS EXPERTS

roof flies off, you don't wonder where the hurricane comes from! It's there, so confront it!

Thabo latched onto the very significant issue of pharmaceutical companies holding a dying populace to ransom with their outrageous drug prices. He pointed out the danger of toxic medication. He said all the right things, but in the wrong order. If he had been given focus by his so-called advisors, who spend more time advising against than informing about, snorting their salaries up their noses, then we'd have had a different story here. Thabo Mbeki could have been the formative energy in fighting HIV/AIDS in the world. Instead the kids in the townships now call him Comrade Undertaker! To the rest of the world he's a mystery.

'Oh! You come from South Africa, where your President has those weird ideas about AIDS? Why?'

Hello? We're not going to go there now. I don't know why he has these weird ideas! Unless his denial is so severe, his refusal possibly to acknowledge his own infection so numbing, that he is living in a fantasy world of gobbledegook? Or is he the most cold-blooded politician we have ever had, knowing that if he ignores the rate of infection among babies and lets them die now, there will be no unproductive army of orphans to feed in a few years? Does he take too much notice of the chanting of traditional healers and sangomas, who see AIDS as a First World racist plot against blacks? Or is it all just to give vent to his favourite byte that talk of a sexually transmitted virus is a smear on the character of the black man, by blaming his suffering from AIDS on promiscuity?

I don't know, but my potential material was there! Already in 1999 I had started toying with the idea of a show about the dangers of unsafe sex. It was called *For Facts Sake*, and I tried out various structures and sketches at the Perron during the months leading up to the new millennium. The title worked, the concept worked, the message was there, but there was no substance to the show. It ended up as a collection of jokes about penises and erections.

My terror of confronting AIDS had also put me in a major confusion. The shock of a close friend who went to have his blood checked for diabetes, to be told that he had full-blown AIDS, was the Damascus Road moment. It was during those long conversations with him, trying to help him come to terms with something he had never even suspected, that I was forced for the first time to articulate my fears. I had to think about AIDS as part of life, because Ronald wanted to live. He didn't succeed for long, which is maybe a relief, as a long period of suffering would have been even more tragic. At the height of his talent and passion for life, his light fused and Ronald was no more. So quick and so unexpected, and yet why the surprise? We were all stunned, shocked and frightened, but not surprised. Too often it is an unspoken thought of not IF, but WHEN? But there's always someone left behind having to face their fear.

I looked at *For Facts Sake* again and realised what was missing. It didn't confront the main issue but skirted around it. I was hinting at a battle while still hiding under the bed with my hands covering my eyes. So I had to go to war. How could I reflect the state of mind of South Africa through humour if my own fear refused to allow me to confront the major issue facing me? AIDS.

Inspired by the energy that the Trek unleashed in 1999, it was obvious that a theatre show was not the answer. Again I had to take the entertainment to those who didn't come to the theatre. When I was at school at Hoërskool Nassau in Mowbray in the early 1960s, local theatre company CAPAB would send a group of actors who, once a term, would entertain us on a Wednesday afternoon in the school hall with a two-hour concert based on our setwork books, bringing them to life through performance and drama, comedy and costumes. I think those experiences had a lot to do with sharpening my taste for what I do today. I never forgot those afternoons, the vivid memories of magic and how easily I was educated and inspired through entertainment.

How could I contact schools in order to take them a show about something they might want to avoid? I phoned the provincial Department of Education in Cape Town. Lists of schools were a problem and cumbersome, and not all schools had faxes or even phones. But there is a 'generic' e-mail address that goes to 400 schools in the Western Cape. This was a start.

I drafted a letter:

Dear School

I have an AIDS-awareness entertainment of sixty minutes, which I am offering you free of charge to help your young people confront their fear of AIDS, mainly through humour and laughing at our fears. There are so many ways to inform about the dangers. This is only one, and even though I do not pretend any medical insight, I have seen what humour can do in tense and fearful situations. It helps us come to terms with issues. While there are as yet no answers or cures, I hope to ask many questions and maybe open doors for future frank discussions. My entertainment is not everybody's cup of tea. The language is very to the point and in some ways impolite. But AIDS is not a polite disease and the urgency surrounding the rate of infection demands radical ways to inform. All I need is a table, microphone and a glass of water.

Looking forward to hearing from you.

I pressed SEND and waited. Within twenty-four hours I had thirty-five answers, from schools I knew by reputation and places I'd never heard of. Most of them were established and wealthy – they all had computer facilities. Although I instinctively knew my future battlefield was among the sprawling township communities and their countless schools, I had to see if this thing would work. So I structured a two-week local tour of schools on a first-come-first-served basis. My most important homework for days was studying the map of the Cape Peninsula and finding out where each school was and how to get there. Then how to get from the 10 o'clock appointment to a 12:30 performance.

I structured an hour-long entertainment, borrowing heavily from the most accessible material in *For Facts Sake*. I realised that if anything was going to work, I would have to be totally honest about me: the mature me, the fat me, the gay me, the bald me, the frightened me. I was then fifty-six years old, probably older than most of the teachers in the hall and most of the parents of the learners. But with kids aged between twelve and eighteen, I had to become a teenager! This was going to be quite an acting feat!

Trekking to Teaching

I started on Monday 8 May 2000. My first school was an ironic kickback to the past: Voortrekker Hoërskool in Wynberg. When I was at Nassau in the sixties, one of our rivals in rugby and athletics was this sister 'Afrikaanse skool'. This was a traditionally conservative Afrikaans place of learning. Standing on the stage in the hall, surrounded by the achievements of the last forty years, I was terrified. Rows of Retiefs and Van Rooyens and Van der Merwes and Bothas and Van Bredas on lists of rugby heroes and head boys and head girls – enough to make your head spin.

I had already decided, if anything, that the message was to be very simple: confront the fear by laughing at it. From my past experiences of using humour to fight an apartheid regime that also had lists of Retiefs and Bothas and Van Bredas in its ranks, I knew that if I say certain things, people will react. My confidence was very low, and so I presented some sketches that had little to do with the issue, although they featured examples of fear. From *Dekaffirnated* I brought out the former apartheid policeman now protecting Nelson Mandela at a music concert in Pretoria, and meeting a former detainee he had once tortured. I think it was too complex for the kids, although surprisingly the dark humour got laughs.

I told them about my childhood as a young Afrikaner in the sixties and seventies, a time of survival based on fear. How I used humour then to fight the fear of guilt and paralysis during apartheid, 'the first virus'. And that the minefield had now moved from politics to sex. I described my first sexual experience in 1959 and how it had happened without me even knowing what it was! This was a first for them too. I doubt if anyone had ever been so frank about sex on that stage. Certain things were said that day, and the echo of shocked laughter still rings in my ears. I broached the subject of condoms, much to their horror and amazement. Of course, as soon as I could, I fell back on Evita. She was someone everyone knows, so I put her together for the kids.

That first show was a mess. I was everywhere and nowhere. I just knew: whatever you say, be clear about the message – the safest sex is no sex. But if you have sex, protect yourself.

To add to my discomfort, the whole hour was in Afrikaans! Not an easy language to ad-lib in, especially when you've planned and structured it all in

English. At last it was over and the kids mobbed the stage for autographs of Evita. Some of them spoke under their breath and said how much they'd enjoyed it. Enjoyed what? The dressing up? The frankness? Or the confronting of the fear of AIDS through laughter? While it all looks so clear-cut now from a distance, it was an adrenaline-soaked nightmare.

I was invited to the staff room by a pale headmaster. He was very friendly, but when we walked into the room, half the staff turned their backs and carried on drinking tea and reading *Die Burger*. The headmaster and I made small talk about my old school and his old school, and then I realised he was younger than me! He then said: 'I'm glad you came to us today, Meneer Uys. I'd never be able to say those things, but at least now we can say to the children: Remember what Oom Pieter said the other day? We're going to talk about those things …'

Opening a door. Yes, that's all it had to be. This was going to be a painfully slow work in progress. Every school would demand a new approach. Every audience was different. Not only in background, but in culture, language, prejudice and fears. It would take many improvised performances to find the ideal balance in the structure, making it entertaining as well as informative. It could never be acting, always *re*-acting!

My next school was deep in the townships on the Cape Flats. Glued to my map, I negotiated my way from the First World via freeways onto main roads and into cul-de-sacs, round rubbish dumps and broken car graveyards, up gravel roads and down grass tracks. I found the school, and it was a world three times removed.

While Wynberg was middle class, this was lower working class without jobs. A dilapidated school building with peeling paint and cracked windows. And three times the number of kids. Small children with old faces. Unsmiling boys with scars and frowns. Nervous girls giggling under Muslim scarves. And no hall! The presentation was in the veld! The mike was faulty, and every time the wind blew, the words flew away. Evita's hair nearly blew away. I forgot everything that had worked an hour before and found myself drowning once again. There was no glass of water to help the dry mouth. I saw a battery of suspicious Muslim parents sitting to one side. The kids were sitting on old chairs, cross-legged on the gravel, perched on mounds of earth, lying on the grass. Once again Evita left me defenceless, and I found myself dropping my Pretoria Afrikaans and getting into the Cape dialect, which was the sound I grew up with. Suddenly we spoke the same language. I told them how frightened I had been when I was their age because I'd never been told about sex.

'Yes, they did once come and give us a talk about sex. We were all trooped into the school hall and Miss Reid came onto the stage and clasped her hands together and giggled nervously.

'"Children," she said, "today we are going to talk about the facts of life. I'm going to tell you about the birds and the bees."'

The township kids laughed. They'd also heard about the birds and the bees that lived in the First World. Here some of them were raped at the age of five.

'The birds and the bees?' I shrugged. 'I've never worked that out? How does a bird fuck a bee!'

Fuck! The word was out! I'd passed the test to join the gang! Not a new word by any means, but certainly the last one they'd expected today! It suddenly made us the same age and we spoke the same taal.

'At least today, with the danger of HIV/AIDS, you as young people will not grow up in the same cave of terror and fear as far as sex is concerned. You must know everything now. Not tomorrow. Today! Because there's always tonight!' And their laughter made me realise that they knew that I knew that they knew!

I demonstrated how to put a condom onto an erect male penis, with the yellow banana standing in for the real flesh and blood.

'This is not a penis? What's it?'

'A baaaannnnaaaannnna!'

'Ja, but you know how many young people like you who see demonstrations like this think they can put a condom on a banana and then they'll be safe? Condoms don't go on bananas? Condoms go on …?'

And out came the pink penis! It wobbled in my hand. The kids screamed. The smaller boys frowned.

'Toemaar, don't look so worried. Yours will grow,' I whispered, as boys fell about in disbelief. I think it was the first time some of the girls were seeing something like this.

Then it was over, and a boy ran after my things as they blew across the veld and brought them back with a huge toothless smile. A Muslim mother came to talk to me. Muslims make me nervous, especially when I know I've been treading on dangerous religious ground with my words. She shook my hand and held it.

'Yes, I'm shocked. Yes, I'm offended. Yes, I wish I'd never come today, but the truth is: it happens. I also have children. I know they say that word. But let them rather say "fuck" than do fuck!'

A group of older girls gathered round. They wanted autographs of Evita. They were interested in theatre and two wanted to be actresses. I asked them what they thought of the show.

'No,' said a pretty girl under her scarf. 'It was shocking but that's good.'

The others nodded. One girl was frowning.

'Ja, but you go too far,' she said sternly. 'When you took out that big penis? Sis, that was obscene.'

They all laughed and shook their heads in disbelief.

'Well,' I apologised, 'I need to make a point that condoms don't go on bananas.'

'No, I agree,' my critic nodded, 'but I thought that was obscene.'

Silence, as everyone thought about what they thought.

Then one girl cleared her throat.

'Ag rubbish man, Ramona!' she said. 'A penis is not obscene. A gun is obscene!'

In those first two weeks of May 2000 I have four days per week and manage to fit in three schools a day. It's almost too much. The strain of adrenaline-fired performances starts to tell. Also the disorientation of having repeated something twice before, and yet was it today or yesterday? Or have I said that already now? So much of the structure is dictated by what I sense from them. Often I start into an area and realise they have no references there, so I change to something more familiar. The message is like a jacket on a hanger. In each session I have to find a different place to hang it.

Step by step I learn my trade. From a boys' school to a girls' school to a mixed school where boys and girls sit together. I also start realising how much I can learn of a school audience by being on stage as they come into the hall. So from then on I get to the venue fifteen minutes before the time, put out the props and settle down with my paper. Imagine the scene: middle-aged man with knitted beanie covering bald head sits on stage as the kids come in. Sometimes they don't even know why they've been herded into the hall. Or they've been told 'Pieter-Dirk Uys is coming'. Who the hell is Pieter-Dirk Uys? Or that 'Tannie Evita Bezuidenhout is going to talk' to them? But this is not Tannie Evita on stage. It's an ou balie!

Their body language is fascinating. Some slouch in, already bored. Some wrestle and push, laughing and full of energy. Some take their seats meekly. Some can't find a place to sit and stand around. One or two twinkle like small fans and wave and wink. If the crowd makes a roaring noise, that's a good sign. That means

there's energy and relative balance. If they're quiet and sullen, that's usually a reflection of some sort of negative peer pressure, maybe punishment threatened.

Even after two years on the road and 400 000 kids later, I still know nothing. It's so complicated and so fragile, so impossible and so impenetrable, that from a distance it often looks like a lost cause. Yet every time one sits on a stage, on a box, on a table, on a mound of dirt, and all that energy and expectation fills the air, you know: it's showtime, folks! You summon up all the spirits of inspiration, because this is the most important performance of your life.

When I had SACS school for boys at ten o'clock and a Hanover Park school at noon on the same day, I took Marianne Thamm along. An old friend and sounding-board, she is also one of our best journalists, as well as a very funny stand-up talent. I needed her feedback. I also wanted someone I knew to see what I was doing!

Her story was published in the *Cape Times* on 19 May. It was the first public notice of what was happening out there:

It's 8:15 am and an orderly stampede of navy blue blazers heads towards the cavernous Hofmeyr Hall at SACS High School in Newlands.

'Ah, the smell of testosterone in the morning,' a teacher, caught up in the throng, quips with a smile.

Within minutes the 800 boys are seated. Those in the front rows are young, fresh-faced and attentive, while the older boys at the back appear nonchalant, aloof, more worldly-wise perhaps.

They look like a tough audience. These are children of the Information Age, an over-sexualised world in which there are few taboos or surprises left, where the President of the United States makes the six o'clock news because of a semen stain on a blue dress.

How on earth is a 50-something theatre icon with a paperbag full of costumes and wigs going to make them sit up and take note of the threat of HIV/Aids, a subject that, like drugs, more often than not provokes instant MEGO (my eyes glaze over)? But there's a master on stage and within minutes they're captivated.

Aids, Pieter-Dirk Uys tells them, is the new apartheid, the new threat to our young democracy.

'I don't want to frighten you, I want to terrify you,' he warns them gently.

Linking HIV/Aids with apartheid provides Pieter-Dirk Uys with a opportunity to recall the horrors and fears of the not too distant past. As he slips into the sinister but powerful character, Hendrik Goosen, a security policeman testifying at the TRC, the young men are transfixed. It is the language of fear and ignorance and the power it has over this character that has gripped them.

Everyone breathes easier when Pieter-Dirk slips back into his own skin.

'The thing about fear,' he says, 'is that if you forget about it, it comes back. Fear is the most terrifying thing in the world. The moment you are frightened you can't think. But if you laugh at your fear it becomes less fearful. Fear makes you think nothing!' And it is the fear of talking openly about sex, the risks around it and HIV/Aids that will enable the disease to thrive and survive.

After an hour the boys are sick with laughter. Pieter-Dirk has told them frankly about his own first sexual experience while reading a vampire story, he's brandished an enormous gelatinous dildo on stage, he's said the words 'wank' and 'penis' and the roof hasn't fallen down.

He approaches the subject of sex with gentle humour and remarkable honesty. He's never clichéd, prissy or vulgar. He uses words the young men clearly understand, but that their parents or teachers might be too embarrassed to use themselves.

'I don't want you to be taken by surprise,' he tells his audience. 'Sometimes sex comes by surprise and you must know what it is; you must be prepared.'

An hour later, before he leaves the stage to thunderous applause, he reads out an advertisement that has appeared in several local papers stating that more than 50% of South Africans under 25 today could die of Aids before they are 35 years old.

'Ag, no man, let's prove them wrong,' he says. 'It would be a tragedy if half of you didn't make it.'

Twenty minutes later we're in another world. Mountview High School is situated in Hanover Park, surrounded by dusty open fields and drab council flats. Six months ago, armed guards would have met us at the heavy metal security gates, but today, thanks to principal Archie Benjamin, co-ordinator of the Safer Schools Project in Athlone, a lone woman volunteer, Rosie Gertze, unlocks the padlock and waves us through with a smile.

There is no hall here, so the 900 excited schoolkids create a spontaneous amphitheatre in the dusty playground, warding off an unusually harsh autumn sun by balancing newspapers on their heads or draping their jackets over them.

'Ag dis mos Evita,' a young girl whispers to a friend.

Pieter-Dirk reads the audience well and, as at SACS, within minutes the kids have all been won over, laughing spontaneously and gleefully checking their teacher's reactions when the dildo appears or he calls a penis a penis. Here, instead of pulling Dr Hildegaard Grumm, a German sex therapist, out of the bag, Pieter-Dirk conjures up Mrs September, Mitchell's Plain gossip and busybody, a character everyone clearly recognises.

An hour later, a throng of young boys and girls crowd around Pieter-Dirk with scraps of paper, wanting his autograph. Principal Benjamin believes that today's performance has been of enormous value and thanks Pieter-Dirk for his frankness. The teachers at Mountview have a special surprise gift: a black, clay penis that they hand over amidst much raucous laughter in Benjamin's office.

For Pieter-Dirk this free schools tour is part of his six-month renewal of his 'love affair with South Africans' and just one of the many of a variety of community projects. The last time he got to get down with the people was with Evita's Ballot Bus. For Pieter-Dirk, meeting ordinary South Africans is what life is all about, the soulfood that keeps this pessimistic optimist going.

Ruffling Some Old Feathers

Set under the ancient oak trees of Newlands, within hailing distance of the famed sports grounds, Westerford High School has a reputation for excellence and pride. While I was snarled up in Christian Nationalist Education at Nassau, my sister went there, and she seemed to be able to explore new horizons and issues. Westerford was never just sommer any old school! So off I go to present my piece to them early the next week.

It seemed to go off well. The usual reactions – some more, some less. But a major blast resulted from this session. I received a personal letter from the guidance counsellor there, who found the whole exercise uncalled for and obscene. Some of his comments were upsetting, but then again, not unexpected. I prepared to answer him point for point. When he went public with his letter in the next morning's newspaper, I decided it didn't warrant a detailed private explanation. This was a good turn of events, because I knew what I was doing wasn't everyone's cup of tea, and some had angry and justifiable criticisms and dislikes.

From the *Cape Times*, 2 June 2000:

Marianne Thamm's perception of the effectiveness of Pieter-Dirk Uys on HIV/Aids may have been clouded by the ready laughs he got with his vulgarity and phallic humour. It is easy to get adolescents revved up with obscene jokes.

The same presentation at our school was cheap, crude and mostly not about Aids. It was destructive in some respects. Sex was portrayed as something to snigger at, as a variety of sexual practices was paraded for commentary, largely in the genre of boys' locker-room smut.

What was meant to be an Aids programme failed to educate or enlighten. Because humour and satire often depend on stereotypes, some of these myths were, in fact, entrenched.

Girls as young as twelve were exposed to vulgar, intimate sexual nuances about which they were previously ignorant. This came to light in subsequent remedial guidance sessions with them.

What an ugly depraved manner in which to be informed!

It verges on child abuse! Parents of schoolkids need to be more alert to the values being taught at their schools. The new education dispensation is creating a values-void in which unsound morals can easily become the norm. Public school governing body elections are currently taking place.

Parents should be taking an interest. Do we want young people to learn about sexuality in an obscene, tacky and blasphemous way?

Uys is in a powerful position to make a life-changing contribution with a sensitive, educationally sound programme. Letting him address sexuality as an open agenda … next we will have the minibus taxi chairman giving us road safety lessons!

John Broster

P.S. I am head of guidance at Westerford High School.

My first reaction was to blast him off his high ground with every bitchy bullet in my bibliography! But then, once I'd written it all down, I tore it up and let Libran balance dictate:

From the tone of his letter John Broster himself could benefit from remedial guidance. It tells me more about his state of mind than my state of play. To balance his opinion, here are comments from headmasters of three other major Cape schools I visited:

'Your presentation was brilliant, the message was loud and clear, so perfectly executed and revealed. We thoroughly enjoyed your jokes and impersonations and thank you for your openness and realism.'

'Your presentation was informative, to the point and sincere; and, of course, your combination of a serious as well as a humorous approach proved more than effective.'

'The feedback from the learners has only been positive. One child hit the nail on the head: "He spoke to us as if we were people … adults, not children." Quite a compliment coming from a very critical age!'

And among the many from young members of the audiences:

'I am thirteen years old. I would just like to thank you for your inspiring message today. It was funny and interesting.'

I shall be doing another season of shows for Cape Schools from 14 to 25 August. It is self-financed and free of charge. Any interested senior schools can contact me on e-mail.

I gave the address. A flood of reactions to the *Cape Times* letter arrived via the e-mail.

A girl in Grade 10: 'I would like to respond to his letter that I thought your talk was informative and brilliant. It went over the topics that our teachers and other speakers in the past were afraid to say and it's ridiculous because it happens and people try to hide it … also after the talk our teachers started talking about sex and AIDS … it was a door that needed to be opened at Westerford.'

From a parent: 'If Mr Broster is so concerned with youngsters learning about sexuality in such an "obscene, tacky and blasphemous" way, then pray how does he suggest we educate them?'

From a former student of the school: 'If we wait till we are past puberty to learn the honest truth about the situation, then it is just too late!'

There was also a battery of letters published in answer to the counsellor's broadside. Many of them were from his own students. I also received more e-mails and letters, from parents and scholars, as well as from members of staff, which were not published. The cat was well and truly among the pigeons now, and the publicity encouraged others to add their loud voices. Most of the subsequent letters came from those who'd never been to one of the sessions. They reflected a very prominent point of view: don't talk about sex to children!

I'd rather talk about a million other things! I hate having to dive off the high-board into the murky water below and try to find diamonds in the slush. But that's the nature of this beast, and no pretending will make it go away. Yet the criticism was also just an example of the fear we were trying to fight. I have to consider all points of view, and where I can learn, absorb. Take for example the ever-present accusation of blasphemy. Every organised religion has very specific attitudes towards sex. Afrikaner Calvinism pretends it doesn't exist! Catholics cannot use condoms for protection. Muslims, Hindus, Jews, probably even Scientologists, have iron-clad rules about the dos and don'ts, and here I come and open the zip! As the experience grew and I was confronting more schools, with many obviously religious pupils, I made a point of addressing faith as soon as possible.

'One has great respect for what your religion teaches you and demands of you as far as sex is concerned. But this is not about morals. It is about hygiene! It's like cleaning your teeth. Save your life through protection against disease!'

Afrikaners didn't care for it at all. After a visit to the Stellenbosch High School, the Broederbond phones started ringing and the few other Afrikaans schools all cancelled. One principal was distraught.

'I know we have to confront this thing, but the parents won't allow you near their children. They say you encourage them to have sex.' Were I a sixteen-year-old pop star, this would be a compliment! 'They also say you use bad language and pornographic objects.' He's right; they're right!

I assure the distraught servant of his people that I will no doubt be around for some time to come. The cure for AIDS is sadly not round the corner. He can phone me when he feels more confident. 'But please, find an acceptable way to put across the message to your learners! Afrikaans kids also do it, sir! Afrikaanse kinders naai ook!'

The Westerford outing certainly made the project public domain. The negative reactions were to be expected, but I was very encouraged by the mass of positive support that flooded in through e-mail, fax, phone and in envelopes addressed to 'Pieter-Dirk Bezuidenhout, Darling'. It made the big black hole out there a little less empty. Inspired by the good news, I soldiered on. But even I was compromising for the sake of good manners, and thereby giving wrong clues. At one school I was talking about the different types of sex.

'Sex is very inventive. New names for old things. So how will you be able to say no, if you don't know what it is? So find out! Don't be shy to ask! It's cool to ask questions! Unprotected vaginal sex can give you a baby. Even protected anal sex can be a real pain in the arse! It's dangerous because that's a Disneyland for AIDS: blood and semen!'

These comments take on new urgency as I meet more young girls who opt for anal sex to prevent pregnancy, but without condoms. They didn't know of the dangers! Oral sex seems to be the most popular way to do a lot while risking a little. Many questions about the safety of oral sex crop up all over the country. The only answer I have is: 'They say it's minimal risk, but if you have cuts and sores in your mouth, the virus has an easy route into your bloodstream. So don't take a chance! And if you do: don't swallow! Spit out and rinse your mouth with clean water, or mouthwash containing chlorhexidine, which you can get at the chemist!'

Oral sex is one thing, but what is a blow job?

Thank God for Bill Clinton! Everyone now knows what a blow job is, because Bill Clinton did it on the news. Imagine Grannie sitting with the grandchild watching the Teletubbies on TV, and there comes the news: 'President Bill Clinton, the most powerful man in the world, had oral sex in the Oval Office with Monica Lewinsky!'

And the child looks up at Grannie and asks: 'Grannie? What is oral sex, Grannie?'

I can assure you Grannie won't know. She'll probably pat him and say: 'Never mind, aural sex happens in your ear!'

After one performance, two pimply boys with worried teenage faces came up on stage as I was packing.

'Mr Uys? Can we ask a question?'

I said yes.

'Okay. Just now you said: oral sex. You said oral sex?'

Yesss …?

'Does that mean: you talk it?'

I couldn't believe it. There I had explained so obviously that oral sex was a blow job! And everyone knows what a blow job is. 'You do know what a blow job is?' I asked.

The pimply boys shook their heads in unison.

'No.'

Shit! Now I must explain? Of course I must explain. I've opened a tin; they don't know what's in the tin. I must tell them. So there I explain in graphic detail to the two pimply boys what I meant by blow job.

When I am finished, they look perplexed, then nod slowly.

'Oh. Cock-sucking! Why didn't you say so?'

P.S. Don't Forget
Your Penis

The new generation doesn't know what apartheid is. Why should they? It died almost a decade ago, and although the smell still tends to linger, the fear of legalised racism is gone. But once the kids realise that apartheid also killed and that there was no cure except democracy, which was seen as 'toxic', and that the older generation were also faced with a terrible fear, somehow it unites children, parents and teachers. Even when I then do President PW Botha with his wagging finger and lolling tongue, to demonstrate how I used humour to confront my fear, they all laugh. The teachers remember the old crocodile and the kids laugh because a stupid face like Botha's would make even an Eskimo smirk!

'But now the virus of apartheid is gone. Politics no longer kills; it just irritates. And that's what democracy means: it's never perfect, but we have all got the right to change it through our vote.

'And always remember, in a democracy, you are the most important person in South Africa. Each one of you is important! You are protected by a Constitution and a Bill of Rights! No one can force you to do anything against your will. You are in charge of your life!'

One has to go there! One has to remind them that they are free! That they are responsible for themselves. That they have the right to life. That they can make their dreams come true.

'Nothing comes from nothing. If you work and empower yourself with knowledge, anything can happen. You can become whatever you want: a doctor, lawyer, businessman, trapeze artist, hip-hop star, housewife or president! That's freedom! But if you make one mistake tonight at the party, you won't get there. If you are careless with sex, you endanger yourself and your partner. There is no second chance here. You make one mistake because you don't know what you're doing, and you get the HI-virus. There is no cure. Your life will change forever. You don't need that!'

HIV and AIDS have had a lot of good and bad publicity, and most South Africans have heard of it.

Few seem to actually understand what it all means. Human Immune Deficiency Virus, HIV, is what you get mainly through unprotected penetrative sex. It can also be passed from mother to baby in the womb, during birth, or by breastfeeding. It invades and eventually disables the body's natural defence against disease, leaving us vulnerable to various infections and diseases that can eventually be fatal. AIDS stands for Acquired Immune Deficiency Syndrome, meaning something you pick up from outside the body that leads to too few fighting cells in the immune system, opening the chance of a collection of illnesses to flourish. A mouthful of explanation. Major glazed eyes material!

I was at a school in a township, talking about HIV and AIDS. Trying to make sense of all the confusions. Afterwards a young girl came to me with a handful of drawings. She was probably twelve?

'Pieter, I made a drawing of AIDS and HIV. Can I show you?'

I said yes.

'I draw the body as a house, because that's what it is: a big house with windows and doors that we can lock from the inside? Ja?'

I said yes.

'So we are safe. It is called the immune system.'

I said okay.

'Because outside on the stoep is a small black cat who wants to come into the house and piepie on the carpet, but it can't get in, because the windows and the doors are locked from the inside.'

Yes, I say.

'But then a strong cold wind comes down the chimney. That wind is called HIV and it blows out the windows and the doors. And now we have no way to protect our house. We have no security. No immune system. So now that black cat can walk straight in and piepie on the carpet. And that black cat is AIDS.'

So simple. So accessible. I decide to stay away from medical definitions. What I must do is hold their attention long enough for them to remember those other 'boring' details from past medical talks and then understand that it's not about statistics; it's about people. It's about life.

'It's about you. And you. And you. We are all in danger. AIDS does not take sides. Anyone can get it. From a teacher, a parent, a president, a pop star, a child. Infected blood is dangerous. Semen is dangerous. And both of them happen during unprotected sex.'

I touch on the dangers of shared needles during drug taking. But the bottom line is: don't think it can't happen to you. It can. So, acknowledge HIV/AIDS as part of life and find out how to handle it without blinding fear.

'The safest sex is no sex.'

Every time I say this, I hear a chorus of my former teachers and preachers and parents and stern boring adults say it too.

'Don't have sex before marriage! Keep yourself pure! No sex!'

It is still being shrieked out from the minarets of morality, but coming from me...? Shockingly, many young people have reacted to it with surprise.

'You're the first person to tell me that,' a girl says. 'Usually they say: if you use condoms you'll be okay. I don't want to have sex, but they force me.'

'Who forces you?'

'Well, not *force*, but when you as a girl say no, the boys say there's something wrong with you.'

'Like what?'

'Well, like, if you say no, they say you're frigid. Or a lesbian.'

'So? Who cares what they say. You know who you are. Protect yourself. It's cool to be alive. No boy has the right to force you. No man can force you into sex. Say no. You have the law on your side.'

While the safest sex is no sex, this might have worked in the movies for Julie Andrews and Doris Day, but we are not in a musical! I use the image of a plane losing its wings and life being saved by the parachute.

'But a parachute is a very fragile piece of silk. And it has to be folded very carefully and correctly. If you fold it just slightly wrong, it doesn't open. That's it – no second chance here. You don't give it to your maid to fold:

'"Sarah, will you fold Master's parachute?"

'"Yes, Master!" giggles Sarah, and ties a knot in the fragile ropes!

'You're responsible for your survival. You check your equipment! Same in life. When the airliner of sex threatens to crash, have a parachute ready. So if you can't say "no", or if you don't have a choice, or if you decide to have sex, protect yourself with a condom.'

In many schools I am aware of posters about safe sex and condoms. In some halls the kids have made their own posters, which are more interesting and arresting in image and copy. Most young people are aware of the need for condoms, but it is extraordinary how many of them have never actually seen one!

'It's a thing that you put on for sex?' asks a teenager, wrinkling up his nose.

What sort of a thing?

'A balloon?'

They all laugh.

Another boy clicks his fingers excitedly.

'It's like a ... like a ... sock!'

'A cock sock!' comes from the back, and everyone is felled with hysteria.

'Is it a knitted sock?' I ask.

'Ja!' says one boy.

'No, man,' says another boy. 'It's plastic.'

'It's rubber!' shouts a girl, who I think knows.

'Like a glove!' agrees another girl.

I hold up a condom in its silver packaging.

They all shout together.

'Condom!'

I hold up an unravelled one. Some nod, others frown, not having seen a real one before.

'Don't be ashamed if you're not sure. I held this packed condom up last week to some grown-ups and a lady thought it was a chocolate I had sat on!'

They all laugh and agree: that's what it looks like.

'So when it's wrapped it looks like this. When you take it out, it is still rolled up. It only looks like a long sausage when it's been used!'

The long floppy condom flaps stickily in my hand. I can see some of the kids are riveted. They've never seen one 'in the flesh' before.

'This is made for the boys. *Die manne*! Young men must have condoms with them just in case. Then you must also know how to put it on properly. They say we must Practise Safe Sex? So practise! Get your condoms, go to your room, lock the door, switch on the light, drop your broeks, think of someone nice – Britney Spears or David Beckham – get the thing up and erect and practise putting on your condom.'

This is greeted by huge laughter and jumping around. Boys box each other with delight, point fingers and shout names. Girls nod wisely, or just shake their heads, eyes closed with embarrassment.

I hold up a very large condom.

'This is a moerse condom! Every time I look at it I want to cry!' Many of the boys appear to empathise. 'But now I find out there are different sizes! Did you know?' They did not know. 'So get different sizes and try them on to see which one fits. If you buy shoes, you don't just say: give me shoes! You say: give me a size 6 or a size 8! So, do your homework so that you've got the right equipment for your equipment!'

The laughter is quieter now because they're all interested in the complications of safe sex.

'No one wants to be laughed at during sex.'

They agree.

'It is personal, special and everyone wants to look their best. And if your condom is too big, it will fall off!'

Lots of reaction here, as many must have been there too.

'And if you get laughed at, you'll never wear a condom again and, I can assure you, you won't turn twenty!'

In most cases I know this is the first time the kids have ever had a chance to react to such details, be it with laughter or shock. I look at the girls, some of whom find the idea of condoms as distasteful as the boys who wear them.

'Just a message to the girls: if you ever see an unwanted erection coming your way, laugh at it loudly and watch it disappear before your eyes.' The girls get the message.

'So, boys, practice makes perfect. You want to be a soccer star, you practise. You want to be a popstar, you practise. You want to live, you practise safe sex so that nothing can go wrong. Remember, it only takes one small mistake and the virus can get to you or your partner. If this parachute doesn't work, there's no second chance. Don't wait till it's dark and you're excited. You'll end up putting the condom onto your big toe, because that's the biggest thing you've got!'

One thing that confuses me is that while 96 per cent of our penises in South Africa are dark brown or light brown, all the condoms are a sickly yellow, especially the free ones handed out by the Department of Health.

I once found a brown condom in Amsterdam at a shop called Condomerie. The owners have been of great help to me in answering the many questions about condoms from kids. These dark condoms were successful in Uganda.

'Are we surprised that black and coloured men are not wearing condoms? Look at the colour!'

A young man tells me he doesn't wear condoms. 'It's ugly!' he says.

I say: 'This is not a fashion statement. This is to save your life!'

He smiles.

'I am a sexy black man with a beautiful black cock. When I put on these yellow condoms, it looks like a vrot mielie!'

The more comments I hear from young men on this issue, the more I realise: fashion has a lot to do with it! Looking good and feeling sexy is hugely significant. The loss of flesh-on-flesh in exchange for sexy, cool safe-sex equipment is still a pipedream!

I hold up a black condom at a township school. The boys whistle and stamp their feet.

'Hey man, I'll wear that outside my trousers!' says a boy wistfully.

Minister of Finance Trevor Manuel stated in his most recent budget speech that 310 million free condoms had been released into South African society in 2001. We've all seen them, at bars, clubs, on counters, next to cash registers. Free condoms? Use them, but check their credentials first!

A recent survey showed how badly researched free condoms were, especially in size. One size fits all and even that size is too small for the average African man. How to check condoms is a constant question.

'If the wrapping is slippery, throw it away. Don't put them in your back pocket, because if you sit on them, you could puncture them. Take a few free ones out of a batch and open them. Fill one with water and one with air and wait. If they don't leak, the batch is probably okay.'

The point is: who can ever be sure? Some years ago a batch of condoms was released, each with a small card explaining their use in eleven languages. Each condom was neatly stapled to the card! The original story stated that these were condoms from Dr Zuma's Department of Health. Recently a member of that department informed me that those condoms did not come from them, but from another safe-sex organisation. Odd that no one from the department found it necessary to inform the public. The fact that 44 million free condoms were released during that period, some with staples through them, surely means there are potentially 44 million death warrants out there! So I warn the kids: 'You never know how safe a condom is! Are there staple holes? Is it damaged? Check! Make sure! If you're not sure, don't take a chance!'

At a boys' school the ultimate safe sex is always the do-it-yourself method. The One Armed Struggle. At a girls' school I don't feel confident enough to venture into those arenas, but make it clear that sex is a normal, natural outlet for all people. It's just how it happens that can cause problems. And with the danger of a virus, masturbation solves many of those problems! Teachers have been seen to pale here, while the occasional nun smiles.

I recommend that girls carry condoms also, because of the danger of rape.

'At least hopefully you'll be able to say: if you're going to rape me, use a condom. If he says: I don't use condoms, then lie. Say: I have AIDS; you'd better use a condom.'

After the talk, one of the counsellors came to me and pointed out that once in court a man would say that the woman agreed to sex by giving him a condom. So the next time I spoke about it, I added that to the thought: 'Of course, in court, if he's caught, he will just say: she agreed to sex because she gave me a condom. Well, get a good lawyer, but hopefully you won't be HIV-positive afterwards.'

I become more aware of the horrors of experience. The countless incidents of daily rape that never see the light of knowledge and yet fester inside like cancer. I realise how dangerous this is, how easily one can trivialise pain with flippancy, or forget that victims are good at disguising their fears. Never underestimate the fact that everything you talk about can happen to anyone. And that those who have been raped need to embrace life after rape. Like those with HIV and AIDS have to be encouraged to believe in life, and not just early death.

It's so fragile, because you know there are many young minds protected by religion and tradition. Usually the ones that look at you with wide-eyed amazement are the ones that come afterwards and earnestly say: 'Am I in danger?'

And you know what she means without further detail. And you say: 'Yes, like me.'

And she says: 'Thank you. Because no one has ever considered that I am in the front line with so many others.'

A girl pushes a note in my hand and runs off. I open it: 'I love you,' it says, and there are little hearts and flowers and a picture of me and a picture of Princess Diana! This is such a reversal of the usual 'black hole syndrome', when the bad news came first: reviews and press comments, all the worst things. Seldom anything good. Yet now all I get are the encouraging notes, the hugs and the embraces, the letters and the e-mails and the notebooks with each page coloured in, as it traces my life as a famous woman! The good news is more shocking than the bad. Good demands everything, and every time a child sees something good in what's being done, the challenge to extend that good is inevitable. This is the ultimate fix. The final addiction. If we can keep these thousands of young people alive, the children of our democracy, we will have the greatest generation the world has ever seen! Keep them alive tonight! For tomorrow!

Even though I'm three times their age, I must keep their trust and never lecture or judge. 'I'm not going to tell you *not* to do it. I know what that means. It means: I *will* do it! Moenie? Waar koop ek "moenie"? You're young and full of terrible energy. Yes, you drink more than Coke and smoke other than stompies. There's Ecstasy pills and poppers and God knows what else you take up your nose or down your throat. But just know that every time you take something that makes you drunk or high or out of it, you don't think clearly and you can make a mistake. Unsafe sex only has to happen once. It only takes one exposure to the virus to make you one of that gang.'

Every time I talk to them about the danger in *their* nights, I wonder if I have practised what I now preach on a daily basis. Do I practise safe sex? In all honesty, my sexual experiences have been severely curtailed in the last decade, purely because of my fear of the virus. Remembering the ease with which I managed to reverse into dingy corners in sauna baths and dark rooms in the eighties, I have tried to keep my very active need for sex mainly 'in-house'. At least you don't have to look your best when you do it, and the imagination does offer great safe choices!

But what about that party last December? I don't often go to parties. Can't hear people talk because of the noise, and, when you can, you wished the noise was louder! Cigarette smoke gets into everything and for weeks afterwards you smell like Chernobyl. However, there are exceptions and this was one. Lots of fun, lots to drink, lots to look at and the next morning I woke up in a strange bed. Not only with a hangover, but with two bronzed bodies on either side. I didn't know who they were. Worse, I didn't remember what we'd done. I woozily looked around the room for tell-tale evidence of common sense, but no squishy used rubbers caught my eye. So I don't know!

'I don't know!' I tell them at the next school. 'So until I go and have an HIV test I will not know. But I'll imagine the worst and probably die of fear. Having an HIV test is not fun. Like anything that has the possibility of bad news. But knowing either way is often better than wondering either way.'

Somehow sharing my life with them makes them feel adult. I have put my cards on the table, shared my feelings and fears with them. Never preach and never be on moral high ground.

The reality of life always anchored me to earth. I received an e-mail in December 2001 with regard to the AIDS-awareness entertainment that has toured throughout South Africa since March 2000.

Dear Pieter-Dirk Uys

Our school is very keen for you to come to us with your Aids concert. Although we are in the rural parts of the Eastern Cape, our children have heard from their cousins in Cape Town that you say important things and that you help us to laugh at our fear. We are very frightened of this HIV and AIDS. So please come and visit us here as soon as you can.

Sincerely

B.K. Hendrickse
Principal

P.S. Don't forget your penis!

From Bishop Lavis to Bishopscourt

I visit an Afrikaans skool in Villiersdorp, across the Hottentots-Holland Mountains. When I was small and wouldn't eat my fish, my Pa would always threaten to send me to the 'verbeteringskool in Villiersdorp'. It became a focus of terror for me. Nothing could be worse than being banished there. Today it isn't a reformatory any more. It's a school like any other, although all Afrikaans establishments carry with them the Calvinist overlay of denial.

'Dit kan nie met ons mense gebeur nie!'

It can't happen to our people!

Things were looking up. This was my second venture into those old familiar territories. Little did I know that very few would be allowed to host me in the future. So from the Villiersdorp laager that Monday to the kugel kibbutz! Off to Herzlia against the slopes of Devil's Peak. What a difference! The show was in English for starters, and there is little fear of confrontation among an audience of Jewish kids. They laughed, they listened and they asked questions! I thought at first this would be an interesting way to end all the performances, with a Q & A session, encouraging some interaction, but too often the kids were inhibited by teachers. Some suggested I ask the teachers to leave, but that would defy the whole purpose of the exercise. We are all in this together. Teachers also die of AIDS!

The trek took me back and forth across the Cape Peninsula, from Fish Hoek to Sea Point, from Table View to Grassy Park. Some schools are like movie sets. Sprinklers whoosh across green lawns, bushes carefully trimmed to stand etched round and sharp against pristine whitewashed walls. Sports fields echoing with the shouts and whoops of youth. The tinkle of a piano from an upstairs music teacher's window. A violin, some drums, cultivated Xhosa rhythms. A timeless atmosphere of controlled peace. And then an hour later, across two freeways, you're in a war zone again, at a school where five gangs rule through terror and among them kill one child a week. I see them sitting in the hall, hierarchy allowing the leaders chairs when the rest hunch on floors. Earrings and gold teeth. A scarf. A cellphone glued to the ear. A smirk and no smile. But gang bossboys also drop the pose and become involved, because they also have a life ahead of them and want their dreams to come true. Different dreams to my dreams, but still hoping for something better.

I discover the concept of crossing gang lines. It's okay as long as I have someone in the car with me who knows what and where. Sometimes it is a nurse from the clinic. On one occasion she sits next to me, her brown knuckles white with tension. I drive through a ramshackle neighbourhood. Cars on blocks. Broken glass on damaged road. Yelping dogs. Small children lolling against corrugated-iron walls. Familiar Third World territory.

'Are we okay?' I eventually ask, after passing a second deserted T-junction.

She nods.

'By now they would've shot at us. We sent out the message. I'm glad they got it.'

Message? 'Evita Bezuidenhout is coming through. She has diplomatic immunity. Don't kill! Wave!' And they do! Gangster boys with orange hair and Mad Max jewellery, grinning with the gap, fingers cocked like guns and pockets fat with weapons of war.

'Hello Tannie Evita!' they wave. I give my best Princess Margaret finger-twiddle. Sister next to me squeaks with discomfort and fear.

One school had radically changed its address. For years it was situated at the corner of two busy township roads, but as the gang warfare took its toll, more of the school collapsed. The windows were gone, doors disappeared. It was hell. One day the principal gathered his 200 pupils.

'Take anything that you can carry and let's get out of here.'

And so, like a latter-day Moses, he led his little troop out of their desert. Small boys were carrying small chairs, older kids each had a desk. They trekked down three blocks and passed a petrol station.

'Hey Salie?' shouted the owner. 'Where are you going?'

Principal Salie stopped, put down his boxes and smiled blearily.

'I'm looking for a school for the children,' he said.

The petrol man waved them in.

'Come in. There's place here for a school.'

And so for a year Salie taught his kids between the old Toyotas and Golfs that were being serviced. Today they have their own building, a patchwork prefab collection of huts. In the centre is a courtyard. I did my show there, standing on some rickety tables. The first thing that struck me on arrival were the rows of pot plants on the veranda. Salie smiled when I asked about them.

'Man, these kids don't even have homes, let alone plants. So every one of them has their own plant in a tin. They must look after that life, as well as their own.'

After the presentation, I was taken on a tour by Janet. She's in Grade 7. She's doing well. She took me to show her little plant.

'That's mine there,' pointing at a healthy collection of leaves. 'And that girl is lazy, because she's got a plastic plant.' Truly, that's what it was, a shiny made-in-Japan cactus with a bright pink flower half broken off at the stem. Janet nudged me gently and pointed at the other end of the veranda with wide eyes. 'And look at the gangs? They also have plants. Dagga!'

I inspected the small yellow plants, distinct and familiar.

Then I joined the principal for a cup of tea. He and I shared an already used teabag.

'Earl Gray,' he winked. 'One bag can make five ordinary Five Roses cups!'

His office was full of boxes and more boxes and other boxes. Memories of a former building that had space but no place. 'Did little Janet show you the plants?' he asked.

I nodded.

'And the gangs? You see their plants?

I nodded.

'You let them grow dagga?'

Salie laughed and gestured towards his desk.

'Look under there.' I looked and saw an old staffie sleeping, head on paws. 'That's Brutus. Every Friday afternoon he pees on the dagga plants. That's why they're so small and yellow. There's no puff left in those leaves!' Brutus opened one bleary eye and gave a small squeaky yawn!

I visit a Waldorf School, where the whole atmosphere is more that of a college, or university residence. The kids don't wear uniforms. They are free of much of the discipline found in other schools. We sit together in a classroom and have a more personal session. The boys are already men and show the arrogance of wealth and position. I can hear my father in my head: 'They all need a good thrashing!'

Didn't do me any harm. But these kids are not used to being curtailed or punished. Maybe their privileged background is punishment enough.

We get to the safe-sex bit and the use of condoms. Two boys slouch in their chairs shaking their heads in contempt. I'm obviously pissing them off.

'You don't use condoms?' I ask.

One of them gives a long hiss as he exhales his frustration. The other raises his eyebrow.

'What for?' he asks.

'Protection against HIV?' I reply sweetly.

He applauds sarcastically.

'I don't wear condoms out of principle,' he brags.

I wait for him to go on. All the kids are now focused on this confrontation.

'I don't like using condoms. It takes away the pleasure.'

'And what if you get infected?' I ask.

'Who cares? I'm sixteen. Within three years they'll find a cure. I'll be cured. Or I'll be dead.'

'Oh? And you don't mind dying?'

'Doesn't matter. If I live, I'll just end up like my father. Maybe death is better!'

Little fucker. He certainly held the floor and his comments reflected a lot of truth. I found out he came from one of the wealthiest families in the country, with divorced parents and a history of tolerated drug-taking at home. It was a scream for help, but he did it so well most people ran for the door. Including me.

I spoke to a school counsellor about him.

'All bravado,' she said, retreading familiar ground. 'Difficult background, brilliant brain, lazy, rich, bored and beautiful. A lethal cocktail. I don't have any answers. One must just keep trying to win his trust.'

The boy was waiting for me near my car. Suddenly he looked younger and quite frail. I opened the boot and put in the bag of props. I felt him watch. Then I looked round at him.

'And?'

'Why do you do this?' he said. 'It's not going to help. We're all going to die.'

'Yes, but not today.'

As I drove away I looked in the mirror. He gave a small wave.

A year later I saw him at a local gay bar. He was too drugged to react when I said hello.

With Devil's Peak disguised in clouds of mist, four buses nose their way through the gates of Diocesan College, aka Bishops. The eager faces of black children are pressed up against the windows, staring at the green grass and the gnarled old pine trees, the driveway that threads its way past playing fields where sprinklers whirl in wet circles despite the soft rain. Whitewashed buildings house study and

168

dreams. This visit was the result of my linking up with Rotary. I met Suzy at the Perron after one of the shows and she wanted to know how they could assist with my schools programme. Knowing how many places I could never get to, I also knew of the many schools around the corner that had no facilities. No hall or classroom big enough to accommodate the whole school. So Rotary sourced those schools, organised transport and found the ideal base at Bishops.

When a small boy, I used to bicycle off to that school from Pinelands to have piano lessons with Dr Claude Brown, a legendary teacher and eccentric choir master. Never mind my having two pianists as parents. It didn't work with me and caused untold dramas, as Pa would scream at me to practise and I'd put hands on hips and lisp refusal. Dr Brown never remembered my name and called me Little Fish. I learnt nothing there either, because I never practised. They said I would be sorry and I am. But the whole atmosphere of Bishops stayed with me forever. It was like the schools we saw in British films, with tradition and culture, discipline and pride amid gorgeous surroundings. Unlike my local school, which was just about rugby and cadets.

Imagine these kids having come from their various schools on the Cape Flats and getting out of a bus in the middle of a British film set? The arrangement was that I would do my show for them. They would then have a break for doughnuts and cooldrinks, after which they'd go off in smaller groups, hosted by senior boys from Bishops and visiting girls from Herschel. There the young people would talk about what they'd heard, and discuss the realities of what was confronting them in life, from violence and crime, to abuse and HIV/AIDS. This would be the first of many such exercises, and each one built up a greater sense of excitement and hope. Let the people lead. The government can follow!

The hall at Bishops is state of the art, with seats that befit so elegant an establishment. Like first-class aeroplane sofas, soft and upholstered. As usual I sat on stage at my table, sorting out my Evita props, wearing my knitted beanie and watching them come in. The group of kids skidded to a halt in the doorways, looking up and around the big hall, impressed. The smaller boys made a dash for the first row as they usually do, so that they can see everything first.

I watched a twelve-year-old in his green school blazer, grey shorts, knock-knees and scrunched-down socks make for a chair and then stop and stare. This chair! What was this chair? He prodded it with a finger, pinched the cushion with both hands. He studied it from below and looked round the back. This was something else, this chair. Then after looking around to make sure no one else wanted to take his chair, he slid himself into it bottom first, curled up and fell asleep! He slept throughout the talk. I kept on looking down at that peaceful little person, curled up like a happy stray cat. Afterwards his teacher came to me and apologised.

'I saw he was sleeping. That's very naughty,' she said.

'Does he usually sleep so well? So soft? So safe?'

She shook her head.

'No, he is one of eight kids in one room with a cold floor. He sleeps on the floor.'

During this session I told them about the possibilities in their lives under a free, democratic system. They could make their dreams come true!

'You can become President!' I said, and looked past the sleeping child at another little boy in the second row. He came up to me after the presentation, a proud, compact little person in his green blazer, holding a squashed tin of what once held cooldrink.

'Bra Piet!' he announced, 'you inspire me! I will always practise safe sex, because you said I would become President!'

Beyond the Playgrounds

I get an e-mail from the Koeberg nuclear power station, which is on the road from Darling to Cape Town. The fact that I have no hair is not their fault! At first I thought they were a high school, and so when they asked what the fee would be, I declined. Once I realised this was not a school, I knew this would be my first presentation to adults. Up to now all my performances had been to children and their teachers. This would be a different kettle of kids!

Getting into the nuclear establishment required a complicated security screening. The workers had been gathered in one of the warehouses. There were close to 400 of them, and when I took to the high platform specially created, I knew they were looking forward to a real show! I was introduced and when the name 'Evita' came up, there was applause and anticipation. I thanked them all. I was thrilled to be here. Baldness is in the family, so don't feel guilty!

'It must be so complicated,' I said. 'What do you have to do to get ready for work every day? And then later when you leave work? Maybe someone can just tell me what the procedure is?'

There was some prodding and pointing and eventually they decided on the actor among them, a young coloured man with a moustache and huge smile. He stood up and they yelled encouragement.

'Okay,' he said, preparing himself to audition. 'This is the procedure I go through from getting out of my car to my place of work and back to my car when the day's done!' He stated meticulously every X-ray, each screening, washing of hands, donning of helmets, dressing up, dressing down, protective this and protective that, checking the whatnot and balancing the whatever. '… and then I'm out of the building in the fresh air and I know I'm safe. The same procedure when I come to work the next morning.'

We all applauded his talent and clarity of presentation.

'Thank you for telling me how you protect yourself from radiation,' I said. 'Now take away the word "radiation" and put in the letters "HIV". What do you do to protect yourself against HIV?'

A deathly silence. No one had an answer. They simply did nothing to protect themselves against HIV.

'Friends, believe me, no one here will die of radiation! Unless there is a catastrophe, and you're also prepared for that. But 40 per cent of us could easily die of HIV/AIDS. That's the catastrophe that is not just isolated to a nuclear power plant. That is an international catastrophe! What are we going to do?'

There was no response. So I took them on the same road as I had their children. A similar path I would in future take corporates, executives, prisoners, parents and workers. Because no matter where they come from, what their culture, how much they earn – old people, black, white, young people – all people meet at the same place. X marks the spot. Sex. The universal crossroads. That's where the Viral Hijacker waits. For everyone!

I was invited to visit a reformatory. This was not a school, but a jail. There were about 150 boys there, between the ages of twelve and eighteen, all in for violent crimes: murder, rape, assault – and many of them also had a virus with no cure. I was warmly greeted by a Dr van Wyk. He was a fan. He introduced me to Mrs van Wyk, who was no relation, and they waved across at Oom Jan van Wyk, who was overseeing the garden. It seemed the Van Wyks bred around this area. There were Van Wyks for Africa. I was invited to join them all for lunch after my talk to the boys.

We went into the prison building and through various locked doors that were unlocked and then relocked. The Van Wyk who led me told how often the boys managed to get out, but how often some just came back. The real world was so terrifying they felt safer inside. We came to a general room, with rows of chairs and six tables pushed together to form a stage. I hoisted myself onto it and arranged my bits and pieces: Evita's hair, her sunglasses, huge earrings, red lipstick, her perfume, her cellphone, a cluster of props that would be Madiba, plus his ethnic shirt, the Tutu drag, and the collection of condoms for demonstration. On one side stood the golden box with the *pièce de résistance*: the big twelve-inch pink dildo, the smaller nine-inch black penis I'd received in Hanover Park from the teachers, and a plastic banana. In *Sarafina 2* terms, probably 10 million rand worth of equipment!

The boys came in. No, there were no boys. Some were as young as eleven, but they'd seen it all. Some were sixteen going on sixty. Tattoos over faces. Gaps between teeth where teeth once were. Sculpted heads with lines shaved pinkly through cropped hair. Half-closed eyes never blinking. Earrings glinting in lobes. Not the best matinée audience. What do I say to them?

'Hi boys, isn't life great?'

Life is hell for them, and being HIV-positive means that there's nothing great to look forward to either. Do I try to remind them that there was a man in jail for twenty-seven years, but he came out and changed everyone's life?

One boy had been arrested the Friday before for stealing a car. By the time it was proved that he'd just borrowed his father's vehicle, it was weekend, and too late to get him out of the place. He was released on the following Monday. He had by then been raped four times and is now HIV-positive.

Everything I have prepared for today feels meaningless, so I chuck it all out and make it up as I go. Language varies from Afrikaans to Cape Coloured to English. And yet no matter where I take this one-sided conversation, I am getting nowhere. I decide to bring Evita in immediately.

'You know Evita Bezuidenhout?' Some nods and grunts. 'You want to see her? Shall I bring you the most famous woman in South Africa?'

The lights in their eyes start going on. They sit up. I take the red lipstick and slowly open it, exposing its bloody little clitoris suggestively. They grunt and snigger. I roll on the Evita lips. Some whistle. I put on the big poncho to give the feel of a cloak. Some applaud. Now come the huge earrings that hang like grapes.

'Hey goose!' comes from the back.

Slowly I put on the blue-tinted Sophia Loren glasses, given to me by the goddess herself, who purred: 'These spectacles for the woman you do!'

Evita is not yet there. It's a bald man with funny glasses and a blanket. Then I pick up the wig and turn my back to them, slowly settling it on my head and fluffing out the curls. The male audience roars its excitement. As I turn to face them, they see Evita Bezuidenhout. Five tatty pieces of costume and a bit of slap and she's there! They applaud and stand up and dance around. They laugh and show me pink gums and shiny tongues.

'Evita, ek wil djou naai!' is a compliment that she takes in the spirit in which it is hurled at her.

The show turns around from being boring lecture to glamorous gossip. Tannie Evita has a son in jail with Eugene Terreblanche. She shares her fears with these inmates. After all, they are there too! Terreblanche is in for six years for assault.

One boy shouts back: 'And I am in for seven for stealing a tin of sardines!' While they laugh with him, I think this is true!

When Evita sprays them with her perfume and announces its name, *Jeau Mour*, we're friends for life. She asks questions and they answer. She warns them against unsafe sex and they nod. She encourages them to read and they laugh. One boy says he loves Shakespeare. The old books. The nice thin paper. So he can roll a joint! Evita promises him old Shakespeare books and makes a deal: 'Read first, then smoke!'

I end Evita and take her off and the boys suddenly realise she's gone, although her perfume remains. Now we can talk and we do. No one has the right to force sex on anyone outside or inside prison. If you have anal sex, use condoms! Semen and blood are the ingredients for HIV! You are also protected by the Constitution that sent you here! Respect life so that you can re-enter society and live!

It sounds naive, but somehow in that strange atmosphere of never-never and nearly, it was possible for a brief moment to forget the reality of hell and pretend that, after all is said and done, people are by nature not all bad. After the session some boys come up to shake hands. Two of them are from the Swartland where I now live.

'Can we come and visit?' one asks.

'Yes, but ring the bell and let me open. Don't come through the roof, or the bathroom window!'

I settle down with the Van Wyks for lunch. The few that were in the room with us share what they heard. Some are still amused, one or two not happy. Then I turn to the man in charge, a Dr Dr van Wyk.

'There's one question I asked in there. I couldn't understand the answer. Maybe you can help, Dr Dr?'

He smiles a Dr-Dr smile.

'Do these young men have access to condoms?'

The sound of the word 'condom' ends the party. Knives and forks in plates, frowns on faces, mouths downturn!

Dr Dr is not pleased.

'We don't talk about those things at table,' he sotto voce's. 'If they must have those things, they can ask Sister van Wyk.'

I look at Sister van Wyk. She looks like Rosa Kleb from the James Bond film. She also has a moustache. She winks at me horribly.

'Oh, I see,' say I, party-pooping even more, 'if the sixteen-year-old boy-man wants to rape the twelve-year-old boy-child, he must first ask her for a condom!'

The good Dr Dr clears his throat.

'We don't believe in condoms. We know condoms encourage sex.'

Picture this: dark dorm, moonlight on boy with erection. He hisses to sleeping boy with sexy bum.

'Psst!'

'What?'

'Do you want sex?'

'No!'

'Are you sure?'

'Yes!'

Boy strokes erection and thinks. Then hisses again.

'I've got a condom.'

'Oh?' sighs sexy bum, 'now I'm encouraged!'

Having visited over 200 schools and a few reformatories, I can tell you that in the midst of an AIDS holocaust, not one of them has got a condom-dispensing machine handy, just in case sex happens and someone needs a parachute!

Do handicapped boys have sex? I never thought about it until the head of a school for handicapped children invited me to come to their hall. It was a grey cold depressing Cape day. The school is somewhere on the Cape Flats, between factories and dumps and swamps. An old building that needs financial help to renovate and bring it into the twenty-first century. As they wheel and stumble into the draughty hall, I see how adept they are with their steering and how quickly they can sidestep on crutches, like ballet. Most wheelchairs are just that: chairs on wheels, but some in the front row are streamlined and complex, like sports cars. The kids are so physically disabled that they need more than just help with movement. A few can't even sit up straight to see the stage, so they watch me through a series of well-placed mirrors. When the other kids laugh, they press buttons and their machines hoot!

They're also scared of getting AIDS! While most of the world sails past them at full speed, giving them a patronising glance and an 'ag shame', these remarkable little humans have to sort out more than just birds and bees.

I moved among them after the show, signing books and papers and a crutch or two. The teacher stopped me.

'You missed Stephen,' she said. 'He so much wants to meet you.'

I looked around. Where could I have missed Stephen? Then I saw his spaceship in the front row, to one side. He was so doubled up I couldn't even see his head. My heart sank. This was too complicated. The teacher led me to him. I touched Stephen's arm. It was shaking. Relieved, I stepped back and whispered.

'No, there's something wrong. I think he's tired ...'

'Nonsense,' frowned the teacher. 'He's fine. He's having a wonderful time. Talk to him.'

Was 'ag shame' so clearly etched on my face? The teacher probably wanted to kick me and I wish she had.

'Talk to him, Pieter, it's okay. You won't catch anything!'

I knelt down next to Stephen's transport and looked under and up into his face. A beautiful young man's face: blue eyes and a sexy Robbie Williams smile. He was laughing at me.

'Hell, Pieter-Dirk Uys, you're so ridiculous, man! You're the first person who's ever been scared that I might get AIDS.'

My mouth went dry.

'But I am,' I stuttered.

'Ja,' he smirked, 'most people think that I will never be able to have sex, but you know what, Pieter-Dirk Uys? One day I'm gonna have sex! And I promise you, I'll wear a condom!'

Report Back from the Frontlines

My visit to some schools encouraged the kids to create their own entertainment about fear. A school in the Cape Flats invited me to come and watch their 'AIDS play'. The school didn't have a hall, so they'd borrowed a church hall for the evening. I hadn't ventured into the underbelly of the Cape Flats without the security of daylight before. It was a dark night as I manoeuvred round stationary vehicles and tried to read signs that were loose, upside down or just blank. I passed the place three times before I realised that the dingy little hall on my left was my destination. Where to leave the car? White fears bubbled to the surface. Hide the radio? Hide the briefcase? Hide the vehicle! Rubbish. I left it locked like anywhere else and no one went near it.

The hall was full of parents and activity. The kids had made posters, and streamers in the colours of the flag brought the ceiling down even closer to our heads. Chairs were set in jagged rows. When I decided to slip into the back and watch without disturbing the preparations, I was discovered and ushered down to the front row where a chair had been reserved for me. 'Pieter-D' it said. The one next to it was reserved for 'Evita B'! The kids crowded round the side of the stage and stared and waved, giggled and showed huge excitement.

It was to be a play about confronting AIDS and other fears. The senior teacher welcomed everyone.

'... especially Mrs Bezuidenhout who came all the way from Darling'.

The empty chair next to me glowed. Everyone looked at me and saw Evita. I waved back.

The first sketch happened. It was about child abuse. There were no microphones and the hall had a typical echo. But once one got used to the pitch of the voices and the accents, the dialogue was clear and shockingly frank. One of the girls had been raped. They discussed it and wanted her to seek help.

'The secret is sometimes worse than the experience,' one girl recited. 'You're not alone, darling. Millions of women share your pain and fear. Share it with them and let your anger help you win.' Then they all looked at me and smiled. A mother leant across my shoulder.

'That's what you said to them, hey?'

Did I? The story unfolded on stage. The person who had raped her was not a stranger. It was her uncle. The atmosphere chilled around me and everyone watched in silence. The small fat boy who was playing the uncle like some pantomime dame didn't raise a laugh. Then I realised why so many in the audience were turning round and staring at a man seated in the middle of the hall. The uncle in the sketch. He didn't flinch and was the only one who laughed loudly at the fat boy's performance. When the sketch ended to huge applause, he suddenly got up and left.

The play also stopped. Everyone milled around and the few chairs on stage were removed and replaced. People in the audience chatted to each other and a few parents came to me and introduced themselves.

The next sketch was about pregnancy in the classroom. It was extraordinary how honest the kids were, and how funny. The more shocking the subject, the further they pushed the envelope with Cape Flats humour. After that sketch the play stopped again.

Then I realised: none of them had ever seen 'a real play'! They'd based their structure on television sitcoms, where a scene is followed by a commercial break. The dramatic unity of a play, with interleading scenes and two or three acts, meant nothing here. It was great! After each sketch everyone discussed what had been exposed. They celebrated their children's talents and showed amazement at the maturity of their awareness. That maturity no doubt comes with experience. I ached at the thought of how many of these wonderful young kids were being subjected to rape, abuse, pain, fear and harassment.

The third sketch was announced.

'This is specially for Mr Uys who seems to be worried about these things.'

It was about condoms and lubricants! Two boys swaggered onto the stage, Jan and Benny. The other kids screamed encouragement. These were obviously the two clowns in school.

JAN: Hell Benny, but I had a nice time last night!

BENNY: Did you have sex with my girlfriend?

Laughter from the kids.

JAN: Yours and mine.

They both get the giggles and we all have to wait for them to recover.

JAN: Ja, but I used a condom.

BENNY: Why bother? That's like swimming in a raincoat!

JAN: Evita Bezuidenhout says you must wear condoms …

He dissolves into giggles. We all wait. I look around. Everyone is watching me with bright eyes. Jan pulls himself together.

JAN: I used a separate condom with each goose.

BENNY: That's good. Evita will be pleased.

They look at me and wait for my reaction. I nod and smile.

JAN: But I have a problem with condoms, Benny.

BENNY: Why Jan?

JAN: I'm so big …

Screams emerge from the wings, denying such an outrageous claim and the whole hall falls about. Eventually:

JAN: I have to use lubricants, but I only have …

He can't remember the word. Someone shouts from the sides:

'Water-based, you doos!'

JAN: … water-based. Is that okay?

BENNY: Ja, Jan, that's very good. Because oil-based lubricants is very bad.

They both turn to the audience and become the typical television salesmen.

BENNY: Let us demonstrate what we mean.

JAN: Here is a condom …

BENNY: Two condoms …

JAN: One on this finger …

BENNY: And one on that …

JAN: I put this lubricant on this condom. It is oil-based …

BENNY: And I put this lubricant on this condom. It is water-based.

JAN: Look what happens!

The atmosphere is electric. Not a sound, as we all strain to look at what is happening on the two fingers of Jan's hand. Then we notice. His pink skin starts to forge through the condom on the oil-based finger!

JAN: See, oil-based dissolves your rubber. It means you are not protected against the virus.

'Or a baby!' comes the prompt from the side.

BENNY: And the water-based lubricant?

They both look at the secure condom.

JAN: Ready for Freddy!

BENNY: Or Joan!

They bow.

As I drove home, passing the huge Lovelife billboards with their incomprehensible safe-sex messages and images, I just wondered what an extraordinary effect Benny and Jan's message would have on national television, exactly as it had been performed. Honest, funny and real. But alas, too good to be true.

After a performance at a school in Atlantis, a former model township in the apartheid dreams of the former regime, an SABC television camera crew interviewed some of the young people. I sat behind a half-open door, hidden so as not to disturb, but wanting to hear what the television reporters were asking. They were not particularly encouraging and seemed to hope the reaction would underline the growing conservative backlash that I was spreading porno-graphic ideas.

A teenage girl answered questions with a smile.

'What did you think of what he did?' the reporter asked.

'No, it was very good,' the girl laughed.

'Yes, but can you make jokes about these things?'

'No,' said another girl of twelve. 'It's not funny; it's true!'

'Oh?' the reporter pounced, 'and what makes you think what he says is true?'

'Because it's free,' the girl said. 'If he was paid, why should we believe him?'

So much for hype. Out of the mouth of a twelve-year-old township child comes the wisdom of this young generation. They're not impressed by any subsidised bullshit. So in future I leave all potential bullshit in the boot of the car.

This production is not *Sarafina 3*. Not another 14 million rand illusion. It didn't cost anyone a cent. And that was the secret of its success. Most of the schools would not have been able to afford even 20c a child. There would always be someone who'd suggest an alternative priority. No government department had put any of its budget into the project, so no one could phone up and suggest other ways of approaching the issues. No censorship, no members of the board, no sponsors, no subsidy. Just me in the little silver car, Tannie in the boot, a map of the area well and truly koki-penned and marked, a phone with a full battery, a cooldrink, a packet of droëwors and the day's newspaper.

'I am not a medical expert like Thabo Mbeki,' I say, and they all laugh, but not with him; they laugh at him! They're pissed off by the confusion and the lies. They know something is killing them. They don't want to be treated like kids. They're sexually active. They're adults. And so I say: 'I'm fifty-seven. You make me feel sixteen and I'll make you feel twenty-four.'

Many of the reactions have mirrored this.

'Thanks for treating me like a grown-up,' a young girl says, and I know that once she's shed her school prison uniform and dressed for the world out there, she is a woman and not a little girl. Although she might only be thirteen.

I meet a boy of nine. He's the father of a child. The mother of his child is eleven. It's a good news tale, because her parents are looking after mother and child and allow the young father visiting rights.

How many other children are not children any more? The eight-year old selling her body for sex to make some money to feed her brothers and sisters, because their parents have died of AIDS and there's no one for them. It took a twelve-year-old small thin boy in a suit that looked too big for him, holding a microphone the size of a magnum bottle in his frail hand, to wake up the world to the plight of our children. Nkosi Johnson appeared on stage at the

AIDS Conference held in Durban in 2000 and made a speech that moved and stunned the watching world. He acknowledged his terminal illness, but underlined his determination to live. The world media were watching his every move, hearing all his carefully pronounced words. President Mbeki was also in the hall, and Nkosi was excited because Thabo was his hero.

In view of the world, the South African President rose and left the hall with his Retex SS. He walked out on a child's plea for understanding. He turned his back on the best invitation he ever had to join the New Struggle on a world stage. Everyone who cared felt sick to their stomachs.

'The President had a plane to catch,' the advisers and bodyguards bleated. One plane that could've been replaced with another plane, one wonders? Nkosi waited for over eighteen months to meet his hero, but never did. When the little boy died of AIDS, not unexpected but still sadly missed, he left an echo that resounds. Nkosi Johnson's heritage gets stronger by the day, as his bravery and presence inspires millions of kids to stand up and be counted. Maybe he is now a haunting voice in Thabo Mbeki's worst nightmare?

Maybe Yes, Maybe No

Meanwhile, on the ANC Olympus, the gods are being led by their Zeus, his Mbekivellian visions stage-managed by Essop Pahad, long-serving chairman of the 'Don't Criticise Thabo' Fan Club. The comrades lose their marbles one by one. Dr Nkosazana has added a Dlamini to her Zuma and is now Minister of Foreign Affairs. The international diplomatic world trembles. Who will inform the good Madame that in order to fly from Pretoria to Harare, she doesn't always have to go via Paris? The new Minister of Health, Manto Tshabalala-Msimang, has a good reputation as someone who has worked with AIDS patients and knows what she's doing. We wait and see what will happen when her foot is cut to fit the party shoe.

While Thabo creates an advisory body stacked with dissidents and cranks, his reputation for leadership evaporates and he becomes the man who believes 'HIV comes from Venus and AIDS comes from Mars'. Our predicament is reflected with withering black humour in the cartoons of Zapiro, showing madness and surrealism going hand in hand with death and suffering. There are no jokes to be made here. There is no inspiration from the wagging of a crooked finger

or the licking of thick lips. There is just sophisticated government spin and easy racist solutions. All criticism of Mbeki's actions is seen as anti-African. All dissent is Eurocentric and colonialist. Ironic that the mouths that utter these words were all educated in the First World during exile.

I ran into a friend who was now closely associated with the Department of Health. She was fascinated by the experiences I shared with her.

'How do I get the Minister to come and listen to a session?' I asked.

She told me to send the invitation via her e-mail address. I found an Internet cafe between schools and sent off a letter to Manto Tshabalala-Msimang. Three weeks later I got an answer. She would try to attend if her schedule allowed. One of the schools planned for that week was Simonstown High. I informed the Minister. Her schedule allowed and she arrived with a driver and an advisor.

'Hello Simonstown,' I started. 'Thanks for inviting me and don't think I know more than you do about life, because I might be older, but not necessarily wiser. And that goes for many of us here.'

I avoided looking in the Minister's direction, but by now the whole school knew she was there, as the headmaster had welcomed us both. Then I left her alone. I could have spent more time reminding everyone of the chaos from government, the denial from the President, the confusion from the Minister, the laughable carelessness that was creating an 'us' and 'them' situation. I could have easily embarrassed her and scored points, but this was not the time or the place. I did the performance and Evita appeared, as did Tutu and Madiba. When it was over, the kids went back to classes and Minister Tshabalala-M stood waiting. She looked great, her plaited hair lying like disciplined bundles of thatch on a perfect dome. She wore her trademark gold-rimmed glasses and a yellow afro-chic suit. Her smile dazzled and her handshake was firm.

'Pity there's not more of you,' she said.

'I'm glad there's only one of you!' I laughed, and her mouth smiled too.

One delinquent high school I knew I had to visit, but hadn't yet approached, was in Cape Town's Parliament Street. Run like a tight ship by Headmistress Frene Ginwala, the South African Parliament was the ultimate audience for an AIDS-awareness entertainment. After the virus itself, they were a second target. It was in Parliament where the gobbledegook around HIV/AIDS was given sense and importance. While as yet no one in their ranks had admitted to having symptoms of HIV, or living with AIDS, the urban legends came thick and fast. That MPs and Cabinet ministers were getting free access to AZT drugs and anti-retrovirals. That a large percentage of MPs were HIV-positive. Even that some ministers had AIDS. Rumours so easy to spread, but then when you realise that the ANC celebrated their victory over apartheid in 1990, in Lusaka and Harare, Uganda and Kenya, without condoms, these stories don't easily dissolve.

So I sent off my letter to Speaker Frene Ginwala. Could I not do a session of what I present at schools to give the MPs some indication of what it entails? They could then encourage their constituents to follow suit, either with a visit from Evita, or any other way of educating through entertainment.

'As with the Election Trek that was so firmly set on its path with your invitation to Evita to visit Parliament,' I wrote, 'maybe this visit about HIV/AIDS will help everyone realise that even gods on Olympus are not immune to this virus?'

Within days I had an answer and a confirmation: Tuesday 20 March at 12:30, in the old House of Assembly where Tannie had waved her kaktus in 1999. This time round, the media were not as welcome. The SABC wasn't present and only a few chosen journalists were allowed to attend. But the house was full!

'You spent R14 million on *Sarafina 2* and got nothing. This is costing you nothing and I hope you get something!'

The big fish weren't there, but I was told that, as before, Frene Ginwala had focused the in-house television on the session, so any government office could tune in and watch. I started with a lit firecracker up my own arse.

'My name is Pieter-Dirk Uys and I'm not a medical expert like President Thabo Mbeki!'

Whereas one was used to laughter in the schools, here was a terrible silence. Gasps of shock and one or two sniggers, but no ha-ha-ha for sure! I took them through the experience of taking bad news to the youth. Of confronting the new generation with the fact that outside the door stood the most sophisticated army of all time, armed to the teeth, with all our names engraved on their bullets, and we couldn't see them. Our Ministry of Defence knew we were in a state of war, but pretended the enemy wasn't actually there. If an army had invaded us from across the borders, and was marching on our cities, we would be mobilised with full powers at our disposal to defend ourselves. All we were doing now was spending billions of rands buying new guns, planes, warships and military hardware. And this to furnish the necessary kickbacks to politicians and their cronies! The arms purchase scandal was now at its height, led by feisty Patricia de Lille of the PAC, who kept biting the bum that tried to sit on her. Why were we spending all that money on war toys, when there was as yet no real physical enemy to fight? While the HI-virus had already killed more people than forty years of legalised segregation and racism ever did, we now had to find the money to pay, not for education and treatment, but for those British guns with French bullets that wouldn't fit and for fancy German warplanes with handbooks in languages that no one here would ever be able to read?

It was a bumpy ride. The temptation to wag fingers was huge. The captive audience of politicians probably deserved a broadside, but 49 per cent anger vs 51 per cent entertainment has always been the sacred recipe, so there had to be more tickles than punches. Hypocrisy, as Evita said, is the Vaseline of political intercourse, so let us not be shy to admit: here people say one thing and do another! The point is: do nothing and there will be no nation left to rule. Ignore the danger and the danger will win. This will become the most beautiful deserted graveyard in the world.

'Let us empower the kids to know they are not children. They are young adults who have to save their own lives. Empower yourself with the alphabet of sex. Know what it is!'

And know that people who should know better put staples through condoms and released them into society! Enter the big cock! After the demonstration of putting condoms onto bananas, and seeing how familiar this was with the lawmakers, out came the big boy. It all went into action-replay slow motion: holding up the twelve-inch pink dildo in the very place where the apartheid government had created the webs of terror that trapped a country for decades, including the Immorality Act, which I had broken so many times without falling to pieces. It was a moment that could not be bypassed without a special little soundbite!

'Comrades, thank you for my Oscar!' I said, and waved the award!

The Deputy Speaker of Parliament had introduced me, and after the talk brought various members of the House to ask about Evita's availability to come to their areas. Cards were swopped, hugs were exchanged, a few photos, and then out I strolled, through security without any suspicion or search. Where else in the world could one walk in and out of the seat of power without at least someone opening That Box and seeing the humungous piepie and saying: 'Anyone we knew?'

The press reaction to the Parliamentary visit was well placed on front pages that also carried the latest statistics of the plague: 'One in nine HIV-positive!' It all seemed to underline the urgency even more, as well as the absurdity of where the confusion and denial had brought us.

As time went by, the confusion became a confrontation, led by people seeing no alternative but to protest loudly and bitterly against the government's carelessness. The struggle continued in the media, the courts and the workplace.

The Minister of Health Manto Tshabalala-Msimang wouldn't even answer a simple question: does HIV lead to AIDS? So what on earth led her to Evita se Perron in Darling?

It was our Youth Festival, coinciding with 16 June, and, as we were a station, it was an ideal chance to invite a train to come for the weekend! Lovelife, an organisation that promotes sexual awareness among the youth, had the train. There was great excitement among the community as Lovelife erected a huge striped tent next to the platform, and when their state-of-the-art train slid into the station, some thought the circus had come to town.

It had! The train had eight coaches, including sleeping quarters, kitchens, a lecture coach and a fully equipped radio station. On a tour of the train by the proud young facilitators, I felt a pang of disadvantage, remembering the dream of Evita's Amachoochoo but not having the bucks. Lovelife had many bucks, and as patrons the Deputy President Jacob Zuma and Her Medical Monstrosity, Manto the Mad!

So she was invited to visit the train. She would do a broadcast from the radio coach and twenty of our local kids would ask the Minister questions live on air. There was great excitement as our Perronistas, the boys and girls from the township, including Evita's three 'grandchildren', prepared their points of view.

The show that Sunday was *Tannie Evita Praat Kaktus*, a perfect entertainment of revisionist South African history with which to entertain a comrade in government! Manto would come to the show and then have lunch.

She arrived in a sleek silver limo with a sullen henchperson in tow. Manto wasn't looking that excited either, but once she had been diverted into our arts and craft hall – 'Tannie Evita's A & C' – she shopped till she dropped and the henchperson paid cash!

Before her excursion onto the platform, we offered her tea and koeksisters.

The Zulu Princess seemed amused by everything, if somewhat distracted. Maybe it was the picture of the Battle of Blood River right behind her? I mentioned a few worrying experiences I had had during the previous months travelling urban areas with my AIDS-awareness entertainment, specifically a recent visit to a country hospital. The nurse there told me of an eighteen-year-old local lad who refused to acknowledge his HIV status. Every weekend she had to watch him

take out another fifteen-year-old girl and seduce her, and she was not allowed by law to warn the girls or their parents of this roving death sentence.

'What do I tell these people?' I asked.

The Minister sniffed and chewed.

'Ag man, they must sort it out,' she sighed wearily.

That was it. Counsel from the highest health official in the land.

They must sort it out.

The hench-honcho escorted her to the train, where a local commercial radio station had linked up for the live broadcast. The kids were nervous, but when the hench-comrade censored their questions, they were devastated.

'The Minister does not have to answer that!' he muttered, leaving the children tongue-tied and inarticulate.

By now Tannie Evita was ready. The theatre was full, including a party from New York University and a film crew directed by Tony Palmer, who was spending the week with me, making a documentary about our struggle to focus on the reality of AIDS.

This was nearly too good to be true. Evita was at her best, demolishing the symbols of her history and bruising the egos of the Zulu visitors. Manto chuckled, or maybe she was choking?

At the end of the show, Evita focused on the Minister for the first time.

'Comrade skattie,' she trilled, 'maybe you can help me? My grandchildren keep asking me this question, but I don't have the answer. You're Minister of Health. You will know. Tell me: does HIV lead to AIDS?'

Everyone held their breath. The camera whirled. Manto rose to her full medium height and wagged a finger at Mrs Bezuidenhout.

'Evita? I'm your friend …!' she threatened with an icy smile. And that was that. No answer. No yes. Just the usual, from Dr No!

A World in One Country

In Johannesburg the schools are obvious and clear-cut. Girls' schools. Boys' schools. The Hillbrow school. The Lebanese school. The ex-Zimbabwe lot. Each one is an hour of energy, delivering a simple message with complex disguises. Lots of laughter, more shock, some facts, many figures, and at the end hopefully a feeling of having won, if not the battle, then at least this small skirmish.

I arrived in the City of Gold at the end of the 1970s, as a theatrical refugee from Cape Town, and lived there for ten years. They were the best creative years of my life, a rollercoaster ride of new plays and dangerous revues, dodging the bullets of official disapproval. Being back in Johannesburg in the twenty-first century with my schools trek rekindled memories, and I rediscovered my old love affair with Egoli, Jozi, the Big Naartjie!

The National School of Arts is a dream destination. We are talking theatre and the kids are all here because they sing and dance and mime and perform. And exactly because of that passion, sex is close to the surface. I know, honey, I'm there too! So we play with emotions and expose pain and secrets. They react with such energy that I leave drained and jealous. If only there'd been such a place for me when I was their age!

Then I'm in a hired car, passing through a landscape dotted with monuments to man's superficial superiority over nature: mine dumps, rubbish dumps, power stations dumping dirty purple and orange filth into the ice-blue sky. The white heat makes the toffee-tarred road melt under the hot tyres.

I'm on my way to Klerksdorp. I received an e-mail from a woman who works as a chemist in the town, telling me of the ignorance and fear that is sweeping her community. The children are not being taught about HIV. They do not understand the need for protection, and they are having sex. As a chemist she knows what she's talking about. Children are in need of help. Klerksdorp is predominantly Afrikaans-Calvinist on the one hand, and African-traditional on the other, and like blood and semen, these are perfect breeding grounds for HIV. Ignorance and intolerance of sexual information go hand in hand. I asked her to help me source schools and set up a two-day visit.

The Milner High School gives me a full hall of boys and girls, and judging from the reactions, one wonders how many live presentations have taken place in this rural metropolis. There is a staged walkout by white girls who belong to a Christian movement. Every ten minutes or so, two of them get up and pointedly leave. It obviously upsets the other kids, but I don't take any notice of the upheaval. I wondered if they'd all eaten the same hamburger and suffered the same cramps! As I'm packing up, a black learner comes to me. I see by his blazer that he is a school prefect. He looks uncomfortable and embarrassed.

'Excuse me, Mr Uys, but I have a message for you.'

I wait for his message. His eyes dart nervously towards the open doors. I see the group of Christian dissidents bunched together, watching.

'Yes?' I ask.

'They said I must tell you that this talk was the most disgusting thing they have ever heard.'

He was not enjoying his job as the messenger of bad reviews.

'Thank them for me,' I said. 'And tell them I agree. It is the most disgusting thing I have ever done. I would rather have spoken about beauty and love and poetry, but the fear of AIDS is a disgusting reality and until we all know what we must do to confront it, I will carry on being disgusting. But thank them and wish them well.'

Thanks to good training in voice projection, the angels in the open doors heard everything. When I looked again they were gone.

My next meeting was at a high school in the township. I drove along a gravel road, zigzagging up and down small rough paths between clusters of tin shacks and tarpaulin-covered huts. In the middle of all this, like a medieval cathedral soaring arrogantly above the primitive cluster of village and town, stood the school. I was late, so the kids were already in the hall. There were thousands, millions, billions of faces all looking alike to me and at me, squashed together on the floor, sitting, crouched, hunched, perched, cross-legged. Nobody in here came from a room of their own with a laptop and a CD player. Few here had a pet dog or cat that lay lazily in the sun on a back porch. Most of them had never heard of back porches. At first I worried about language. Would they all be okay with English? They all have television, and if *Ally McBeal* and *All My Children* are good for them, the basic words I used were familiar enough!

'Nothing is easy! Life is not what we see on television and in the soap operas. Sometimes our lives are better, because our lives are real and those stories are not real! But you all have a chance to make a better life for yourselves and your

191

families! You can lead and people will follow. Education is liberation! South Africa is free and so are you! Free to become whatever you dream!'

A girl suddenly gets up and I wonder if the Christian Society has a branch here too. She stands straight and proud and lifts her arm to hold up a clenched fist. And then she sings:

'Nkosi Sikelel' iAfrika!'

They all get up, a shuddering racket of shuffling shoes and stamping feet and they sing for me the anthem of their freedom and their future.

'Amandla! Awethu!'

They know all the African words, even the Afrikaans ones to the transplanted wagging tail of 'Die Stem', tacked onto the Struggle song through negotiation. They sing in harmonies and add rhythm with their feet and hands. My few hairs stand on end and I cry while smiling.

Afterwards they mob the stage. Typically I think the worst as I'm separated from my carrier bag and all my props. Evita's earrings will go!

The lipstick? The cellphone! And the sunglasses? The caps and the Mandela shirt?

Nothing disappeared! Again I feel so stupid playing out my white fears based on someone else's urban legend.

The next leg of the tour took me to Bloemfontein, the capital of the Free State and a place I knew well from past experience. Ironically, during the 1980s I always felt safe in this boeredorp, even though all the worst elements of Afrikaner Nationalism seemed to have anchored themselves here. Extremists, right-wingers, neo-Nazis, bigots, racists, homophobics. Between 1981 and 1985 my shows all world-premièred in this neck of the woods, up on the hill in the small Observatory Sterrewag Theatre. I remember the second performance of *Total Onslaught* in 1984, with Evita sitting in her white Cadillac after the show. A man waited his turn, and when all the other fans had their gun holsters autographed by the most famous white woman, he leant towards Mrs B and whispered: 'Mevrou Bezuidenhout, u was wonderlik, maar as ek ooit daardie Pieter-Dirk Uys in die hande kry gaan ek hom dônner!' And he meant it.

And so did Evita when she added: 'Ek wens jou sukses!'

The Bloemfontein structure went through the offices of a prominent educationalist, who did things by the book. Permission had to be sought from the Ministry of Education, as well as the parents in each school, and eventually she presented me with a very well-researched programme – First World and Third World schools balanced carefully. My Second World experience was performing *For Facts Sake* at the local PACOFS André Huguenet Theatre. Three performances gave me the trophy of an income cheque for R12,98! After rental and percentages and payments for publicity and the deworming of the guard dogs, there was very little left. Also, the audience had shrunk by half when word got round that the show was focused on HIV/AIDS.

'Sies!' said the public, and cancelled their bookings.

Bloemfontein is proud of generations of South Africans who went to school there. Even in our age of equality, St Andrews, Christian Brothers College and Eunice are famous for their excellence and tradition. I was very pleased to be presenting, firstly at the boys' schools and then at the girls'. All three experiences were in turn attended by various members of the organising Mafia, and included the Minister himself, who said a few words and declared the bridge open.

The other schools were across the line in the other Africa: Dr Blok, Leklulong Senior School and Sehunelo Senior School. In distance they were not far from each other, but each township audience was so different. One was very noisy and full of energy, another quiet and sullen, and the other singing the time away till we started. They say lightning doesn't strike twice? Here it struck thrice! At each venue the microphone system failed. At one school it just didn't work,

193

one school had forgotten to get a mike and the other's mike was stolen an hour before the presentation! That's hell for an actor once in a lifetime, to be faced with a waiting audience and not knowing if the voice will carry. The halls were not built to carry the whispers of opera. They echoed and clanged.

The first session held together, but by the end my voice was raw and my throat sore. I looked forward to the comfort of amplification at the next school. When I got there, no mike! I wanted to run away, but not with kids looking so excited and waiting for a concert! So once again I made a deal with the Muse: give me voice and projection and I'll buy you a chocolate! At least the third school would have a mike? Was that the familiar bolt of lightning striking for a third time? The audience of kids was chatting and yelling and it was impossible to rise above the din. A teacher tried to create order and had to scream to be heard. I felt drops of blood gather on my shattered vocal cords, ready to drop into my heart and congeal!

The introduction led to a deafening welcome. I raised my hands and indicated to them to settle down. Eventually, with some help from the teachers, they all sat more or less quietly. I could croak forth.

'There is no microphone. It was stolen!'

They laughed, and it took another concerted effort to shush them.

'I'm white and we whites have got small voices. You blacks have great big voices!' They showed me I was right. Eventually: 'But I have things to tell you that I want you to hear. Do you want to hear?'

They screamed yes, but calmed down quickly.

'Okay. I also want you to laugh. Do you want to laugh?' They laughed and then became still. 'So this is what we'll do. I can't talk much louder than this. If you want to laugh, I'll let you laugh. But when I do this with my hands, you stop, so I can go on. Okay?'

We practised. They laughed, I raised my hands and then brought them down, and they stopped. Instant silence. It was like a Victor Borge revue sketch. Sound. Silence. Sound. Silence. Talk. Perfection. They heard every word. I never raised my voice. My throat didn't bleed. The voice didn't die. Miraculous! Who needs mikes!

That evening I went out on the town with my cousins who live and work at the university. We went to a steakhouse and were welcomed by a young woman who led us to our table. A young man took the order. They were both very friendly and I wondered if we'd met. Only after the meal did they come and introduce themselves. She was still at school, and I'd spoken to them the day before. He was at the boys' school and I'd spoken to them that morning. Now they looked like real people, not like children. It just confirmed that I was right, warning the kids in the halls about what happens when the sun sets. That's when they change from innocents to survivors, with all the trappings of attraction and the latest in fashion and charm. Beautiful, young, sexy people, sitting targets for HIV, unless they know what they're doing!

A world in one country is how SATOUR once sold South Africa. However, schools straddle many worlds: First World private schools in Gauteng; public schools in the Eastern Cape; primary schools in the Boland; special schools in the Free State; destroyed Third World schools in KwaZulu-Natal. Now it was time to go back to the future. I had done a motivational talk to the sponsors of the Air Mercy Services of the Red Cross and met up with John Stone, who is in charge of this remarkable helping hand. We planned to go together on one of the junkets. I would talk at a school, while their doctors did ears, noses, tits and teeth. And so came about my visit to Rietfontein, deep in the Kalahari.

After a two-hour flight, over mountains, farmlands and glittering dams, shifting sands and clumpy rock towers, we circle Rietfontein twice, mainly to be sure this is not Salt Lake City, but also to alert the transport. The school stands out among the cluster of small buildings like a skyscraper. There are a thousand kids here. Dear God, from where? God can't remember making Rietfontein. Take a rain check. And yes, there's been no rain here for the last twelve years. This is the Kalahari.

The AIDS-awareness concerts take place in the hall, probably the biggest space made by man in a thousand-kilometre radius. There are too many kids in the school for just one show. The juniors come at 9 am and the rest later. And so the two performances bear no relation to each other, except in the context of conversation and the bottom line: 'AIDS is everywhere, even here in Rietfontein. So let's find it in the caves of fear and smoke it out with knowledge!'

I look at the faces. This is one of my youngest audiences ever, and most of them have never seen a tarred road before. The show's in Afrikaans, not deep Taal, but the local dialect, which means I talk to everyone to get the tune of their language and speak to them in their own music.

Between shows we all have a cup of rooibos tea in the principal's office. He is hiding, but lady teachers coyly carry in plates of scones and cookies and stare at me like people transfixed by a vampire. Thrilled but wary. I'm already known as 'that man who uses words'. Some who saw the first show suffer from culture shock. Some can't stop giggling. One woman looks as if she's died with the word 'sies' on her lips.

The second session is more animated. It has got round that 'words are spoken here'. And so they were. All the talk of 'sex' and the 'act of intercourse' was as vague as counting kilometres round a full dam of water, or understanding moon rings. So I use the words they know and understand. I say: 'Naai.'

Pandemonium. They all scream and jump up and down. Aunties have the vapours and grown men cross their legs. The small ones can't believe their ears. The older kids applaud. Liberation in Rietfontein. I wait for them to settle down.

'Excuse me, but what's all this noise? That's the word everyone hears and uses every day. It's not polite, but then nor is AIDS polite. Naai is where AIDS lives. Naai is dangerous!'

The laughter is over. They know where they are. Disguises have been dropped. Now we get on with the business of survival without having to mention the word 'naai' again.

When its over we pile into the hot minibus, Tannie in her bag in the boot. Kids hop on the burning sand in their bare feet, wanting to be around till the end, besotted by the bald fat clown who said naai in the school hall and lived.

We go back to the plane and, even though we are now well over 2000 kilometres from Cape Town, in the middle of nowhere where nothing has a name and empty could mean full, we fly even further over blood-red sand up to the border with Botswana and the Gemsbok National Park. While Germans and Yanks and Japs come and search for buck and cheetah and postcards of elephants, real brown people also live here to cook and clean and keep the wild nice and tame for the civilised to zoom in on. We travel for twenty minutes along the border gravel road to a small compound called Welkom! In a big classroom, filled with locals, the third show starts.

The temperature is in the mid-forties. There are workers from the game park, mothers, aunties and grannies. And ten children to each adult – creatures even smaller than in Rietfontein. Four years old, and Old!

I speak to a tiny person waiting in the doorway to come in, ribbon in hair, barefoot and trying to clean doggie-poo off her sole.

'Are you coming to the show?' I ask.

She doesn't know who I am, and why should she?

'Ja, I'm so excited,' she lisps.

'How old are you?'

Her mother mouths: five.

'Old,' says the little thing oldly.

'Do you now what the show is about?' I ask.

'Ja, sex,' she nods.

'Aren't you too small?'

She looks tearful. 'No, I'm also scared. I want to know.'

There we also soon drop 'sex' for 'naai', and when I ask where a condom goes, they all react with a long word: 'Peeennnnniiiiissssss.'

Except, from the lap of his mother, a small boy with big ears and wide eyes bleats out, 'Nay, dis 'n piel!'

His mortified mother covers his mouth with her hand.

'No, he's right!' I say. 'I also call mine a piel!'

Disguises have been discarded again. The final audition has been passed. They now believe me when I say: 'You are the most important people in South Africa. You must stay alive and build our future! Put your love in a plastic bag! On the Piel! Before you Naai!'

I ended that show with my Desmond Tutu going into the crowd of small people and inviting them to join in a dance. They giggled and cowered. Except for that little monkey child, who slid off his mother's lap and like a small brown hobbit walked towards me with outstretched arms. My Tutu waved his purple and said: 'Dance!'

And in the heat of the Kalahari, the small brown manchild danced the toyi-toyi to the delight of all.

In Denaaial

Afrikaner pig-headedness with regard to the virus was an ongoing issue. I was scheduled to perform on the campus of Potchefstroom University, but this was cancelled at the last minute, as a 'suitable venue' could not be found. Eventually the powers stated their reasons: 'Pieter-Dirk Uys is not scientific in his approach.'

Off-the-record comments ranged from 'It has nothing to do with us,' to 'We are Christians and can't contract AIDS,' and 'We refuse to listen to his smut!'

Minister Kader Asmal flew the tattered flag of freedom of speech in Parliament, and questioned why a university claiming full subsidies was censoring a talk on AIDS awareness. Letters appeared in the Afrikaans press that clearly stated the other point of view. This was pornography and taking freedom of expression too far!

Members of the university contacted me and arranged an alternative venue in the Town Hall. The free show was well advertised and badly attended. It seems that in spite of the fact that 40 per cent of first-year students were testing positive, this was not an issue in Potchefstroom.

Another delicious opus appeared in *Die Burger* of 22 March 2001:

Under the guise of his AIDS awareness campaign, Pieter-Dirk Uys is once again spouting his sick, immoral jokes to anyone who will listen. Anyone who is not interested in this sort of rubbish becomes a target to be humiliated with his derogatory humour. For Uys, nobody and nothing is sacred if they differ from his way of thinking. His wings should have been clipped long ago by those whom he so liberally insults.

He is definitely not an asset to institutions such as Rustenberg High School or the University of Potchefstoom, hence their decision not to allow him and his smut. Why PW Botha did not sort him out years ago, amazes me. His reference to Botha's sex life ('remarried and a sex slave in the Wilderness, addicted to Viagra, because that finger stands up straight like a little stick!') affords Botha enough ammunition to shut up his foul mouth once and for all. I doubt whether anyone with moral standards and an appreciation of talent without filthy implications will support him.

JJH du Toit
East London

Only Evita could answer, and she did on 24 March 2001:

My thanks to JJH du Toit from East London. At last a man with moral standards and an appreciation for talent without filthy implications! It is time Pieter-Dirk Uys's wings were clipped! It is not only Mr PW Botha and decent Afrikaners who had to suffer Uys's sick comments! I, too, am still being insulted and humiliated by his foul mouth. Uys and his filth are only tolerated because of the present democracy. If we were still in power, Uys and his derogatory 'humour' would have paid!

Evita Bezuidenhout
Laagerfontein

Is an Afrikaner reaction that important? To isolate a small minority's negative reaction and go into freeze-frame? Just because I am one of them doesn't mean we as Afrikaners have any special resonance. Like all other compatriots, we are in the same boat, as the captain once said on the Titanic. When there is racism in my thoughts it makes me shudder, but I know why, because as a white South African what else can I be but a racist? Having been educated, trained, streamlined and praised by the apartheid overlords, what came out of the sausage machine? Leni Riefenstahl's blond boy! My greatest contempt is for fellow whites who start a conversation with the words: 'Yes, but I am not a racist.' Rubbish! We are all racists, especially us whiteys, but not just us whiteys. It is the flavour of every nation to have something that makes them stand out in a crowd. The Brits have class, the Americans have cash, the Indians have castes and the Germans have blond hair. Easy to hate any of them if you don't understand them! So now every morning when I wake up, I look in the mirror and say: 'I am a racist, therefore I will not be a racist!' Like an alcoholic who swears never to drink again, but repeats it every day as the drink passes by, so tempting and inevitable.

Support came, however, from the most unexpected source. The powerful synod of the Dutch Reformed Church sent me a letter:

Dear Mr Uys

During the past week our Convocation has gathered amid the green pastures of Darling. Unfortunately we hadn't the time to take in a show, or we would definitely have popped in! Someone even suggested that we elect Tannie Evita as Chairwoman of the Women's Auxiliary Convocation …

On a more serious note: We would like to take this opportunity to thank you for the enormous work you do in bringing the life-threatening disease of HIV/AIDS to the attention of the South African population. You succeed in hitting targets that are out of reach for the Church. For that we are truly grateful. Your work is an inspiration to us and for the task the Church itself has to perform. We would like to assure you of our sincere prayers.

'For facts sake', don't stop what you are doing.

Performing at the 2001 Klein Karoo Nasionale Kunstefees in Oudtshoorn with two cabarets, I offered them the AIDS-awareness entertainment for free. It was scheduled for a ten o'clock slot in a good venue. Thirty people bothered to turn up. There must have been 10 000 around town, half of them under the age of twenty. Not a poster, a banner, a sign to warn them of the danger of HIV. I made a point of mentioning the carelessness of the festival sponsors, who just seemed intent on selling their product and image. Did no one understand that young people came to this glorious Karoo dorp at the height of the good warm weather not just to see plays, to sing and dance, but to naai! Booze has always been easily available at the festival, as one of the sponsors is generous with its products. Drunk kids are part of the scenery. In 2002 I went back to deliver a lecture about 'AIDS and the Afrikaner'. There was nothing really to say about AIDS and the Afrikaner except: yes, even if we still think we're God's Chosen People, who reject gay sex or sex with blacks, we Afrikaners will get AIDS! Yet after a year of reminders, there was still not a poster, a banner, a pamphlet around Oudtshoorn warning the young festos about the dangers. Not preaching, just warning:

'Oppas! Be Careful! It's when you have fun that you make mistakes!' Even in Afrikaans!

How many hundreds of young festival-goers have been infected by the virus in the last five years of djolling, simply because the sponsors, with their smelly old Broederbond links, regard AIDS as a non-issue?

International assistance streams into South Africa. Not a day passes without great donations being made in dollars to fight the scourge of HIV/AIDS. The Nelson Mandela Children's Fund receives its customary millions each month, and Lovelife barely seems to manage on their multi-million-dollar gift from the Kaiser Family Foundation.

They asked if I would be part of their planned campaign to encourage parents to talk to their children about sex. Of course I would.

A date was arranged in Johannesburg during a school tour. It would be a sixty-second bite as PDU, encouraging parents to talk. One camera, neutral background. The location was the grand old Johannesburg Club. Huge film trucks stood on either side of the road, which had been sealed off to traffic. Dear God, were they doing the latest James Bond film here as well? In the beautiful mahogany and leather smoking room, the camera had been set up. There were make-up people and continuity people and props people and scriptwriters and catering and cameramen and stills-cameramen and clients. The place was packed! They gave me a script, suggesting an angle to take, a soft and polite way to gently prod parents into talking to their children. I knew there were some very important South Africans such as Deputy President Jacob Zuma, Desmond Tutu, Tim Modise and Nelson Mandela lined up. They would need this angle and do it magnificently. I had to cut to the car chase and take the script out of experience. We did a long shot, medium shot and close-up on the following:

'Don't talk to your children about the birds and the bees. How does a bird fuck a bee? I know this is not polite, but then AIDS is not a polite disease. There is no time for good manners. AIDS is killing our children! Speak to your kids in a language they understand. Love them enough to talk to them about sex.'

I enquired who was doing it in Afrikaans. No one had thought of doing it in Afrikaans. I translated and did the three takes. I was out of there in less than an hour. It could've been shot in a garage for R12 000. This must have cost a million! The gravy stains remain. When it was eventually released on television, Lovelife had copped out of using the 'fuck' line and used a warm-up take: 'Parents say to me: "Who are you to talk sex to my child? I will talk sex to my child when I am ready." Yes, when you are ready it's too late.'

Mildly effective, but birds-fuck-bees makes a better point! Ironically they did use the 'kinders naai ook' line in the Afrikaans version. Obviously no one at Lovelife understands the language. Or, it seems, what they're supposed to be doing! An organisation that is supposed to alert the youth to the dangers of unprotected sex does not censor the word 'fuck'!

A typical mid-1970s hue and cry ensued. The Afrikaans message was pulled off the air and banned from radio and television because of one complaint. As in 1975, when they banned me for using the word 'Nigel'. I realised that even in a free society, old habits die hard. It achieved just what the message intended. The publicity was more than money or planning could buy. People were talking! That was the point. Even the newspapers had fun with their billboards:

'SABC says Nay to Naai'

'PDU in DeNAAIal'

Life at R50 a Month

A trade union was hosting its annual national congress in Johannesburg. Evita Bezuidenhout was contracted to be hostess for the dinner, which meant hard work: six costume changes and a constant presence moving around the floor from table to table, making Evita small talk and posing for pictures. The fee was huge, and that's the way this cookie has to crumble. At least Mrs B's corporate cabarets bring in the budget to be able to present the AIDS programme as community service.

The afternoon before the dinner, the union was presenting an AIDS seminar to which everyone had been invited. I was asked to give them a background chat on my school programme.

Not many of the delegates bothered to attend. Among those who spoke was a young Johannesburg doctor, who sketched the growing incidence of HIV testing and the negatively positive results. A comrade from the Department of Health presented dusty five-year-old statistics about HIV/AIDS and sang the Mbeki tune. I should have known when I saw her gold-rimmed spectacles and knitted hair. After her recitation, an American businessman took the mike. He was a friend of the union management and an advisor. He gave us a chilling picture of what the world saw in the pot at the end of our rainbow. It was not gold.

'We love you in South Africa,' he drawled. 'We admire what you've done, and how you've done it. We want you to succeed. We want to invest billions in your country. But you're dying. If 40 per cent of your workforce is HIV-positive, within five years you will be paying for their funerals. In order to replace these trained workers, you will employ new people, but you aren't allowed to check their HIV status by law. So possibly 25 per cent of the new workforce will be HIV-positive. Our automobiles will never be built! It's no return on investment. Sorry, South Africa. We have to go to South Korea instead.'

Someone pointed out that if you now give blood in the United Kingdom, one of the questions on the donor form is: 'When last did you have sexual relations with a South African'!

Apartheid made us pariahs; AIDS turns us into lepers.

I was back on the Cape Flats in a poor school with poorer kids and huge problems of survival. So what was a *Vogue* model doing in the third row? A beautiful tall girl with a long, graceful Sophia Loren neck, thin and elegant among the scruff of the suburbs? She looked uncomfortable. Then someone got up and brought her a cushion, and she became less restless. This was not a model, this girl had AIDS! That's why she was so thin and uncomfortable on the wooden bench.

Afterwards I spoke to her. Her name was Christine. She was fifteen.

'No,' she said shyly, 'it's so good that you're here at our school, Pieter. We see you and Evita always on the teevee and never imagined you'd both come here to our school. It's good that we hear these things as part of life. When I hear you was coming, I say to Sister at the clinic: I also want to come. Because I was once at this school, you know Pieter, but now I've got AIDS. But still I think it good to come here, so that kids can see me not living with AIDS; AIDS is living with me! I'm in charge, you know Pieter?'

Her fingers thin, long, beautiful.

'And how is the medication going, Christine?'

The sister from the clinic came back with cooldrinks for both of us. Christine drank hers slowly.

'No, fine, you know, Pieter. The pharmaceutical companies recently got so much free publicity because they give free drugs to AIDS victims, so I get this free pill.' The sister nodded and wanted to say something, but didn't. 'But you know this pill is so horrible, Pieter. I'm so grateful I get something, but it makes me so sick and mad in my head, I think I rather die of this AIDS than take this pill …'

The sister sighed and shrugged. Christine's fingers intertwined with mine.

'But is there nothing else you can take, Christine? Something better?' I looked at the sister, but before she could say anything, Christine grabbed my hand in hers with passion.

'Ja, Pieter, there are three pills you take as a cocktail and that's very effective, because you know it is possible to live with HIV and AIDS if you have the right treatment, but that costs R50 a month, and that's too much, because our Grannie is sick and my three little brothers are still at school, so R50 is too much, you know Pieter …'

R50.

More or less $5.

A month?

For a life?

Thabo Mbeki must know what he's doing. Surely? He doesn't give AZT drugs to raped women or anti-retroviral treatment to AIDS mothers to prevent their babies being born HIV for a good reason. Surely. It is whispered that he gets those drugs to members of his own party and his Cabinet, and judging by their erratic behaviour, many of them are not taking their daily pills! The bottom line is: our President must now find the money to pay for the arms we have purchased from the European Union! The Arms Scandal is now policy and must be paid for! Those British guns with French bullets that won't fit. German warships and Italian jets that no one here can sail or fly! Besides the fact that we have no enemy worth fighting! But we have politicians! Politicians who demand their kickbacks! Their 4×4s! Their percentages! And since our Thabo is so deeply committed to his African Renaissance, when President Sam Nujoma of

Namibia has a .20 jet, and President Robert Mugabe of Zimbabwe has a .50 jet and Gaddaffi of Libya has a .80 jet, President Thabo Mbeki demands a .99 jet! It's called Boeing Envy. And Christine from the poor school on the windswept Cape Flats? Politics before sentiment, darling! Swallow that free pill and have a nice day!

When I was in Holland with a show in October 2001, I was invited by the Dutch Minister for Development Cooperation, Eveline Herfkens, to open an international congress. Its objective was to discuss how Trade Ministers at the Ministerial Conference of the World Trade Organisation due in Doha, Qatar, in November 2001 could reach a consensus on the problem of access to affordable medicines in developing countries. Medical and pharmacological professional organisations, civil servants from several ministries, representatives from the pharmaceutical industry, academic researchers and students, as well as interested individuals would gather in The Hague, and would I open the congress with a touch of humour?

It was held in De Ridderzaal, where the Dutch monarch gives her annual State of the Nation address, a building dating back to the 1500s. I pointed out that, in that very room, white supremacist dreams were born and exported to South Africa to rule for 350 years. I didn't spend much time pinpricking in the direction of the pharmaceuticals. I agree that they are enriching themselves at the expense of millions of sick people. Some are giving their products at cut-rate prices, or even free. It's about time.

'But who do you give those free life-saving drugs to? Politicians. They will then add some fat fee to the original 0 before passing it down the line, and by the time the pill reaches Christine, it has added 50 rand to the original 0.'

I had told them about Christine and her R50-a-month dilemma. Could pharmaceuticals not start at grassroots level, educating the people to distribute and to use the drugs as prescribed? Some drugs need constant reminders and double-checks. Most of our sick people don't understand how they can afford to return to a clinic once a week for these important consultations. Some take a pill once and then stop. Every 1000 people in each community should have a representative in whom they have confidence, who controls information and product. To help the people known to them by name and to become counsellor, friend, advisor, nurse, lawyer. It was once the work of the Church. Churches have become weakened by corruption. Now there is no one. Politicians are not the answer. International conferences don't ask the question: How is all this

going to get down to the people who need it, without percentages being taken for just taking the call? The mother and the child, the father and the son, need to trust in order to tell about their need. That's the missing link.

I ended my little tap dance in the Den Haag Ridderzaal, finishing my Nelson Mandela impersonation by blowing up a condom and, to the echo of 'Amandla', allowing it to fly around the hallowed hall, deflating in circles.

'This has never happened in here before,' the Minister solemnly proclaimed. Her department made a big donation to my collection box for Wola Nani, a Cape Flats self-help charity. The beaded AIDS ribbons she bought were handed out to all the delegates, and for the next few days, television news interviews with important participants showed them all wearing their badge of solidarity.

Which brings me to Nqoepsie Mkwanazi.

Foreign Aids

My invitation to visit St Cyprians girls' school against the slopes of Table Mountain uncovered many little hooks in my past. When my mother Helga Bassel arrived in Cape Town from Berlin in 1938, her first concern was to find a permanent job. She eventually started at the music department of St Cyprians, teaching piano. To this day, there are still many women older than me who remember 'Miss Bassel'. Tessa Fairbairn, who is the exceptional principal of this great school, was at the University of Cape Town with me. She studied and read and worked and has become a major force in education. I didn't study, scarcely read, and loafed, and yet when we hugged after all these years, all we remembered was bunking phonetics and having sausage rolls in the Students Union.

The St Cyprian girls are involved with more than just studying and passing exams. They focus on community needs and actively involve themselves with the poor, the needy and the frightened – the majority of citizens of the Mother City. Because for every one with R100, there are 100 with less than R1!

The girls were just as exciting as I'd hoped they'd be. We shared fears and hopes and plans to conquer the world and make it a better place. And then I met Nqoepsie. She had just turned sixteen and was in Grade 11. She gave me an AIDS ribbon, an African brooch of coloured beads shaping the red symbol of care. She thanked me for my speech with flawless casual confidence. Although by then I had already met 300 000 young South Africans, there was something about this young woman – a sense of humour, an earnestness, and yet a maturity that matched my years! We talked and immediately found common ground. She told me about the Wola Nani project, which was involved with self-help groups among those less fortunate.

'I'm lucky,' she said. 'I have education. I have parental support. I've travelled. I've been blessed. I don't have to be ashamed of that. I can use that to help others!'

She has been committed to projects where she visited orphanages and hospitals to entertain the children. She became involved with the Wola Nani project for HIV-positive teenage mothers in Khayelitsha, and was so impressed that she raised funds for hampers for the women. In the shelters and self-help units looked after by Wola Nani, she met up with mothers and babies: women with AIDS and their children born HIV-positive. Some of them were making the beaded AIDS ribbons, but not with much enthusiasm.

She said to them: 'Let's make more and I'll sell them to shops in Cape Town.'

So they made more, and Nqoepsie sold them to shops in Cape Town and collected R1000! I asked her if that money was used for medication. She suddenly lost her childlike innocence and looked at me cynically.

'Medication for R1000? Hello?' Then she smiled. 'No, we could buy shampoo for the mothers, so that they could wash their hair and smell nice for their babies, and the sixteen-year-old girls with full-blown AIDS could get beautiful red nail polish and Britney Spears sunglasses and feel like women and not like victims!'

And I thought: Yes! Yes! This is what I've been waiting for! It's about life, not death. It's about care, not cure. It's about dignity. Nqoepsie has probably been the most rewarding friend I have made during this experience.

When I went over to the Tricycle Theatre in London NW6 with my new one-man show *Foreign AIDS* for a six-week season in the middle of 2001, I took a few thousand AIDS ribbons to sell for Wola Nani.

I told the audience: 'Schoolgirls are doing what a government is failing to do. A sixteen-year-old girl is showing that in a healthy democracy, the people can lead and the government can follow. Nqoepsie has encouraged me to look and believe that in South Africa we are not just dying. We're also living!'

Foreign AIDS was the result of my experiences on the road. After months of *For Facts Sake* on stage and the schools tour during the week, I knew what I had to prepare for my London season.

'Uys gets us laughing,' wrote Lyn Gardner in the *Guardian* of 7 July 2001, 'not at death, but at fear, ignorance, complacency and drug companies, as well as the curious head-in-sand mentality of President Thabo Mbeki. Uys's comedy is ruthless. The show has as much to do with campaigning as comedy. But I have never had a more enjoyable time being soap-boxed. Laughter alone may not change the world, but Uys knows how to use it as a weapon to start the revolution.'

The first thing I noticed in London was the lack of focus on the dangers of HIV/AIDS. No posters, no articles in the press or magazines. Condoms were freely available, accompanied by clear, concise pamphlets echoing the warnings and suggesting the protections. No panic. No issue. When I visited a few high schools in the Borough of Brent and presented them with my experiences travelling through South Africa, the response was shocking. Most of the kids weren't that sure where South Africa was. They had no knowledge of HIV/AIDS! A young black girl asked if skin colour changes with HIV.

'Because in Africa so many blacks get it. Were they white?'

Could this be a joke? Trying to hold the attention of a class full of London youth was also a new experience. Even though I had been into the pits of South African education, I had never been confronted with such dismissive rudeness. The secret was to focus on the loudest punk with the spikiest hair and make him a spokesperson. This didn't always work until it was too late. The bottom line was: here in the First World there is no issue. AIDS was here and HIV existed, but the National Health Service could supply the necessary drugs. The plague had been tamed. Soccer hooligans were more dangerous!

By starting with the audience in the bar of the Tricycle Theatre, I had a chance to introduce the conversational style from the start. No pretence, no theatrical fourth wall. I pointed to those South Africans I'd met in the foyer: 'So easy to find you. Just have to hear a wail: "Oh, my God, it's all so expensive!" to know here are holders of rands in a place where it's worth less than a cent!'

London is full of South Africans! In the audience were young West End waiters and waitresses originally from Joburg and Durbs, on their night off, bringing their British pals to see their old African queen! They got more than they bargained for. I'd put on make-up while talking. False eyelashes and gashy red mouth. This was not the woman they were expecting. This was Tannie Evita's sister, Bambi Kellermann, a character new to most members of the audience. Bambi knew London well, having lived in Neasden with her husband Joachim von Kellermann from 1964 to 1975.

'It was sehr gemutlich here. The weather was terrible, but we were safe from Simon Wiesenthal! Thank God you Brits are so rude, you never look anyone in the eye. And so no one recognised my Nazi husband!'

Bambi has got AIDS, but enjoys getting her drugs free on her NHS card. She recalls an experience in Paraguay, where her husband eventually became Minister of War in the fascist government of Alfredo Stroessner.

'The weather was so lovely in Paraguay! Not horrible like here in England,' Bambi would purr in her Dietrich-accented tones. 'But I don't suppose you can have everything? Good weather, old Nazis; bad weather, new Labour? We were sitting on our patio in the hills above the capital Asuncion. It was a warm night. Martin Bormann was with us on his way back to Brazil after a face-lift in Los

Angeles. Dr Mengele also popped in on his way to Argentina. We would sit for hours and talk, wondering how come, during the 1930s, when there were so many good, decent British and American politicians and social leaders, who already knew then that Jews were being rounded up by the Nazis and murdered, none of them ever said anything?

'Then Adolf Eichmann, who was writing a book in the cottage, came out. He was always so dour – no sense of humour at all. He said: "Maybe the world wasn't that worried about the prospect of losing a few million Jews? Maybe the civilised world said: No, let's wait a few years and then we can take notice and be appalled?"'

Which is what happened. The First World would eventually take on the Third Reich, six million Jews later. And today in Africa? With Africans dying in their millions? Maybe history is repeating itself in the small talk?

'Yes, shame, poor blacks, but don't rush here. Let's give AIDS a few more years? A few million less starving, warring, demanding Africans? Then we can do our International Live Aid appeal and wheel Sting out to sing.'

The South Africans didn't laugh. Bambi would leave the audience with a question.

'And here you are, the converted, sitting comfortably in a theatre in NW6, feeling bad about the blacks on a continent far away? No problem here in the United Kingdom, you say? Really? Are your kids okay? Tonight? Out there, in a city teeming with sex? My darling, while you are here thinking your kids are watching television, they might be having unprotected sex with a South African!'

The structure of the show was anchored in the South African experience of HIV/AIDS, but reflected the British political pizza of concern and involvement. Sketches in which characters would put across a certain point of view were balanced with my experiences from the schools road show. Whereas audiences in South Africa would laugh readily at the familiarity of our dark humour, British audiences were shocked, and in some cases moved. They in their First World security, looking across the barbed-wire fence at a foreign battlefield, where a Third World was fighting its losing war.

It was also important to remind the comfortable chattering classes that this was a virus that didn't give up. Already there were reports of a new strain appearing in the United States, where the young generation was being sexually careless. A form of HIV that was immune to current anti-retroviral treatments.

'It's on its way back through your lives, and this time there'll be no Diana on television hugging a dying man and proving that without a cure there can still be care! You will have to start caring now!'

They did care! I'd sit in the foyer after the show with an empty plastic bucket and a yellow Checkers bag full of beaded ribbons. The members of the audience threw money into the bucket. Five pound notes, ten pound notes, fifty pound notes! Between the London and Dutch seasons, we raised half a million rand for Wola Nani, exciting so many caring people with the realisation that they could make a difference.

'Where can we send our cheque?' they would ask.

I'd give the addresses of a few charities and explain: 'Your cheque will be great. But remember that a huge percentage goes towards admin costs and I doubt if your money will reach the ground. Why don't you get on a plane and go to Cape Town, hire a car and drive out to meet a family and get to know them, take them to the movies, open a bank account for the kids' education and become one of the family? Educate them. Entertain them. Send them postcards from Alaska and Disneyland! Help them with care and love and a name that they know. Learn their names in their language. Not statistics. Real people.'

One British couple came to the show three times.

'We've changed our holiday plans. We were going to Tuscany. Now we're going to Cape Town and visiting Wola Nani.'

SA Tourism should cater for the people who want to come and help. Not exploit the reality and suffering of AIDS, but support those who want to come from other places in the world to assist and be part of the healing process. So that a tourist can visit any bureau and source contacts to a self-help group, a clinic, an orphanage or a hospice. The AIDS gravy train is getting longer by the day. We need focused support to point people in the right direction, so they don't get ripped off by shysters and crooks trading under the mantle of official blessing.

Nqoepsie is now head girl of St Cyprians, and her first decree was to appoint me as head boy. I returned to do a session with parents about HIV/AIDS and how to confront fear, and afterwards the new head girl asked me to accompany her to the Quad.

'Just something I want to show you,' she mumbled uncharacteristically.

The Quad was lined with balconies and verandas and on them stood the whole school. I was inducted as head boy of St Cyprians by Nqoepsie. The girls made me feel like one of them! I told them about my extraordinary association with St Cyprians.

'My mother came to Cape Town, having left her beautiful city of Berlin, because of lethal racism. Her first job here was at this school, as a piano teacher. Sixty years later her son becomes head boy! This is one of the best days of my life!'

180 Degree Turn?

What will happen to South Africa when Nelson Mandela is no longer here as our guardian angel? A question that most of us dread to answer. The country will be forever poorer without Tutu and Mandela, but their imprint is so strong that we can follow the path of their leadership even when they've moved on. But if we lose our children to AIDS, we're finished! They are the only future for South Africa. No matter how much gold and diamonds in the earth, how many drumbeats and kwaito rhythms win the hit parade, how many white, blond, blue-eyed Africans fly into space, without the living energy of youth, we're a rainbow museum.

The guardian angels of the Mandela heritage were giving little reason for smiles. The confusion about the link between HIV and AIDS was deepening every time Thabo Mbeki answered a question with a question. The circle of buddies drew closer around him and there was no hint of humanity to remind us that once, not so long ago, a real person was called President.

I kept sending an e-mail to Mbeki's office: THABO COME IN PLEASE ALL IS FORGIVEN I KNOW YOU ARE THERE OVER?

Nothing. Starship Amandla was gone, off the face of the screen.

The need to treat pregnant women with AIDS to prevent their babies from being born with HIV became the primary concern. The drug Nevirapine had been proven to work with few side effects. Government focused on the side effects to open the next chapter of the farce. They branded it toxic. Various clinics and hospitals were allowed to become test areas for the drug, but it was not made freely available to pregnant women on request, or through prescription. The Treatment Action Campaign (TAC) took the Ministry of Health to the Supreme Court and, after many tangos, foxtrots and twists, won the case. The Department now had to give pregnant mothers the drug. The government appealed. Tensions grew and the state of paralysis extended into weeks and eventually months.

Wherever the President of South Africa went, the AIDS issue tripped him up. He was seen as the one obstacle towards a clear and logical policy to confront the plague and find ways of turning the tide of infection. Minister of Health Manto T-M refused to answer questions either with a yes or a no. Senior members of the ANC were dying of 'backache', soldiers of 'toothache'. Headlines alerted us

214

to the fact that we were losing many teachers to AIDS. Were teachers exposed to HIV more than other members of society? No, it's just that their absence was noticed by all. When a child loses a favourite influence in the classroom, everyone suffers. But accountants, builders, technicians, drivers, policemen and women, tramps and burglars were all being infected.

Too few of us were affected. Too few were aware of the battle. Too many ignored the war. Too many had no knowledge of the struggle.

'What's that pretty beaded badge you're wearing?' a woman asked me in the queue at Pick 'n Pay.

'The people at Wola Nani make it,' I explained.

The woman was clearly in love with the little badge. I took it off and gave it to her.

'No! I can't take it!' she protested, taking it. 'It's so beautiful. What does it mean?'

I waited for her to laugh and expose the joke, but she was serious.

'Don't you know what the red ribbon means?'

'Red ribbon? Oh. No ...'

'It's to promote awareness of AIDS,' I said.

Her face fell. She pushed the badge back into my hands and took a step back in the queue as if she'd catch AIDS by just being there.

'No, thank you,' she stammered, and took her trolley to another cashier.

Doesn't she watch television? Doesn't she see all the Hollywood stars wear the red ribbon at the Oscars and the Golden Globes and wonder what it means? What planet is this lady living on? But when Thabo and Manto and all the leaders also wear the red ribbon without commitment, why should anyone take it seriously?

Just when one thought there was no hope, a sudden turnabout in policy took place. From one day to the next, Mbeki's denial became Thabo's surprise.

'Me? Say that HIV doesn't lead to AIDS? I never said that? Moi?'

The Retex PR machine went into overdrive. The President was now prepared to take the lead in the fight against HIV/AIDS! How? Would he take an HIV-test and set an example? Would he give weekly radio talks and keep us all in the loop? Would we at last become a representative democracy? And what had caused this sudden rash of common sense?

It's Nelson Mandela, stupid! Up to now he had carefully been kept in the background, opening schools and making sweet speeches. But it obviously became too much for him to swallow, and eventually Nelson Mandela stepped

into the arena and added his opinion. This would carry weight worldwide. His comments reflected so much of what had been hoped for. The acknowledgement that HIV leads to AIDS. The need for medication for all. The end of the constant confusion and denial.

Within twenty-four hours there was a retraction. He had been misquoted. The media had taken him out of context.

'We in the ANC are a collective leadership ...' droned the party machine.

The 4×4s were reparked in a laager and the Xowboys hid behind the party lines. President Jimmy Carter visited South Africa and took Nelson Mandela to Soweto, where they hugged babies and posed for pictures. The message was clear. Confront this thing with honesty and courage. Within twenty-four hours there was a new explanation. Jimmy Carter was speaking in his personal capacity and off the record. He had been misquoted. All Mandela said was that, no, he was not criticising Mbeki.

A flood of newspaper articles written by journos with tongues deep up the party cracks hailed Thabo as the great leader who no one understood because he was so special! No reference to Mandela. But good ol' Jimmy Carter wouldn't stop hucking Thabo's attitude. Within days, local media reports isolated Carter as a former president without much clout, a has-been.

It was then that our leader came from behind his barricades and waved the red ribbon flag. The country was bewildered, but relieved. At last, screamed the media, common sense! At last a united front against HIV/AIDS! In the background the dark smirk of Minister Essop Pahad added to the discomfort of those who saw his spin in the fabric of Thabo's speech. Why the sudden change of heart? Was it just the concerns of Nelson Mandela?

No, it's also the Earth Summit, stupid!

In August 2002 some 160 world leaders and 65 000 participants attended the World Summit on Sustainable Growth in Sandton, Johannesburg. It was structured as a major all-singing, all-dancing, all-green production of the ANC. In the preparation for this UN-sponsored event, the issue of HIV/AIDS was absent, to say the least. But then, if the South African government had committed itself to confronting it, as it seemingly had, was there any need to put a virus on the agenda?

The Summit ended with no mention of the holocaust on the doorstep. The Retex spin doctors had succeeded beyond their wildest dreams. On the one hand they were giving in the light of world publicity, but on the other they were stalling in the dark. All this made no difference to what was taking place in real life beyond the Summit. Anti-retroviral drugs were still not being made easily accessible to people who needed them. Education about the dangers of unprotected sex took third place to the hotbeds of *Big Brother*. Sex was happening among people who had no knowledge of the dangers. Truckers were racing their behemoths through the country and stopping for sex en route, giving the virus a free ride.

Vuk'uzinzele

The twenty-seventh of April was a day that changed so many lives. Each anniversary is a celebration not just of a victory, but a rebirth. The first Freedom Day had changed her life in more ways than one, Renate told me. We were sitting at Evita se Perron in Darling. Her two small children were playing with the cats and eating ice cream. Memories of that 1994 celebration are still fresh in many minds. The end of the beginning, when the sun finally set on the 1000-bylaw Reich. Expecting the worst, we were not just given the best, but also a chance to make some of our dreams come true.

Renate had worked for us briefly as a waitress but stayed a friend, especially after the birth of her two babies. She often visited me, and I became involved in her problems. The children loved coming to our place because the cats didn't mind that they had AIDS. None of the other kids wanted to play with them. Their mother was still beautiful, in spite of her weight-loss. Here was a young woman whose life had changed radically from one day to the next. As a coloured person she'd been, for so many years, neither white nor black, just not allowed.

We laughed as we remembered how frightened everyone was in the run-up to the first election. Urban legends fuelled the panic. There would be riots, revolution, violence. Food must be rationed. Supermarkets would fall prey to the communist torch.

'And so we coloureds also stocked up on tuna, just because you whites did!' she giggled. 'I think there is still a tin or two in the shed.'

She looked at her small kiddies pulling the cats' tails. They could both be born free after that day in 1994. They would never be burdened with the baggage of a suffocating past.

'They even have little plans, you know?' she said. 'My little boy wants to be a fisherman. And the girl ...'

We'd been here before. I waited for her to sip her rooibos tea.

'That April 27. You weren't here in Darling then?'

I shook my head. I was buying tins of tuna in Cape Town.

'Man, you should have been here! We had a celebration party after we went to vote. Imagine, all of us in the same queue? Whites and browns and blacks. The Oom and the Tannie, next to the Jong and the Meid. It was so exciting!

There was wine and dancing. Everyone was happy. Then three boys came round, the Bruwer brothers. I couldn't believe it! My mother was once their nanny. Typical Afrikaans boys, usually rude and racist. They brought me flowers.

'"Hey Renate, now we can do it legally!"'

'It sounds worse when I say it. It was then quite sweet. It would also be my first time with a boereseun. The younger Bruwer boytjie? Sexy. We were a bit drunk. I don't think he was the only one that night. It was 1994. Who thought of protection? And anyway, after all us coloureds have been through, God would give us a break on Election Day.'

She wiped her sick child's ice-cream-covered hands. The cats purred and rubbed themselves against the children. Renate sighed and brushed her daughter's neat ponytail.

'Yes, my dear, 27 April 1994 gave me the two things that changed my life for sure: it gave me the Vote, and it gave me the Virus!'

Today, Renate and her kiddies don't come to have ice cream and play with the cats at the Perron any more, because they're dead. Victims of the invisible killer that always comes uninvited to every party. And stays.

Being an optimist in the present South Africa is unfashionable and even suspect. The old warriors are no longer strong enough to govern, or healthy enough to lead. They had a lifetime in prison to watch how a country should not be ruled. They could plan what had to happen. They turned the ship of state around and prevented it from being wrecked on the rocks of revenge. The foot soldiers of the Struggle, those brave kids who in the 1976 Soweto Riots unleashed a wave of change, are no longer young and angry and lionised. They are middle-aged and uneducated. Empowered by the slogan 'Liberation before Education', fed to them by an impatient regime in exile, the children's revolution of the mid-1970s eventually resulted in the inauguration of Nelson Mandela on 10 May 1994. The millions who cheered saw their dream come true, but couldn't spell it. They have no jobs. They cannot run a country. The old white bureaucracy is retired in boere-baroque splendour, living in huge Lenasia-type mansions squeezed onto smallholdings. The present reins of power are in the hands of those returned exiles who sat out the big rumba in order to enjoy the last waltz. An elegant educated alien elite, who have no idea of who we are, or how we function. Their obsession with grand design world politics – an 'African Renaissance', a 'NEPAD', the proposed 'African Union', with its proposed redrawing of the borders of a continent – underlines an ambition that focuses on a world stage, not a local canteen. But that's what South Africa is, and all it needs to start a day is a job to go to, a home to come back to, and the occasional cup of hot coffee, a sticky bun and a nice hug. Like the thousands of hugs I've had from thousands of kids! But Retexes don't hug. Never mind, soon they will also go.

Most of them will jump ship and get involved with lucrative private enterprise. Some will go down the foefie-slide of scandal and end up as ambassadors to Bali or Malawi. A few will make their mark before retiring ill and insane. Then we must be ready!

I tell the kids: 'Not only must you stay alive! You must be awake – always! You will come out of school into a graveyard! Don't expect a country! You must find that dream among the graves! It is up to you to become the New South Africa!'

Within a few more years that new generation of Amandla will be ready to rule. Among the 400 000 faces I have seen, a few will one day grace our stamps and coins. Already, at the age of sixteen, some of the youth are doing more than entire government departments to improve the lot of the people. The leaders of tomorrow who were born and bred in the New SA! Each one of them can be felled by a virus tonight! Assassinated by HIV!

In time for the opening of the South African Parliament in early February 2002, Evita Bezuidenhout wrote this open letter to the man she calls Comrade President. It was published in the *Sunday Independent* and then in the *Cape Times*.

I want President Mbeki to feel better.

Thabo skat, not everyone regards you as a pretentious, arrogant, para-noid, heartless, ruthless Stalinist! My son Izan, who is in jail with AWB leader Eugene Terre'Blanche, says you are his hero. In fact, the whole Afrikaner Resistance Movement is inspired by your brilliant leadership. Izan says that thanks to you, Afrikaners will soon rule South Africa again.

I did point out that we have a very large black majority in government, but Izan just laughed.

'Mama, not for long!' he said, and explained. Because there is so much official confusion about what causes this AIDS, black men refuse to wear condoms to protect themselves against HIV. So they infect the black women, who then infect their black children. And because they are refused anti-retroviral drugs on a national level, they will all die!

AIDS will succeed where apartheid failed.

Izan says soon there will be so few healthy blacks left in South Africa, that he looks forward to a democratically elected white majority government, with Terre'Blanche as president!

So don't feel too bad. I know many citizens of our rainbow nation are wondering how long they can support a party whose leadership persists in condemning their children to death. But not all South Africans feel like that.

The AWB loves you!

Evita Bezuidenhout

Darling

There was a copy of that *Cape Times* on his desk as he rose to speak to the nation and the world.

Thabo Mbeki delivered his Opening of Parliament speech brilliantly, and, like a world-class surgeon, avoiding the cancer, just stroked the silicone. He left one gem on the carpet, one word.

'Vuk'uzinzele!'

Arise and act! Do something! Volunteer and assist to make this a better place! No one picked up on that doctrine. The AIDS denial factor is still the strongest magnet to attract the bits of media tin. Yet surely if everyone put aside an hour a month, a day a month, a week a year to assist someone in need, it could only build a better future? My greatest wish is for a cure to be found for HIV/AIDS, the reason for our terror. So that we can get on with building a future and not only burying a past. That one morning in the headlines we read: THABO FINDS CURE FOR AIDS IN DEEP-FREEZE! I love being proved wrong. I'm quite happy to say sorry. But until that moment it is essential that those who cannot deliver must make way for those who can. There are people in South Africa who can. They must stop sitting on the fence. Their window of opportunity will only come by once. Miss it and they become another footnote.

It's taken over a year for my little footnote to take shape. Feedback from those in the audiences who reacted to the Konsert. Bad news always travels first via the media, but when the people who clean the streets and build the walls tell you that their kids have been affected by the concert, then at least you know something has worked. The letters don't stop coming, from all over the land.

From a fourteen-year-old: 'I feel that you go by your speeches the right way because most of the girls in our school will remember all you said and will probably think before they drank or smoked or did something stupid they would regret for the rest of their lives?'

'All I have to say is you showed me you can never be too old or young to say no, to talk, or educate people about sex or HIV. May God bless you. You're the new Diana.'

From the Free State: 'People with AIDS are normal and very intelligent and should make their life worth remembering. I hope you will soon come back to our school and talk to us once more but until then keep well.'

'Many adults think that children know absolutely nothing about sex and the complications that follow, and they think that if they don't tell us we won't find out,' says a teenager in Randburg. 'How very wrong they are! As you obviously realised finally that if we aren't told about sex, we go exploring and thus mistakes happen.'

A card covered in drawings and words in Zulu carried a message to me too: 'I love the joys of being young, carefree and without any major worries; yet I realise that with an attitude like this I could become another number on the HIV/AIDS statistic charts. I love my youth, and responsibility is one of the words that I've come to incorporate into my language and style. Thank you for increasing my awareness, letting me see the rude, crude fact of how it is.'

From Pretoria: 'I've been having sex education at school since the beginning of Standard 6. I must tell you it has been quite explicit but NEVER has anyone gotten through to me the way you did this morning. I'm sure I know just about everything there is to know about sex. I've experimented very much with oral sex in the past year with different people and my best friend in Grade 11 has been sexually active for the past year now. It was never really a big deal how many guys I had. It wasn't the highlight of my life really. You today explained to me in myself why the fear is so great. It's not the pain of the first time, it's the consequences of every single time. Yes you are rude, crude and REALLY funny, you made people think and people talk (a lot of people) – and you made ME think more than anyone has. More than my mother and we have these talks quite often.

'P.S. You will continue to make a difference I know.'

I still don't know, but if only a few young people have been stimulated to think, to ask, to decide, then it has made all the difference. One is not just a number. One is a life. One life is all that needs to be extended for caring to be a success.

And so, recently on a cold, windswept midnight, at a petrol station somewhere on the road from Cape Town to Darling, I stop to put petrol into my car. The south-easter shakes the car. Papers fly around. A tin advertisement bangs against the wall. The black man holds onto his cap. He leans against the wind and fills the tank. I hand him my garage card and he goes off to process the transaction. He comes back and knocks on the window with his pen. I open it.

'Are you Dirk Uys?'

'Yes?'

'Pieter-Dirk Uys?' He points at the initials on the petrol card. 'The one who came to the Khayelitsha school and told them about this AIDS? Hau man, my child is at that school and he came back and told me all about this AIDS. I did not know. Now I know!'

He wants to shake my hand. I get out of the car and shake his hand too. I sign the petrol chit and get back in the car. He stands to one side. As I drive off, I hear his words come through the window on the wind.

'Now I also know ...!'

Abbreviations

ACDP: African Christian Democratic Party
AIDS: Acquired immune deficiency syndrome
ANC: African National Congress
AWB: Afrikaner Weerstandsbeweging; Afrikaner Resistance Movement
BBC: British Broadcasting Corporation
CAPAB: Cape Performing Arts Board
CNN: Cable News Network
DP: Democratic Party
FA: Federal Alliance
FAK: Federasie van Afrikaanse Kultuurverenigings;
    Federation of Afrikaans Cultural Organisations
FF: Freedom Front
HIV: Human immunodeficiency virus
IEC: Independent Electoral Commission
IFP: Inkatha Freedom Party
MTN: Mobile Telephone Network
NEPAD: New Partnership for Africa's Development
NHS: National Health Service
NNP: New National Party
NP: National Party
PAC: Pan African Congress
PACOFS: Performing Arts Council of the Orange Free State
PFP: Progressive Federal Party
PT: physical training
RDP: Reconstruction and Development Programme
SABC: South African Broadcasting Corporation
SACS: South African College School
SADF: South African Defence Force
SATOUR: South African Tourism
TAC: Treatment Action Campaign
TRC: Truth and Reconciliation Commission
UCT: University of Cape Town
UDM: United Democratic Movement

Glossary

ag: oh
aikôna: no way, no
aluta continua: the struggle continues
amachoochoo: train
amandla awethu: power is ours
ander dinge: other things
baas: boss
bakkie: light delivery vehicle
bedonnerde: angry
bek: mouth
bene: legs
berge so blou: mountains so blue
bergies: hoboes
biltong: dried meat
blaf en byt: bark and bite
boekie: little book
boer: Afrikaner
boeredorp: Afrikaner town
boerekos: Afrikaner food
boereliedjies: Afrikaner songs
boeremeisie: Afrikaner girl
boereseun: Afrikaner boy
bokkie: term of endearment, literally
    'little buck'
boytjie: boy
bra: brother
braaivleis: barbecue
broeks: pants
Broerderbond: literally 'brotherhood';
    secret society formed for the advance-
    ment of Afrikaners
daardie dônner: that arsehole
dagga: marijuana
Die honde blaf maar die karavaan
    gaan aan: The dogs bark but the
    caravan continues!

die manne: the men
Die Stem: 'The Voice', the old South
    African national anthem
dierbaar: loveable, precious
djol: party
djolling: partying
dominee: reverend
donga: ditch
dônner: hit, punch
doos: arsehole
dorp: town
droëwors: dried sausage
Egoli: Johannesburg
foefieslide: a slide
fundi: expert
Geloftedag: Day of the Vow
gits: goodness!
gogga: bug
Gogo: Granny
gril: shudder
hau: hey
heldersonop: bright sunrise
hoer: whore
hoërskool: high school
hotnot: derogatory term for coloured
    person
indaba: meeting
ja: yes
jong: derogatory term for coloured man
Jozi: Johannesburg
kaffir: derogatory term for black person
kaffirboetie: someone who likes black
    people
kak: crap
kaktus: cactus
karnaval: carnival

227

kinders naai ook: children also fuck

Klein Karoo Nasionale Kunstefees: Little Karoo National Arts Festival

koek: cake

koeksisters: sweet, syrupy confectionery

konsert: concert

koppie: small hill

kragdadig: forceful, strong

kugel: Jewish princess

kultuur: culture

kwaito: African music

laager: circle of oxwagons

langbroek: long trousers

lekker: nice, pleasant

liewe: dear

liewe aarde: good heavens

magtig: damn it

meid: derogatory term for coloured woman

meneer: mister

mevrou: missus, madame

mielie: corn cob

moenie: don't

moerse: huge

moffie: gay man

muti: magic potion

my skat: my dear

naai: fuck

naartjie: tangerine

nee: no

nie waar nie?: not so?

Nkosi Sikelel' iAfrika: 'God bless Africa', the liberation anthem

nooit: no, never

oom: uncle

oppas: be careful, watch out

ou: old

ou balie: old fart

ouks: guys

piel: dick

piepie: pee, penis

Pietertjie: little Pieter

plaas: farm

poep: crap, fart

poephol: arsehole

rooibos tea: indigenous South African tea

rooinek: redneck

sangoma: traditional healer

selle ou storie: same old story

sies: term of disgust

siestog: term of sympathy

sindroom: syndrome

sis: term of disgust

skat, skattie: dear, lovey

slegs blankes: whites only

sommer: just because

sonskyn: sunshine

spruit: brook, stream

sterkte: strength

stoep: veranda

stompies: cigarette butts

suster: sister

taal: language

tannie: auntie

Tannie Evita Praat Kaktus: Auntie Evita talks cactus

tata: father

toemaar: don't worry

toyi-toyi: dance

Uit die blou van onse hemel: 'From our blue heavens', the first line of the old South African national anthem

verbeteringskool: reformatory

verboten: forbidden

verjaarsdagkoek: birthday cake

vieslike woorde: dirty words

vrot mielie: rotten corn cob

Vrystaat: Free State

vuk'uzinzele: arise and act

wena: hey

Translations of Afrikaans quotes

p. 30 Ons mense is nie so nie.
Our people are not like that.

p. 75 Hey? Djulle? Fok off!
Hey, you, fuck off!

Kom kindertjies!
Come little children!

Sien, ek't gesê dis mos 'n fokkin man!
See, I told you it's a fucking man!

p. 90 Marthinus Skattie, Tannie gaan in Engels skryf sodat jy jou Ingels kan oefen.
Marthinus, lovey, Auntie is going to write in English so you can practise your second language.

p. 117 Pik? Is jy wakker? Ek wou jou faks, maar ek was bang iemand sou dit sien. Hierdie e-pos is beter. Maar in watter taal? Ek dink Afrikaans is nie 'n goeie idee nie – te veel van 'hulle' verstaan! Dus: vieslike Engels!
Pik? Are you awake? I wanted to fax you, but I was afraid someone would see it. This e-mail is better. But in which language? I don't think Afrikaans is a good idea – too many of 'them' understand. Hence: horrible English!

Hier kom Allan! Daar gaan Bantu! Oppas vir Winnie!
Here comes Allan! There goes Bantu! Watch out for Winnie!

p. 149 Ag dis mos Evita.
Oh, it's just Evita.

p. 154 Afrikaanse kinders naai ook.
Afrikaans children also fuck.

p. 163 Moenie? Waar koop ek 'moenie'?
Don't? Where do I buy 'don't'?

p. 165 Dit kan nie met ons mense gebeur nie!
It can't happen to our people!

p. 173 Evita, ek wil djou naai!
Evita, I want to fuck you!

p. 193 Mevrou Bezuidenhout, u was wonderlik, maar as ek ooit daardie Pieter-Dirk Uys in die hande kry gaan ek hom donner!
Mrs Bezuidenhout, you were wonderful, but if I ever get hold of that Pieter-Dirk Uys, I'm going to beat him up!

Ek wens jou sukses!
I wish you success!

ZEBRA PRESS
supports
book*eish!*
South African International Festival of Books

Cape Town 27 February to 1 March 2004